I0094479

ecpr PRESS

Series Editors:
Dario Castiglione (University of Exeter) and
Vincent Hoffmann-Martinot (Sciences Po Bordeaux)

coercing, constraining and signalling

explaining un and eu sanctions after the cold war

Francesco Giumelli

ecprPRESS

First published by the ECPR Press in 2011

The ECPR Press is the publishing imprint of the European Consortium for Political Research (ECPR), a scholarly association, which supports and encourages the training, research and cross-national cooperation of political scientists in institutions throughout Europe and beyond. The ECPR's Central Services are located at the University of Essex, Wivenhoe Park, Colchester, CO4 3SQ, UK

Typeset by Anvi Composers
Printed and bound by Lightning Source

British Library Cataloguing in Publication Data
A catalogue record for this book is available from the British Library

Paperback ISBN: 978-1-907301-20-9

www.ecprnet.eu/ecprpress

To Melissa

Endorsements for the book

In his important contribution to the field of UN and EU targeted sanctions, Francesco Giumelli provides an excellent conceptual account of the challenges this strategic tool confronts in today's world. He does so by providing both an excellent theoretical as well as methodological analysis, especially with regard to strategies of coercing, constraining and signalling. What more is that Dr. Giumelli also provides scientific recommendations for how to move the field forward. In short then, this book should be a required reading for anyone interested in the state of the art of sanctions.

Dr Mikael Eriksson,
Researcher at the Swedish Defence Research Agency

"Francesco Giumelli's analytical distinction between the different purposes of sanctions – to coerce, to constrain, to signal – introduces an innovative way to think about and to evaluate the effectiveness of sanctions."

Prof. Thomas J. Biersteker,
The Graduate Institute, Geneva

"This is a thoughtful study of economic sanctions as instruments of statecraft together with other forms of statecraft in pursuit of a variety of foreign policy goals. To his credit, the author neither dismisses nor ignores signaling as a foreign policy device."

Prof. David A. Baldwin,
Princeton University

| contents

| list of figures and tables

| acknowledgements

First and foremost, I have to thank the person that I love the deepest, and to whom I dedicate the entire text: my wife. Melissa walked step by step through the hurdles of my research and her support has been a constant. Simply put, she made everything possible.

There are several people that I would like to mention and gratefully thank. Prof. Filippo Andreatta and Prof. Leonardo Morlino should be mentioned for their unconditional support to this project despite my initial doubts. Their insightful advice and confidence in my work have given me the motivation to complete this research. Prof. Michal Klima, Dr. Oldrich Bures, and Dr. Mitchell Belfer from Metropolitan University Prague provided me with the best environment for the publication of this book.

Numerous friends stood next to me in this journey: Marcelo, Nicola, Nino, Andrea, Octavio, Nicoló, Michele, Tommaso, Ruggero, Giovanni, Massimo, together with my loving family. A long list of scholars participated in various ways in the elaboration of this work: my sincerest thanks go out to Prof. Pascal Vennesson, Prof. Donatella Della Porta, Hon. Sue Eckert, Prof. Lisa Martin, Prof. Stanley Hoffmann, Dr. Claudius Wagemann, Prof. Sebastian Royo, Prof. Suzanne Berger, Prof. Meghan O'Sullivan, Prof. George Lopez, Prof. Thomas Biersteker, Prof. Martin Beck, Prof. Vittorio Emanuele Parsi, Prof. David A. Baldwin, Prof. Andrew J. Bacevich, Prof. Fulvio Attina, Prof. David Cortright, Prof. Mathias K. Archibugi, Dr. Mikael Eriksson. Prof. Peter Wallensteen, Prof. Luciano Bozzo, Prof. David W. Ellwood, Prof. William Long and Prof. Roberto Belloni for their help and advice. Many thanks also go out to Krystof Krulis and Petr Slowik for their assistance in preparing the data for the news coverage of the crises.

I would like to acknowledge the institutions that provided resources and support to this study. First of all, it is important to mention the Robert Schuman Center for Advanced Studies at the European University Institute where I am currently working as a Jean Monnet Fellow. The onset of this study took place at the Italian Institute of Human Sciences in Florence, but important steps were taken at the Massachusetts Institute of Technology (MIT) and at the Kroc Institute for International Peace Studies at Notre Dame University where I was hosted as Visiting Fellow. Finally, the cooperation of the UN Sanctions Branch and of various EU officials from the Council, the Commission and the Delegations was a fundamental asset to this research. This research would not have been complete without these experiences.

Many thanks go to Prof. Dario Castiglione and the Committee of the Jean Blondel Prize, which shortlisted my work, and ECPR Press for receiving positively this manuscript. I would like to acknowledge the anonymous reviewers who provided suggestions and contributed to the improvement of the book. Mark

Kench has been a tireless and precise editor and I strongly appreciated his working ethics and his dedication.

Last, but certainly not least, a special thought goes out to my nonna Luisa, for being so truly unique. Her grit and serenity, happiness and strength, affect every decision of my life. Her greatest teaching is that success is possible under any circumstance if you work hard for what you want and that life's many challenges can be overcome with joy and tranquillity.

These outstanding people and places have helped to reduce the mistakes in this book. The errors that still remain are all mine to account for.

| list of abbreviations

AMG	Advisory and Monitoring Group
AMISOM	African Union Mission in Somalia
ASEAN	Association of South East Asian Nations
AU	African Union
CBC	Cross-Border Cooperation
CFSP	Common Foreign and Security Policy
COREPER	Committee of Permanent Representatives
CPP	Cambodian People's Party
Cs-QCA	Crispy Set-Qualitative Comparative Analysis
CTC	Counter-Terrorism Committee
DPRK	Democratic People's Republic of Korea
DRC	The Democratic Republic of the Congo
DV	Dependent variable
ECHO	Humanitarian Aid department of the European Commission
ECOMOG	Economic Community of West African States Monitoring Group
ECOWAS	Economic Community of West African States
EEAS	European External Action Service
EU	European Union
EUBAM	European Union Border Assistance Mission
FATF	Financial Action Task Force
FRY	Former Republic of Yugoslavia
Fs-QCA	Fuzzy Logic-Qualitative Comparative Analysis
FUNCIN-PEC	United National Front for an Independent, Neutral, Peaceful and Cooperative Cambodia
FYROM	Former Yugoslav Republic of Macedonia
GATT	General Agreement on Tariffs and Trade
HSE	Hufbauer, Schott and Elliott
IAEA	International Atomic Energy Agency
ICAO	International Civil Aviation Organisation
ICC	International Criminal Court
ICTY	The International Criminal Tribunal for the former Yugoslavia

IGADD	Intergovernmental Authority on Drought and Development
IIE	Institute for International Economics
IMU	Islamic Movement of Uzbekistan
INTAS	International Association for the promotion of cooperation with scientists from the independent states of the former Soviet Union
IV	Independent variable
JCC	Joint Control Command
JEM	Justice and Equality Movement
MONUC	United Nations Organisation Mission in the Democratic Republic of the Congo
MPLA	Movimento Popular de Libertação de Angola - Partido do Trabalho (National Union for the Total Independence of Angola)
NLD	National League for Democracy
NPT	Non-Proliferation Treaty
OAS	Organisation of American States
OCHA	UN Office for the Coordination of Humanitarian Affairs
OFAC	Office for Foreign Assets Control
OSCE	Organisation for Security and Cooperation in Europe
OSCE/ODIHR	OSCE Office for Democratic Institutions and Human Rights
P5	Five Permanent Members of the UN Security Council
PDK	Party of Democratic Kampuchea
PSC	Political and Security Committee
QCA	Qualitative Comparative Analysis
R2P	Responsibility to Protect
RUF	Revolutionary United Front
SADC	Southern African Development Community
SLA/M	Sudan Liberation Army/Movement
SLORC	State Law and Order Restoration Council
SPDC	State Peace and Development Council
TACIS	Technical Aid to the Commonwealth of Independent States
TFEU	Treaty on the Functioning of the European Union
TFI	Transitional Federal Institutions
UN	United Nations
UNAMIC	United Nations Advance Mission in Cambodia

UNAMIR	United Nations Assistance Mission for Rwanda
UNICOI	United Nations International Commission of Inquiry
UNITA	*União Nacional para a Independência Total de Angola* (National Union for the Total Independence of Angola)
UNOMIL	United Nations Observer Mission in Liberia
UNOMUR	United Nations Observer Mission Uganda-Rwanda
UNTAC	United Nations Transitional Authority in Cambodia
WBO	World Border Organisations
WTO	World Trade Organisation

chapter | introduction
one |

This book is a comprehensive study of the logic of international sanctions defined as 'how sanctions influence their targets'. As the world moves towards a new era in which sanctions play an important role in conflict prevention and foreign policy, a fundamental flaw in the current literature still prevails in their respect, namely that sanctions must necessarily impose a cost on their target in order to bring about a change of behaviour. This logic was already defined as naïve by Galtung in 1967 (Galtung 1967), but it persisted in most of the studies on sanctions undermining the usefulness of their conclusions. Indeed, the expectation that sanctions should determine the behavioural change of a target is a central pillar of many investigations on the effectiveness of international sanctions (Doxey 1987; Hufbauer *et al.* 2007; Baldwin 1999/2000). This understanding is also part of the discussions regarding the policy objectives of sanctions when measures that do not have an impact on their targets are downgraded to the status of merely symbolic in nature (Brzoska and Lopez 2009; Cortright and Lopez 2002a). The interest of this research is fuelled by the empirical evidence that points to the fact that sanctions are only one foreign policy tool available to policy makers and that the causal mechanism portrayed in the syllogism 'economic pain leads to political gain' is too much of a minimalist approach to understand sanctions.

When the United Nations (UN) imposed sanctions on Serbia, a parallel military campaign was prepared and eventually launched. Similarly, Iraq was hit by a total embargo when the Security Council also authorised the use of force to liberate Kuwait. The European Union (EU) decision to impose sanctions on certain individuals in Uzbekistan was accompanied by a set of foreign aid and diplomatic initiatives organised towards the government in Tashkent. Multiple foreign policy tools were also used when the EU's Council of Ministers decided to freeze the assets of certain individuals in the Former Yugoslav Republic of Macedonia (FYROM). In all of these cases, the use of sanctions took place within a larger foreign policy strategy that involved other forms of coercive and non-coercive diplomacy. So, how can we analyse sanctions if we do not know the exact role they play? Strategies are a multilevel and multidimensional aggregation of policy tools, and within them each use of any foreign policy tool is an exercise of power. As such, sanctions can influence targets in multiple ways that we should be able to distinguish and to conceptualise. This step is crucial in order to understand how sanctions work even before knowing whether they work.

Indeed, sanctions do differ from each other in more than just subtle ways. The sanctions of the UN against Iraq in 1991 share certain characteristics with the ones imposed by the Security Council in 2005 on those responsible for the Hariri murder (a former prime minister of Lebanon who was assassinated on 14 February 2005). Certainly, both of them are characterised by a global action towards important events and they indicate an interest by the Security Council to contribute to world peace, stability and security. However, the international community mobilised enormous resources to impose and implement the embargo on Iraq, which also had tragic consequences on the civilian population in the country. Contrarily, little or no resources were requested in order to implement the measures on those responsible for the attack in which Rafic Hariri lost his life along with other twenty-two people. The difference in these fundamental aspects forces us to wonder whether their imposition was moved by a similar inspirational logic.[1] Interesting conclusions could be drawn by comparing the UN sanctions imposed on Liberia and those on Rwanda, or the UN counter-terrorist measures with the ones taken against Libya, since there was very little in common between them. The form taken by sanctions can vary greatly across time and space, complicating any attempts to create typologies that encompass a large range of possible behaviours. The endeavours to create typologies based on policy objectives also ended up in lengthy lists with scarce analytical value. On the contrary, the menu of logics available to policy makers is short and useful.

The objective of this book is to classify sanctions according to their dominant logic and to test a systemic explanation for such logic. The context in which sanctions are imposed is a potent explanatory variable and the creation of a theoretical framework to reach this conclusion relies on two different lines of investigation. The first touches upon the problem of identifying sanctions and of creating a useful typology to be added to the literature. The second regards the causal links between the context of sanctions and their dominant logic.

The logic of sanctions

Sanctioning is a foreign policy decision put into action and every decision in foreign policy is an exercise of power. Power can be exercised in different ways and such 'ways' are defined as 'logics' in this study. There are three logics identified in the literature (Berenskoetter and Williams 2007: 1–22).

First, power can be intended in the classical definition of A makes B do whatever B would not do otherwise. Taken directly from Dahl, Baldwin, Lasswell and Kaplan's work, the concept of power has also differentiated between power and influence, which is an important distinction that will be useful to this study. The second dimension of power captures the ability to ensure that certain decisions may not take place at all. In other words, this dimension of power was named 'the agenda-setting power' by Bachrach and Baratz (Berenskoetter and Williams 2007: 7). Finally, the third dimension of power attempts to capture the relationship of power even when there is no conflict of interest, and identify a form of power that prevents conflicts from arising. In other words, this dimension of power works with a different internal logic than the previous

---

1.   Logic is used as synonym of mechanics and it refers to how sanctions are expected or supposed to influence their targets.

two since it neither coerces an actor to act in a specific way nor does it modify their agenda, but rather it shapes the interests and the knowledge of the actors.

These three dimensions of power in international relations can be translated in terms of winning conflicts, limiting alternatives and shaping normality. To this extent, sanctions can coerce ('win conflicts'), constrain ('limit alternatives') and signal ('shape normality') in international relations. The first type has been labelled *coercive* because it has the objective to impose a cost on misconducts aiming at affecting the costs/benefits calculation of the target so the latter will have an incentive to modify its behaviour. The second type of sanction has the goal of limiting the capabilities of the target in pursuing its aims, namely a *constraining sanction*. Finally, sanctions can simply send a message to certain targets, and these can be either domestic or international, or both (Giumelli 2010b).

This approach solves a series of problems in sanction debates and offers a number of opportunities. Sanctions are commonly linked to specific foreign policy objectives, but this approach could generate tensions between the expectations of what a foreign policy tool can achieve and its capabilities to do it. For instance, the UN employed multiple tools to deal with the crisis opened by the Iraqi invasion of Kuwait: but how can we know whether it was the military tool, the economic sanction or the other decisions that affected the behaviour of the government of Iraq? Foreign policy tools can only contribute to foreign policy objectives. A similar reasoning applies to EU relations with Belarus, where a wide range of economic incentives and promises have been used parallel to the imposition of sanctions. The approach adopted in this investigation could help to clarify EU and Belarus relations as well, since we would be able to distinguish the effects of each foreign policy instruments and to verify whether they are in line with the expectations of the senders.

A systemic explanation

What determines the logic of sanctions? The objective of this study is to test whether the different environments in which sanctions are imposed (also called the 'context' of sanctions) can be an explanatory variable for the logic of sanctions. The diverse contexts are identified thanks to three different variables:

- the level of threat to the sender;
- the salience; and
- the complexity of the crisis.

The combinations of these three variables constitute the different 'systems' of sanctions.

The underlying hypothesis that the context provides the actors with constraints and opportunities to their freedom of action was confirmed by the empirical analysis of seventy sanctions episodes. The findings show strong relations between specific contextual configurations and the three types of sanctions. Coercive sanctions appear to be more likely when there is a threat to senders and the crisis is not complex. The second recurrence relates constraining sanctions to high levels of threat and complexity. Finally, signalling sanctions are more likely when the level of threat is low and the crisis is not salient. In other words, if we know the context of sanctions, then we have higher probabilities to know what type of sanction will be imposed.

The theoretical framework constructed and tested in this study would be useful from both theoretical as well as policy perspectives. Proving the connections between the type of sanctions and the context in which sanctions are imposed would be fundamental in confirming that the 'system' matters. Sanctions would not be independent from their context and any relevant study on this subject would have to consider this aspect. The centre of the analysis should then move away from the simple interaction between two actors, sender and target, but it would widen the focus to include the environment in the picture.

Another relevant aspect is linked to the difference between the variable of threat and salience. The two independent variables (IVs) originate from two competing theoretical paradigms, respectively realism and liberalism, and the empirical test would verify the different effects they have on the dependent variable (DV).

The establishment of a comprehensive theoretical framework would create the opportunity to accumulate knowledge in the field of sanctions. One of the most serious shortcomings of the debate on sanction is the lack of coherence and communication among sanctions scholars. Looking for an explanation of why scholars reached such divergent conclusions on whether sanctions work, Baldwin wrote in 1999:

> A [...] potential explanation is that scholars are talking past one another because they ask different questions, use different concepts, and set the discussion in different analytical contexts. In short, they are talking about different things.

(Baldwin 1999/2000: 80)

The need of a theoretical conceptualisation of this sort arises from Baldwin's concern. In fact, this concern linked to the fruitless debate on effectiveness is expandable to most of the debates on sanctions. If the theoretical framework passes the empirical test, then it would provide the participants of the sanctions debate with common language and analytical tools for constructive discussions that could sustain the accumulation of knowledge in the sanctions field.

Finally, the theoretical framework proceeds from the context and takes account of variance.[2] Usually, studies on sanctions do not take into consideration this external dimension, therefore certain sanction cases become comparable even if, in fact, they differ substantially. Two events can be compared if they are different cases of the same phenomenon (e.g. two democracies, two wars, etc.), and the environment can be exogenous to the theoretical model if it does not affect the events that are on the focus of the study. However, the context appears to be a

---

2. Variance here refers to the dependent variable, which can be of three types. Therefore the variance is that the dependent variable can be of one type in one case and of another type in a different case. The variance is that the dependent variable changes across cases.

determinant of sanctions so that similar cases of sanctions could become different if the environment varies between the two. Indeed, a cross-section comparison is possible only if the environment does not change across the sample, otherwise the hypothesised causal link would be biased by the variation of the environment. The assumption that the context does not matter is one way to solve the problem, but the utility of the concepts used in these analyses would inevitably decrease. A comprehensive theoretical framework would allow for reliable comparisons across time and space.

On the policy dimension of the theoretical framework stands the mutating utility of sanctions and a renewed criterion for effectiveness. The analysis of the environment of sanctions enhances the capacity to discern among different crises and to discover what sanctions can do under what circumstances. Indeed, sanctions should not be intended only as a pain-causer, but the changing context would render sanctions able to contribute in at least three different ways to influence the behaviour of targets.

Finally, the fact that sanctions do not only aim at changing the behaviour of targets inevitably modifies the method to evaluate their success. Here, there are two added values enshrined in the theoretical framework. On the one hand, the tripartite typology based on the logic of sanctions leads us to look at whether the mechanics of the restrictive measures worked as expected. On the other hand, the knowledge of the context contributes to the discussion on the comparative utility of sanctions. This concept was developed by Baldwin (1999) and it refers to the idea that the effectiveness of sanctions can be assessed only if it is known that other policy measures would have yielded better results. This evaluation cannot be carried out if the context is not comprised in the framework.

The structure of the work

The research is divided in three parts. The first part is more theoretical, it presents the fallacies in the literature and designs the framework used to justify the expected associations among the variables. The second part focuses on the presentation of the dataset and on the results of the comparative analysis. Finally, the third part presents the case studies used in this investigation.

Chapter 2 underlines the two wrong assumptions at the base of the sanctions debate and highlights the need for a comprehensive theoretical framework. The erroneous representation of how sanctions work and the lack of contexts in sanctions analyses undermine seriously our understanding of sanctions. The perception of the utility of sanctions is altered by mistaken assumptions on how they work, which undermines how we understand success and widens the expectation-capability gap between what sanctions can achieve and what they actually achieve. A systemic comprehensive framework is needed to move the debate forward. The final section of the chapter presents the methodology adopted to answer to the research question.

Chapter 3 presents the theoretical framework and illustrates the expected links among the variables. The base of the framework is set with the creation of a typology based on how sanctions influence targets, namely through coercing, constraining and signalling. The second level includes the definition of context as the IV of the framework, which is operationalised with the variables of threat, salience and complexity. The concluding part of the chapter summarises the hypotheses of the associations between the independent and the DVs that will be tested in the following chapters.

Chapter 4 opens the empirical part of the book by introducing the database of sanctions to readers. The method adopted to complete this mission is to provide an overview of the seventy episodes covered in the dataset by presenting the descriptive data of the variables considered in the theoretical framework. The presentation of the aggregate variables as well as specific indicators is supported by the historical narrative of episodes taken from the dataset. This chapter is essential to confirm the idea that sanctions can be distinguished systematically from one another and that the context cannot be assumed to be static across time and space.

Chapter 5 runs a crispy-set qualitative comparative analysis (Cs-QCA) of the seventy episodes of sanctions and it tests the hypotheses elaborated from the theoretical framework. First, the individual associations between each IV and the DV are measured and the results seem to suggest that the correlations are solid. Second, the three IVs can be combined to represent eight different configurations of the environment in which sanctions are imposed and also under this perspective the presence of certain context configurations increases the probabilities of specific outcomes. The results would confirm the assumption according to which the context affects the type of sanctions by reducing the range of options available to policy makers.

Chapters 6 and 7 present case studies selected from the database. Chapter 6 is devoted to the United Nations as a global sanctioner. The opening section briefly summarises the main procedural aspects of the UN sanctioning policy that are crucial to assess the different indexes and to study the relevant episodes under scrutiny. The chapter focuses on three episodes of UN sanctions on Libya, on the Taliban and Al-Qaida, and on Rwanda; these are selected to represent the three types of sanctions: coercive, constraining and signalling. The case studies unveil some causal mechanisms that increase the probabilities that the sender would resort to one specific type of sanction over the others.

The EU as a regional sanctioner is the centre of attention in chapter seven, concluding the empirical and the final part of the investigation of this study. After the description of the EU sanctioning policy, a further three case studies that represent the three logics are examined. First, the episode of coercing sanctions looks at Belarus and President Lukashenko since 2007; secondly, the constraining measures are the ones imposed on Transnistria from 2003 to 2007; and, thirdly, the signalling sanctions selected are those imposed on Uzbekistan from 2005 to 2009. The analysis of the EU is an important step that confirms that every actor suffers similar pressures in the international system: different actors behave similarly under similar systems, and the same actors behave differently under different systems.

Chapter 8 is dedicated to the final remarks of this effort in advancing knowledge on international sanctions. The chapter summarises the research question and the reasons to support the decision of creating an alternative theoretical framework for explaining and understanding sanctions episodes. The main findings of the model are presented in this final part of the study with particular stress on the correlations between the external context and the logic of restrictive measures that emerges from the empirical investigation. The chapter underlines the achievements of this theoretical enterprise and the contributions to the literature of sanctions, and in light of these accomplishments, it sets forwards policy recommendations for the future of the UN and the EU sanctioning policies. Finally, although the mission is still far from being thoroughly accomplished, the chapter emphasises how this research represents a step ahead in explaining and understanding sanctions, and concludes by indicating how further studies could contribute to fill in the remaining gaps between theory and practice of international sanctions.

chapter two | framing the problem: the fallacies in the debate of sanctions

The centrality of sanctions in foreign policy has been acknowledged by a rich debate among political scientists, historians, policy makers and members of the civil society that has lasted for centuries. Since the times of city-states in Greece, sanctions were officially a policy option at the disposal of the authorities of political communities. However, the length of a debate does not always match the level of understanding of the topic at the centre of the discussion, and this is definitely the case for international sanctions. The lack of certainties arising from the debate about the effectiveness of sanctions is telling about how little we understand of sanctions.

The objective of this chapter is to point out to readers the barriers that prevent the accumulation of knowledge in the study of sanctions. It does this by setting the terms for the creation of a comprehensive theoretical framework that would solve two fundamental flaws in understanding sanctions. First, sanctions are assumed to be equal, when in reality they are different. Secondly, sanctions are not imposed in a vacuum and their context may play an important role in their imposition.

The existing literature has either simply documented new sanction episodes or looked at the problem from a micro level of analysis. By micro level, I intend issues such as the use of sanctions as a complement to other foreign policy tools, their effects on authoritarian regimes, their general effectiveness, their actual humanitarian impact or the response of targeted actors. However, a macro, or system, level of analysis has been seldom undertaken. This book intends to fill this gap by testing a 'systemic' explanation for the logic of sanctions.

This chapter introduces the concepts and the problems addressed by this book. The first part is a necessary premise to this elaboration. It presents a brief overview of the evolution of sanctions from 'comprehensive' to 'targeted' and provides the definition adopted. The second part introduces the reader to the problem of debate inconsistency by focusing on the little knowledge accumulated about sanctions effectiveness. The third part tackles the problem of distinguishing the different episodes of sanctions by presenting the efforts to create a typology based on policy objectives and other methods. The fourth part highlights the problems encountered in these definitions and argues for the need of a systemic approach introducing the reader to the basic concepts. The remainder of the chapter is devoted to the research design and the methodology used to answer the research question.

The historical evolution of sanctions

Many studies recall the embargo that Athens imposed against Megara through the Megarian decree before the outset of the Peloponnesian wars in 432 BC as the first sanction episode ever recorded (Tsebelis 1990: 3). Although strongly illustrative, Thucydides' analytical description of the famous war that set in motion the decline of Athens is not the sole example of a sanctioning method in ancient times. The tactics of the warrior peoples that inhabited the steppes in the Far East consisted of cutting off supplies in order to force the surrender of villages during their horseback raids (Keegan 1994: 153–234). History certainly abounds in cases wherein political actors have decided to deny resources or expected gains to other actors for a number of reasons, and it could be plausible to claim that this practice is as old as the existence of the international system as we define it today. The attention devoted to this subject by newspapers in the twenty-first century (e.g. Iran, North Korea, Guinea, Zimbabwe, Lebanon, etc.) confirms that sanctions remain relevant today.

Imposing sanctions is a political decision available to any units of a system. It is believed that sanctioning is a foreign policy decision in the hands of the strong versus the weak, but, in fact, every unit of the system can impose sanctions on others. In a remote past, the units were mostly cities, realms and kingdoms. In the past, the main actor of the system became the nation-state; therefore it was common to see states imposing sanctions on each other. The units today can be international organisations, nation-states and non-state entities. Since the end of the Cold War, a normative change seems to have modified the concept of sovereignty as international organisations and nation-states can impose sanctions on individuals and non-state entities as well (Cortright and Lopez 2002b).

Historians have consistently described sanctions throughout their war narratives since this method was used to undermine enemy economies by helping to curtail their capacity to organise an efficient military apparatus. Total embargoes were the rule rather than the exception when the organisation of political authority was structured on city-states and fortresses. As kingdoms expanded they cut enemy cities off from their supply routes, which explain the technological innovations that led to food and water self-sufficiency as a means to strengthen their resistance to sieges.

The use of force is the ultimate form of foreign policy and sanctions are usually associated with wars in international relations. An interruption to trade often resulted in accompanying military campaigns and, ironically, the continuation of commercial relations may have strengthened targets and enhanced their capacity to resist an assault. History provides a plethora of examples of such practices. For instance, the Roman siege of the city of Masada against the Zealots (or *Sicarii*) was a due complement of the military campaign (Hoffman 2006: 43–62). The hostile relations between Germany and England were characterised by a history of embargoes that date back to the fifteenth century (Fudge 1995) and all the way to World War II, when Hitler interrupted commercial relations with England after attempting to invade it (Keegan 1994). The NATO air campaign on Milosevic was the one with the prohibition to sell military equipment to Serbia that could have enhanced its capacity to respond to the bombing campaign (Minear 2000). Another relatively present day example is the UN's decision to impose a total embargo on Iraq after the invasion of Kuwait in 1990 as the military option was soon taken into consideration to restore the *status quo ex-ante* (Cordesman and Hashim 1997).

In other words, sanctions and war have coexisted and their relationship has shaped part of their history. Sanctions went from being considered a complementary measure of war to an alternative to the use of force in international affairs with President Wilson. After the end of World War I, Wilson hoped to inaugurate an era where collective responses to common threats in the form of sanctions could have avoided the use of force. Wilson talked about a 'peaceful, silent, and deadly remedy' that the members of the League of Nations could have resorted to where international law was violated. In his mind, sanctions would have eradicated the need to wage wars, preventing thus the violation of the international order (Foley 1923: 71).

This ambiguity has endured to the present day, when the recent development in the use of sanctions has led pundits and scholars to study the so called 'targeted sanctions'. While sanctions used to be imposed on entire political communities – as seen above in the case of fortresses, city-states and entire nations – were called 'comprehensive', the UN established the praxis of imposing sanctions on individuals and non-state entities, which gained the new appellative of 'targeted'. It has been argued that all sanctions imposed after the mid-1990s are to be considered targeted (Cortright and Lopez 2002b: 1), but this seems to be more of an etiquette than an empirical reality. Sanctions were imposed against individuals and non-state entities – the formula in Latin *persona non grata* (unwelcome person) is precisely because the practice of keeping certain individuals outside of one's own territory is a principle enshrined in the Vienna Convention – or targeted against specific commodities already in the past – such as the grain sanctions on the Soviet Union in the 1980s (Martin 1992). However, the novelty is that multilateral organisations are doing it now officially. Targeting specific individuals inside the territory of one state would have meant disregarding the authority of the sovereign ruler, something that would not have occurred a few years ago.

The multilateral efforts to focus on targeted sanctions observed in the acts of the Security Council are an important innovation in international law (Cortright and Lopez 1995). From the mid-1990s, three forces contributed to this: the need to make sanctions more effective, the need to lower their humanitarian impact, and the establishment of the international individual responsibility principle (Giumelli 2009). These factors shifted the attention from the foreign policy of a state to what was happening inside the targeted state, the so-called 'microfoundations approach' (Morgan and Schwebach 1996: 252):

A microfoundations approach looks not at economic sanctions in general, but at the differences between various forms of economic statecraft. Instead of considering how those sanctions hurt the target state, this approach emphasises how groups within the target are affected differentially, and how these consequences change with the form of statecraft chosen.

(Kirshner 1997: 33)

The end of the Cold War inaugurated an era in which the actions of individuals became accountable before the international community. This is the justification that led to the creation of the Special Tribunals in the former Yugoslavia and

Rwanda, and the one that eventually led to the establishment of the International Criminal Court (ICC) in 1998 (Sadat 2002; Ralph 2005). Other principles, such as the growing importance of the doctrine of the responsibility to protect, brought attention to the consequences that the actions of states may have outside of their own borders. This is precisely when the humanitarian impact of sanctions entered the debate (Clawson 1993; Weiss *et al.* 1997; Mueller and Mueller 1999; Naylor 2001).

Already in 1992, the UN Secretary General Boutrus-Ghali urged the Security Council to prevent sanctions from hurting innocent people (von Braunmühl and Kulessa 1995), and in 1997 the Economic and Social Council of the UN stated that the states that signed the International Covenant on Economic, Social and Cultural Rights (1966) would be held responsible for human rights violations provoked by sanctions. The Committee concluded:

> While sanctions will inevitably diminish the capacity of the affected state to fund or support some of the necessary measures, the state remains under an obligation to ensure the absence of discrimination in relation to the enjoyment of these rights, and to take all possible measures, including negotiations with other states and the international community, to reduce to a minimum the negative impact upon the rights of vulnerable groups within the society.

> (United Nations, Economic and Social Council 1997)

'Who suffers' rather than 'how much does a state suffer' became central. In a 1995 report released by the Red Cross, Peter Walker wrote that sanctions against Iraq, Haiti and Serbia-Montenegro 'have paid only minimal political dividends at a very high price in human terms' (Walker 1995). Sanctions have proven to be more harmful to civilians than to the targeted elites. The Iraqi case stood out as a clear example of this failure as a widely reported study held UN sanctions responsible for the death of 500,000 children (UNICEF 1998; Ali and Iqbal 2000; Alnasrawi 2001).

Sanction practices needed to be changed because in contexts such as Iraq and Haiti, they were worse than the disease that they were required to fight (Mueller and Mueller 1999; Cortright and Lopez 2002b). The frequent alarms raised by many led the Swiss, the German and the Swedish Governments to cooperate on refining this foreign policy tool in three international conferences. The first conference on how to make targeted financial sanctions more effective was held in 1998 and 1999 in Interlaken, Switzerland. 'The result of the Interlaken process significantly advanced the collective understanding of the promise and feasibility of targeted financial sanctions.' (Wallensteen and Staibano 2005: 16) To maximise the utility of the two sessions of the conference, the Swiss government began a cooperation with the Watson Institute to develop a manual for practitioners – *Targeted Financial Sanctions* – that was submitted to the Security Council in 2001 (http://www.smartsanctions.ch). This research group released a subsequent manual with a variety of proposal to improve the effectiveness of financial targeted sanctions (Biersteker and Eckert 2006).

Interlaken paved the way for other similar events, one of which took place in Bonn-Berlin and another in Stockholm. The former aimed at improving the effectiveness of sanctions tailored against individuals or specific groups. The results of this conference have been published in *Design and Implementation of Arms Embargoes and Travel and Aviation Related Sanctions: Results of the 'Bonn-Berlin Process'* and were presented before the Security Council in 2001 (http://www.smartsanctions.de). Finally, the Swedish Government funded the Stockholm Process, a large international conference that was held in Sweden, wherein the activity was divided into three groups which provided recommendations on the implementation process of sanctions, the challenges posed by the legislation of nation-states, and on the opportunity to evade the sanctions from the targets. The results of the meeting were published in *Making Targeted Sanctions Effective: Guidelines for the Implementation of UN Policy Options'* (http://www.smartsanctions.se).

These international meetings, years of procedures and court rulings (as targeted individuals began to appeal against the decisions to sanction them) led to very elaborated procedures to list and delist individuals and groups that will be described later, but here the problem at hand is accurately defining the subject of this investigation since sanctions have evolved throughout the years.

What are sanctions today?

When one talks about sanctions, the almost immediate image is of an embargo, even though sanctions today seldom take the form of comprehensive economic blockades. The European Union indicates a list of restrictive measures that can fall under the category of sanctions:

- diplomatic sanctions (expulsion of diplomats, severing of diplomatic ties, suspension of official visits);
- suspension of cooperation with a third country;
- boycotts of sport or cultural events;
- trade sanctions (general or specific trade sanctions, arms embargoes);
- financial sanctions (freezing of funds or economic resources, prohibition on financial transactions, restrictions on export credits or investment);
- light bans;
- restrictions on admission.

(European Union, E.C. 2007)

This list can be further reduced to four categories: arms embargoes, travel bans, financial restrictions and commodity boycotts (Cortright and Lopez 2002b).

Arms embargoes encompass the decisions to ban the sale of weapons to a certain country, region, group or individual who may use them to carry out actions against peace processes, to undermine the stability of regimes and to violate human rights. These decisions may be directed to dual-use goods, related *matériel*, and services, such as training or technical support, to the targeted actors (Brzoska and Lopez 2009; Cortright and Lopez 2002a: 153–180; Bondi 2002).

Travel bans refer to the prohibition imposed on certain individuals to enter a given territory. This aims at causing discomfort or preventing banned individuals from carrying out actions. A simple example pertains to the new worldwide threat of terrorism. Of course, it would be easier for members of terrorist organisations to organise attacks in cities and other sites if they were allowed to travel in the targeted areas. Travel bans can also include aviation bans, which are prohibitions of commercial flights to operate across certain countries. Travel bans have been criticised as they would violate the human rights of blacklisted individuals in case they had to travel for medical reasons or they would undermine peace processes in a case where government leaders would not be allowed to take place in international meetings. Therefore, exemptions and exceptions are usually considered when the official decisions are made (Cortright and Lopez 2002a: 133–152; Cosgrove 2005).

Financial restrictions can take several forms, from the seizing of bank accounts, to the prohibition of financial transactions, to the prohibition of lending money to central banks of targeted countries. There is a lengthy list of measures that would fall under this category and they are imposed with the double objective of undermining the capabilities of targets and creating a personal discomfort that would, possibly, affect their decision-making (Cortright and Lopez 2002a: 93–114; Cortright et al. 2002; Newcomb 2002; Biersteker and Eckert 2008).

Commodity boycotts pertain to the action of banning trade of specific products, such as timber, copper and diamonds. This type of measure is imposed to create discomfort, but especially to alter the domestic distribution of power among actors. It is common for an authoritarian regime to enjoy the support of a strong group that exploits one particular market, so affecting that market can have an impact on the calculations of the elite and on the groups that support the ruling power (Cortright and Lopez 2002a: 181–200).

Comprehensive sanctions have evolved to target measures to avoid unintended consequences, but the problem is still present. For instance, aviation bans can affect the delivery of foodstuff or medicines whereby innocent civilians would suffer the most. The freeze of financial assets would affect creditors of blacklisted individuals. Commodity boycotts would affect the firms of the targeted sectors, which would balance their economic losses by decreasing the number of employees. Arms embargoes as well can have a perverse effect when the weak party cannot acquire weapons in the international market to protect itself from a stronger party. This can also be the case when denying training to police forces of certain countries, resulting in a force with lower skills and unable to limit the number of casualties or human rights violations in operations in urban centres (Doxey 2002; Weiss et al. 1997; Mueller and Mueller 1999).

Defining sanctions

Even if the new form of sanctions seems to be radically different from the previous one, the very act of sanctioning should be described by the same concept, whether the targets are individuals or nation-states. The act of sanctioning is an important sociological and legal behaviour and the definitions used in these two disciplines will help to clarify the object of this study.

In sociology, sanctions are seen as means to bring and ensure behavioural conformity among the actors of a political community, and they can be either positive or negative (Giddens 1994: 125). The former 'are defined as actual or promised rewards to B' (Baldwin 1971: 23) and they can be translated in incentives to targets, e.g. development aid or diplomatic statements (Baldwin 1985: 41). Instead, negative sanctions are viewed as 'actual or threatened punishments tó B' (Baldwin 1971: 23) and they come usually as a consequence of an action committed by a target that is deemed disputable by one or more senders. In a nutshell, sanctions play the role of fighting deviance in the system.

In law, a sanction corresponds to a negative sanction in sociology. The concept of positive sanctions has not been developed as much as that of negative sanctions, mostly because of the analytical difficulties in operationalising the separation between the two (Baldwin 2004: 13481). Having clarified this aspect, this research adopts the legalistic approach, and therefore the word 'sanction' – or 'restrictive measure' – refers to negative sanctions only, while the concept of 'positive sanctions' is expressed with the term *incentive* hereinafter.

The focus of this research is on international sanctions as a foreign policy method, but what exactly does that mean? Elaborating a clear definition of what sanctions are has been a daunting task in political science – finding a balance between extensity and intensity for this concept appears to be quite complicated. Similar to the concept of 'terrorism', for which over one hundred definitions have been identified (Schmid and Jongman 1988), sanctions encompass sieges and embargoes, but also travel bans and the freezing of financial assets of private citizens. For clear reasons, there are evident problems in conceptualising under the same term the three-month blockade of Masada by the Roman army in the spring of AD 73 (Miklowitz 1998) and the UN assets freeze of Charles Taylor's supporters (Boulden 2003).

Another important distinction that has to be made is that the term 'sanctions' has been associated with the one 'economic sanctions'. In broad terms, 'economic sanctions are generally seen as a foreign policy option that resides somewhere between diplomacy and military engagement' (Askari *et al.* 2003: 1), or as 'the use of economic measures directed to political objective' (Barber 1979: 376). In one of the most cited analysis on economic sanctions, Hufbauer *et al.* 'define(s) economic sanctions to mean the deliberate, government-inspired withdrawal, or threat of withdrawal, of customary trade or financial relations' (1990: 2).

However, the confusion between the terms 'economic sanctions' and 'sanctions' can be misleading. Indeed, economic sanctions have been used to refer to non-economic sanctions, such as travel bans or arms embargoes, but this is a vital mistake in the study of sanctions. Sanctioning is a method of pursuing objectives in foreign policy and sanctions can take the form of cultural, diplomatic, economic or military measures. Limiting the study of international sanctions to economic measures alone means to reduce the value of the findings of any empirical research. For instance, those who analysed the Hufbauer, Schott and Elliott (HSE) dataset to extrapolate general assessments on sanctions were, in fact, referring only to economic sanctions and were, therefore, committing the mistake of generalising their findings from biased sampling.

Since a definition of international sanctions is required in this investigation, the starting point for this reflection is provided by Nincic and Wallesteen, who have adopted the following definition:

> Economic sanctions (coercion) are actions initiated by one or more international actors (the senders) against one or more others (the targets) with either or all of two purposes: to punish the targets by depriving them of some value and/ or to make the targets comply with certain norms the senders deem important.

> (Nincic and Wallensteen 1983: 7)

This definition presents four elements that need to be evaluated. First, the confusion remains between 'economic sanctions' and 'sanctions'. Secondly, this definition does not include imposed sanctions that do not have a material impact on targets, leaving a few crucial aspects unclear. For instance, under which category should a sanction be when no material impact is expected? Would that be supposed to 'punish the target' or to 'make the target comply'? In the former, the sanction cannot punish the target if it does not have an impact and in the latter, it cannot make the target comply since the sanction does not have an effect on its costs/benefits calculations.

The third ambiguity is the uncertainty about whether sanctions are punitive or coercive tools, when the first element is always present (Nossal 1989). Sanctions are intended 'as penalties threatened or imposed as a declared consequence of the target's failure to observe international standards or international obligations' (Doxey 1987: 4). Logically, from this definition it can be argued that sanctions are, at least partially, effective by nature (Nossal 1989). As defined by the Longman English Dictionary, a sanction is 'an action, such as the stopping of trade, which is taken against a country that has behaved in an unacceptable way', or 'something that is intended to force people to obey a rule or moral standard'. In other words, a sanction comes always after an act of wrongdoing – defined on a case-by-case basis by senders and it is treated as exogenous in this study – and the nature of the sanctions (punitive or coercive) should not be mentioned in the definition. Finally, the definition also includes two purposes (or logics), but a definition of a policy tool should only say what it is, and not what it does.

In light of these considerations, international sanctions are defined here as politically motivated penalties imposed as a declared consequence of the target's failure to observe international standards or international obligations by one or more international actors (the *senders*) against one or more others (the *targets*).

This definition encompasses all the positive actions taken by senders to sanction targets, such as the League of Nations' measures against Italy after the invasion of Ethiopia in 1936, the UN's sanctions on Southern Rhodesia in order to force the white minority to accept the establishment of universal elections, the EU arms embargo on China after the events in Tiananmen Square, and also the more recent targeted sanctions against the military junta in Burma/Myanmar or the North Korean elite.

Identifying the problem: little understanding of sanctions

Although this research does not intend to contribute directly to the debate on the effectiveness of sanctions, the presentation of the discussion about whether sanctions work serves the objective of showing the low level of understanding that we have of international sanctions, despite this being the subject that received most of the attention in the past decades. The three answers available in the literature to the question of whether sanctions work, in fact, lead neither to any accumulation of knowledge nor to the creation of analytical tools to understand how sanctions do work. The presentation of this debate highlights two fundamental flaws in the literature of sanctions. First, there is little conceptualisation of sanctions and, secondly, there is barely any research on how the context influences the decision of policy makers to resort to different type of sanctions. These two are the issues that I intend to tackle in this book.

The widespread belief that the literature holds a negative evaluation of sanctions (Drezner 2003a: 10–11; Rogers 1996) does not seem to be accurate as the discussion offers many positions that can be organised in at least three different groups. First, there are the 'optimists' who think that sanctions work often enough to be considered as a valuable tool of foreign policy; secondly are the 'pessimists' who hold that sanctions are not effective; and thirdly are the 'relativists' who maintain that sanctions may work under certain circumstances.

Hufbauer, Schott and Elliott (HSE) stood up as leaders of the optimists when they challenged the generally accepted negative view of sanctions with their extensive empirical analysis of international sanctions that was first published in 1985.[1] In the second edition, published in 1990, the scholars of the Institute for International Economics (IIE) proved that economic sanctions were partially successful in 40 cases out of 115, that is to say 34 per cent of all the cases (Hufbauer *et al.* 1990). HSE reached their conclusions by using a qualitative comparative case studies approach. The updated research goes up to 2000 and identifies more than 200 cases of economic sanctions, but the result does not change that much: in April 2006, Elliott held that 80 cases out of 211 were considered partially successful (Elliott 2006), and the third edition of the HSE updated maintains that 70 out of 204 were successful (Hufbauer *et al.* 2007: 159).

Even though a 34 per cent rate of success seems sufficiently high to boost the enthusiasm towards this foreign policy tool, *Economic Sanctions Reconsidered*

---

1.   The 2nd edition was published in 1990 and the 3rd edition in 2007.

has been questioned for its prudent approach that underestimates the success rate of sanctions. Indeed, if senders threaten to impose restrictive measures on targets and the latter comply before the actual imposition, then sanctions should be deemed as successful (Smith 1995; Drezner 1999; Nooruddin 2002; Miers and Morgan 2002; Lacy and Niou 2004; Li and Drury 2004; Drury and Li 2006; Blake and Klemm 2006). From this perspective, sanctions would have a much higher rate of success than the 34 per cent stated by HSE.

The second group lies at the opposite end of the pole, claiming that 'sanctions do not work' (Pape 1997). One of the pioneering studies pertaining to the lack of effectiveness regarding economic sanctions belongs to Johan Galtung. Not only does the author claim that 'the probable effectiveness of economic sanctions is generally negative' (Galtung 1967: 409), but Galtung also sustains that the target could even be strengthened by sanctions. Accordingly, restrictive measures trigger hidden forces – adaptation to sacrifice, restructuring the economy to absorb the shock, smuggling, the collectivity being strengthened by the external threat, no identification with the attacker and a firm belief in one's own values – eventually reinforcing the will of the target in pursuing its policy, which is also referred to as 'the rally-around-the-flag effect' (Galtung 1967: 393). Other scholars reached the same conclusions by analysing the HSE database: only 5 of 115 attempts were successful according to Pape (Pape 1997; Pape 1998). Margareth Doxey wrote in 1987 about the impotence of sanctions in changing the behaviour of targets without the adoption of other measures (Doxey 1987: 92).

The group of the relativists is the last of the three and it is also the more complex and diverse, since it sustains that sanctions may not be a panacea to solve international disputes, but that they can be very useful under the right conditions (Hovi et al. 2005; Blanchard and Ripsman 1999; Cortright and Lopez 1995). For instance, Hovi, Huseby and Sprinz suggest that sanctions work only when the negotiation process fails because the target underestimates the real intention of the sender (Hovi et al. 2005: 480), and Blanchard and Ripsman believe that the effectiveness of sanctions is linked to the cost of non-compliance: if compliance is more harmful than non-compliance, then the target is not likely to yield (Blanchard and Ripsman 1999: 225).

Cortright and Lopez have on several occasions (1995, 1997 and 2002) stressed that the objective of sanctions may also be limited to making life harder for targets and that the signalling effect can be at times the most important objective. It is evident that these instances would require a careful evaluation of success irrespective of the behavioural change of targets (Brodie 1946; Liddell Hart 1947; Schelling 1960; Jervis 1970; Sagan 1993).

Another contribution to this discussion is represented by those who believe that in order to assess the effectiveness of sanctions, their objective should be looked at. The golden rule would be that sanctions work if they achieve the objective for which they were imposed. Daoudi and Dajani wrote that:

> sanctions may not have the power to topple governments, change political system or even induce drastic foreign policy changes, yet they have the power

to cut fresh inroads, impose heavy sacrifices on the target, and inflict deep internal cleavages in the political fabric of the target regime.

(Daoudi and Dajani 1983: 160–161)

They conclude by stating that '[we cannot ask] the pistol to inflict damage of which only the cannon is capable' (Daoudi and Dajani 1983: 168).

This brief presentation could proceed, but little would be added as this debate lingers in a limbo created by the lack of generally accepted concepts that are held together by loose assumptions based on empirical evaluations. Sanctions can reach a variety of goals, but this implies also that sanctions differ from one another and a proper classification is strongly needed. The contextualisation done by Doxey, Daoudi and Dajani also directs the attention towards another problem, namely the fact that sanctions are not imposed in a vacuum and the context in which senders decide to impose them may be essential to understanding why one type of sanction has been favoured over another. The aim of this work is to deal with these two problems by creating a systemic theoretical framework that can tell us more about how a specific system affects the selection of one sanction type over the others.

Not all sanctions are equal

Sanctions differ from each other and this fact is confirmed by the multiple attempts to create typologies of sanctions based on their objectives. The problem was treated in the literature in two ways: either sanctions can achieve foreign policy objectives or contribute to their achievement. The two debates that sprang from these two perspectives on the problem have failed to produce a shared conceptualisation to classify sanctions. While the first were based on the assumption that sanctions determine the achievement of foreign policy objectives, the latter did not specify how sanctions can contribute to foreign policy objectives. Common concepts are instrumental to cross-case comparison and knowledge accumulation, and a functional typology is strongly needed in the sanction literature.

James Barber (1979) created the conditions for a debate on the objectives of sanctions. Basing his analysis on the sanctions of the League of Nations on Italy, the US on Cuba and the British sanctions against Rhodesia, Barber listed a series of policy objectives that were pursued – the protection of the weak against the strong, the reduction of the will of ruling elites, the societal support for the imposition of the measures, the symbolic value of fighting against certain ideologies and the deterrence of similar actions by other actors – creating an interesting typology of primary, secondary and tertiary policy objectives.

There are 'primary objectives' which are concerned with the actions and behaviour of the state or regime against whom the sanctions are directed-the 'target state'. There are 'secondary objectives' relating to the status, behaviour and expectations of the government(s) imposing the sanctions-the 'imposing state'. And there are 'tertiary objectives', concerned with broader international considerations, relating either to the structure and operation of the international system as a whole to those parts of it which are regarded as important by the imposing states.

(Barber 1979: 270)

This classification is very effective, but it is not a typology of sanctions. Instead, this seems to be more about the 'targets' of sanctions rather than the objectives. More specifically, primary, secondary and tertiary refer to the spatial area where targets can be founded, and not to what sanctions are supposed to achieve.

The objectives of sanctions were not properly classified until 1986, when Lindsay (1986) suggested five categories under which sanctions could fall:

- compliance;
- subversion;
- deterrence;
- international symbolism; and
- domestic symbolism.

Lindsay constructed these categories on a database of 18 cases taken from previous contributions by Wallensteen (1968, 1983) and Hufbauer and Schott (1983, 1985). The five categories are not mutually exclusive as made clear by the author, an aspect that does not undermine the validity of the typology given that foreign policy instruments can commonly have multiple consequences that are readable through a variety of foreign policy aims.

Other attempts were made to conceptualise more intensively the objectives, but little results were achieved in this direction. For instance, Brady listed six goals for international sanctions:

1. To bring about a diplomatic loss of face.
2. To signal the target country that the resolve to resist its aggression is not lacking.
3. To signal the target country that its conduct is considered unacceptable by some and to raise the possibility that others will condemn such behaviour.
4. To reduce the possibility of a military conflict.
5. To alter the status of the target country as a dominant supplier of critical resources to friends and allies.
6. To reduce other forms of economic leverage that may be used by a potential adversary to harm the national interests of the initiator.

(Brady 1987: 298)

The possible interdependence between the objectives is not analysed and the classification is also undermined by confusion between means and ends that weakens this approach. For instance, is a 'diplomatic loss of face' an objective or it is the means to reach a behavioural change? Or is it deterrence? Is altering the status of the target country as a dominant supplier the final objective (end) or a way to discourage the target country from embarking on unwanted policies (means)?

Lindsay goes a little further than Brady as the categories refer to the final end of sanctions and Lindsay also indicates how the categories relate to each other:

Three results emerge from this analysis. First, trade sanctions rarely force compliance or subvert the target government and have a limited deterrent value. Yet they often succeed as international and domestic symbols. Their success in achieving these two goals explains why states continue to employ sanctions. Secondly, sanctions pose costs to the country applying them. They often reinforce the target state's behaviour and forfeit the initiator's future economic leverage over the target. Third, the goals of international and domestic symbolism undercut the goals of compliance and subversion.

(Lindsay 1986: 154)

The list of objectives was complemented by Nossal who noticed that 'if, however [...] sanctions are policy responses to acts perceived by the sender to be acts of moral wrongdoing, it is difficult to exclude the punitive objective of sanctions: in other words, the goal of punishing an act of wrongdoing' (Nossal 1989: 308; Doxey 1987: 93–94).

Barber did not create a typology of sanctions objectives, but the author brought to attention the domestic component of sanctions, which is also partly incorporated in Lindsay's typology, that is to say that lobbies and pressure groups are determinant in the decision-making process that leads a government to impose sanctions more than specific actions that have to be prevented (Kaempfer and Lowenberg 1992; Kaempfer and Lowenberg 1999; Shambaugh 1999; Fearon 1994; Fearon 1997). There may be little care for what the target does as: 'Sanctions are symbolic policies to please some interest group or divert attention away from the inability to really do something about the problem' (Dorussen and Mo 2001: 397). There are two types of domestic factors that can justify the imposition of international sanctions. The first is referred to in the literature as the 'audience costs' (Fearon 1994; Fearon 1997) or the 'agent veto' (Putnam 1988; Mo 1995) when internal actors determine the imposition, or the lack of imposition, because of particular interests. The second is referred as 'rent-seeking' (Dorussen and Mo 2001), which is when senders decide to impose sanctions to please the requests of internal lobbies.

Following Barber's typology, the tertiary category is also very interesting. While most of the empirical evaluations do not include this aspect and most of the bureaucrats working for international organisations would not agree with this statement, sanctions can very well be imposed to uphold a norm or to shape the international environment. These types of sanctions have been treated in the debate and they are usually referred to as 'symbolic measures' (Schwebach 2000). Lindsay himself used this term to label two categories out of five possible types, which indirectly confirms that the symbolic aspect of sanctions could hardly be explained in a similar way to other types of measures. Symbolic sanctions can either show that the sender is really committed to engage with targets or it can also indicate that the sender is not willing to commit resources on a cause that may not be worth fighting for. Indeed, whether symbolic or not, the imposition of sanctions could be the last step before the decision to use force to settle the dispute or the crisis as mentioned above.

While Barber was unsuccessful in creating a useful classification of sanctions, Lindsay's typology is often used to interrupt any discussion on the objectives that sanctions can achieve and on the need of creating a more useful categorisation. This observation emerges from my experience in conferences and in reading reviews of articles submitted for publication. Reviewers often consider Lindsay's views as definitive, so little contribution is brought to the debate when scholars attempt to move away from that categorisation. Despite the apparent consensus, I would like to disagree with Lindsay's categorisation, which suffers from three main deficiencies. First, the typology is generous: five categories appear to be too many to allow for any analytical utility originating from the adoption of the typology. Secondly, there is little effort in making the typology operational and therefore the research is not replicable. These two elements together would explain why this typology has received very little empirical follow-up since its creation. The third aspect is highlighted by those who think that sanctions do not have 'individual' objectives.

Instead, sanctions can only contribute to the achievement of overall policy objectives of political actions. For instance, an interesting approach has been developed through the lenses of the 'bargaining model' (Wagner 1988; Cortright and Lopez 1995; Morgan and Schwebach 1997). The underlining concept of this model is that sanctions are only one aspect of conflict management and their use can grant the sender greater leverage over the target in order to extract better concessions (Morgan and Schwebach 1997). In other words, sanctions are only one of the variables among many that can influence the outcome of an interaction between two actors; therefore, it would be more appropriate to reason in terms of gaining or losing 'bargaining power' rather than in terms of success or failure of a sanction (Baldwin 1985; Cortright and Lopez 2000). As Elliott wrote, 'Analysing whether and how sanctions *contribute* to foreign policy outcomes, rather than whether they *cause* them, leads to important differences in research method' (Elliott 1998: 51).

Bargaining theory provides further clarifications on this. Wagner defines bargaining power in the following way:

> If two individuals bargain over the division of a sum of money, how the money is divided provides an unambiguous measure of bargaining power: to say that Bargainer 1 is more powerful than Bargainer 2 means simply that Bargainer 1 receives more than half the sum of money to be divided.

> (Wagner 1988: 468)

If sanctions are to create bargaining edges, then knowing the overall policy objective does not tell much about what sanctions can or cannot do as a bargaining advantage is, by definition, short of reaching the full political objective.

The scholars who adopted the spatial theory model of crisis bargaining to analyse sanctions raised the same point and concluded:

Sanctions can be useful under fairly restrictive conditions and perhaps may enhance the impact of other policies. [...] In most cases, a state imposing sanctions on its opponents can expect an outcome that is just about the same as would be obtained without sanctions.

(Morgan and Miers 1999: 46)

This approach contrasts with the efforts to identify the objectives of international sanctions and the epistemological trap is set. If we are to analyse sanctions looking at their objectives, we are then confined to analyse them with the expectation that they will achieve the objective assigned to them. On the contrary, if sanctions are only one of the ways that the sender can use to achieve political objectives, then a typology of sanctions based on policy objectives would not provide any useful analytical tool to study real world cases. In brief, Lindsay's typology is not sufficient to understand sanctions and this book proposes a solution to the fallacies in the literature with the creation of a typology based on how sanctions influence their targets, as illustrated in Chapter 4.

The missing piece of the puzzle: explaining the variance of sanctions

If it is acknowledged that not all sanctions are equal, then the literature should flourish with research aiming at explaining the variance of sanctions. Surprisingly, this question has received little attention so far, but knowing why one type of sanction is imposed over others would allow for better designing and better understanding of the conditions under which sanctions can achieve what objective.

There are virtually no systemic (system approach) and systematic (based on large and comparative analysis) studies on this subject. There are only loose associations that were not tested empirically on a wide range of cases, such as the assumption that light sanctions are imposed when governments do not intend to commit in specific crises, so they have to compromise between the unwillingness to pay any costs and the reputational damage of inaction. Sanctions imposed by the UN to halt the genocide in Rwanda would fall under this category. It was clearly too late and the sanctions were too light to have any valuable impact on the events, but the Security Council was under strong pressures to do something about it.

The form taken by sanctions has been sometimes associated to the actions of internal economic lobbies. For instance, companies and firms may play a crucial role in shaping sanctions, as documented in *Feeling Good or Doing Good with Sanctions* on the case of the US (Preeg 1999). An example of this instance is the episode of the sanctions on Haiti in 1993, when a series of US-owned industries in Haiti were exempted by the ban on trade imposed to force the military junta to return power to President Aristide (Gibbons 1999).

Other loose associations have been established between specific forms of sanctions and the type of behaviour that is intended to be punished. For instance, during an interview with an EU official working for the Council of Ministers it emerged how EU members imposed arms embargoes and a travel ban when the violation was less serious, and a freeze of assets and a commodity boycott for more serious violations.[2] This point is also expressed in the book by Wallensteen and Staibano (Wallensteen and Staibano 2005) on international sanctions. However, the former (expressed in the anecdote) reports an inductive lesson, while the latter (expressed by the authors) throws the concept out there without going into details.

There are two obstacles for those who want to tackle this challenge: first, a functional and operational typology of sanctions has to be created; secondly, a systemic approach should be preferred to an analytic one in order to approximate the creation of a theoretical framework that would help in understanding the constraining factors that are conducive towards one specific type of sanctions. These two tasks will be carried out in chapter three, but as the ambition of this study is to create a systemic theory of sanctions, it is necessary to present what it is meant by that.

Reductionist v Systemic Theories: a neorealist foundation for sanctions

Reductionist (or analytical) analyses of international politics focus on the interactions between the units of the system, while a systemic approach focuses on the pressures that contextual frames exercise on the units in order to reduce the range of possible behaviours. This second approach, which is based on the one elaborated by Kenneth Waltz in his Theory of International Politics, is adopted here and adapted to the cluster of sanctions episodes that is isolated and analysed as if it were a system on its own. The stated aim is to develop a systemic theoretical framework of international sanctions.

Waltz drew a line between reductionist theories of international politics, which concentrate causes at the individual or national level, and systemic ones, which conceive of causes operating at the international level (Waltz 1979: 18). Instead of writing about the relations among the units of the system, I would like to focus on how the structure of the system affects the interacting units (Waltz 1979: 40). Waltz justified the need for a systemic approach after 'the repeated failure of attempts to explain international outcomes analytically – that is, through examination of interacting units' (Waltz 1979: 67), and the justification follows similar lines in the field of sanctions.

Theories are a set of laws – namely empirical associations – that 'explain regularities of behaviour and lead one to expect that the outcomes produced by interacting units will fall within specified ranges' (Waltz 1979: 68) and a systemic approach focuses on '[...] how much of the outcomes their [units] actions and interactions produce, can be explained by forces that operate at the level of the system, rather than at the level of the units' (Waltz 1979: 69).

The concept of explanation defined by Waltz is adopted in this research so as 'to say why the range of expected outcomes falls within certain limits; to say why patterns of behaviour recur; to say why events repeat themselves, including events that none or few of the actors may like' (Waltz 1979: 69).

---

2. Interview with official at the European Commission, carried out in Brussels in April 2008.

Hence, by looking at the structure wherein sanctions are imposed we can 'describe and understand the pressure states are subject to'. However, it cannot predict and tell how states will behave. Instead, 'System theories [...] are theories that explain how the organisation of a realm acts as a constraining and disposing force on the interacting units within it. Such theories tell us about the forces the units are subject to'. The outcome becomes than more predictable, but this would not be a theory of foreign policy, where it is explained why the interacting units decide what they do.

> Systems theories explain why different units behave similarly and, despite their variations, produce outcomes that fall within expected ranges. Conversely, theories at the unit level tell us why different units behave differently despite their similar placement in a system.
>
> (Waltz 1979: 71–72)

Therefore, one important premise is that units are taken as unitary actors here and a structure only 'designates a set of constraining conditions':

> Agents and agencies act; systems as wholes do not. But the actions of agents and agencies are affected by the system's structure. In itself, a structure does not directly lead to one outcome rather than another. Structure affects behaviour within the system, but does so indirectly.
>
> (Waltz 1979: 74)

This is indeed an adaptation of the systemic approach to the compromise of the middle range theory requirement. In a way, this book aims at the creation of a systemic middle range theory of sanctions that could shed light on the elements that pressure the units to impose different types of sanctions in different contexts.

The methods: classificatory typology, QCA, and case studies

This book will adopt a systemic approach to the study of sanctions. One of the shortcomings of this undertaking is the limited usable knowledge that can be extrapolated from a study that does not focus on explaining the interactions of the system's units. The limitations of such a study are reduced by a middle range approach. Basically, this occurs by narrowing down the focus of investigation to a more specific 'policy-contingency'. This means that if an episode of sanction is intended as a system of the matter that we intend to study, then the focus of a theory is narrowed and the insights from its use could generate usable knowledge (Keohane 1986: 188).

The concept of a middle range theory combined with the intention to take a systemic approach makes this study a unique experiment of theoretical innovation. The system would be limited to the context in which sanctions are imposed, thereby isolated from 'higher' structures, and the middle range scheme is motivated by the narrower focus of the research on sanctions: 'deliberately limited in [its] scope [in order] to explain one subclass of a general phenomenon' (George and Bennet 2005: 266).

The relations between the context and the type of sanctions are sought in three different steps. First, the creation of the theoretical framework will depend on the construction of a classificatory typology of sanctions and on the definition of the system. Secondly, the first empirical evaluation will be done with a crispy set-Qualitative Comparative Analysis (cs-QCA) to prove the plausibility of the model and to verify that the expected associations hypothesised by the theory occur. Thirdly, typical case study designs are adopted in the final part of the book in order to complement the shortcomings of the qualitative comparative analysis.

The ideal type of classificatory typology is characterised by mutual exclusiveness, namely that one entry cannot belong to more than one category at any moment. This will be limited to the primary, or dominant, logic at work identified for a sanctions episode, but it is acknowledged that in the real world some overlapping is expected, especially if one considers secondary and tertiary logics.

The selection of the cs-QCA method, pioneered by Charles Ragin in 1987, has a two-fold advantage. On one hand, it allows the adoption of medium N samples, as in this study. Both statistical and case-study methods are not appropriate to deal with fewer than 50 and more than 10 cases. Originally, the number of episodes taken into consideration did not pass this threshold, but the development of the database led to exceed this limit, which does not undermine the importance of the finding in any way. Furthermore, statistical methods acquire utility for the analysis of databases with large N and when the main intent of the research is theory-testing (Ragin 1987). With a focus on theory-making, this research has favoured QCA and case-study methods.

The second major advantage is the possibility of using Boolean logic, which 'allows us to examine the possibility that X has a different effect on Y when combined with the presence of absence of other variables' (Gerring 2001: 207). QCA serves the purpose of theory development because it allows the researcher to test the causal effect on the DV of several IVs and their combinations. Each IV is codified in high and low terms and the causal link between the variables will be explored. QCA encompasses the principle of causal complexity, which implies that events do not have a mono-causal explanation, but rather that they can be explained only by looking at multiple IVs.

Despite these positive aspects, cs-QCA presents two problems that have to be addressed. The first one is the loss of information through dichotomic operationalisations. Political phenomena cannot be represented in black and white terms, because reality lies always somewhere in the middle. Since the purpose of a theoretical framework is to provide an analytical tool that may contribute to explaining and understanding international sanctions, and not to picture every single nuance of real world events, a process of simplification is necessary and also desirable. However, the simplification of the world is a double-edged sword: the more it is simplified, the less accurate is its representation. Charles Ragin was aware of this problem and developed a more complex version of QCA where the variables are presented with a 'fuzzy-logic' – named fuzzy set-QCA (fs-QCA). This means that a variable is no longer represented in black and white terms, but it can be rather described in degrees of strength (Ragin 2000). Even though this study appreciates this further development of QCA, a crispy-logic QCA is adopted here for the sake of brevity. Furthermore, a theoretical framework should make the reality intelligible, but the inevitable loss of data is counterbalanced by the employment of the case-study method in the last part of the research.

This method has also been criticised for its deterministic character (Goldthorpe 1997: 4; Mahoney 2000: 391; Wagemann 2008: 6). Since the Boolean logic does not tolerate exceptional cases, sanctions episodes that deviate from the patterns of expected associations adopted may be left out from the sample. However, this is a false problem, because it is possible to interpret the results through probabilistic lenses, as shown by Ragin himself in a later work based on: 'a) the degree of membership of a case in a category (which can be scored, and correspondingly weighted) and b) the frequency with which a designated causal path can be found' (Gerring 2001: 209; Ragin 2006). This is precisely the intention of a systemic approach. Hence, given certain combinations of IVs, a certain outcome is more likely to happen.

The last step of the research design is to analyse typical case studies of sanctions in order to verify and further examine if both the hypotheses and findings from the QCA analysis are the product of causal mechanisms. A QCA analysis can provide correlations at best, but it is only with within-case analysis and in-depth process tracing that an expected association from deductive theorisation can be properly explained. Six typical cases from the experience of the UN and the EU will be used. A typical case study maximises the representation of specific categories to which the case belongs, it is supposed to epitomise the most usual case of a particular population so to represent it at best (Gerring 2001: 218–9; Bennett and Elman 2007).

The UN and the EU have been selected for specific reasons. First, the systemic theoretical framework is based on the assumption that the actors are unitary. Thus, selecting the cases according to the least-likely case criterion would lead to the following conclusion: if the analysis works for multilateral organisations, then it will work for nation-states as well. Secondly, the UN and the EU are at the forefront for innovating sanctions from comprehensive to targeted. Therefore, studying these cases since the beginning of this evolution consents to have a wider variance in the forms of sanctions imposed, which would result in a stronger empirical testing for the theoretical model. Additionally, the UN and the EU resorts to targeted sanctions more frequently and more commonly than nation-states. This ensures that the analysis and the framework are tested with the greatest degree of variance. Third, the real novelty in the sanctions field, as illustrated in the chapter, is that international organisations are resorting to sanctions in a way that used to be carried out by nation-states. It is more relevant to see how models and concepts drawn from the analysis of nation-states apply to international organisations, rather than to states themselves. While the enlargement of the database is certainly desirable, given the three justifications presented above, it would not be appropriate to extend the database in this study in order to maintain the added value of cs-QCA method that is well achieved with a medium N. The inclusion of more cases could water down the findings and dissipate the efforts of theory making and concept formation.

A final methodological note regards the process of data gathering: the findings published in this book are the result of three years of secondary and primary source research. It is important to point out that the information disclosed in the text is non-confidential since there was little need for the use of undisclosed documents to support the testing of the theoretical model. Interviews were conducted with officials at the United Nations and the European Union headquarters in New York (May 2008) and Brussels (April 2008, May 2009, February 2010) and their accounts are included without revealing their personal identities solely based on the institution that they represent and the general period of the meeting. Finally, sanctions episodes are presented with labels that contain information that helps to distinguish them from one another. Labels are presented as the following: sender/ country in which targets operate/year of imposition of sanctions/year of sanction lifting (the term 'present' is used for sanctions in force in December 2010). For example, UN sanctions on Rwanda (from 1994 to 1995) are labelled as UN/Rwanda – 1994 to 1995 or EU sanctions on Guinea (still in force since 2009) are labelled as EU/Guinea – 2009 to present.

chapter three | a systemic approach to sanctions

This chapter aims at defining the conceptual bases for a systemic theoretical framework of sanctions. In other to reach this goal we must take a two-step procedure. First, we need to classify sanctions in categories that can be useful to highlight their different logics at work. Secondly, the 'system' of sanctions needs to be defined and limited as required by the characteristics of a middle range approach.

The DV will be the mechanic, or logic, of sanctions at play. Instead of classifying sanctions according to their objectives, I look at how sanctions influence targets. To this extent, sanctions can coerce, constrain and signal primary and secondary targets. This typology is operationalised with two dimensions that entail the feasibility of the demands attached to the sanctions and their direct material impact. The IV is the 'system of sanctions' and it is constituted by three elements: the level of threat to the sender represented by the targets or by the crisis, the salience of the crisis and its complexity. These three variables together account for the interests of senders (threat), the normative and social pressure on senders (salience) and the will/capability gap (complexity).

This theoretical framework allows us to formulate expectations on the constraints and opportunities created by the context on policy makers when they decide to impose sanctions. Thereby, in general terms, higher values of threat would most likely lead to coercive or constraining sanctions; higher values of salience would most likely lead to constraining sanctions, and higher values of complexity would lead to constraining or signalling sanctions. The IVs that characterise the context or the system of sanctions are dichotomous in this research; therefore, eight specific hypotheses are possible and will be described in this chapter.

Sanctions are used even if it is not clear why. This study focuses on the logic of sanctions through the development of a conceptual framework that could make the understanding of sanctions episodes easier and the explanation of their purpose possible.

The chapter is divided in three parts. The first part describes the DV and the three ways how sanctions can influence their targets. The second section presents the IV and introduces the three elements that constitute it – threat, salience and complexity. The third part summarises how the variables are expected to relate to each other; in other words, this part deals with the hypotheses of the research.

The theoretical framework: the dependent variable

Not all sanctions are created equal, so we need a functional typology that would guide us to understand their differences. The creation of a typology is possible only if sanctions are broadly defined and if the classification can be replicable and operationalisable. By 'broadly defined' it is meant that any classification of sanctions must acknowledge that sanctioning is only one of four foreign policy methods and they are never imposed alone, which means that sanctions can always and only contribute to foreign policy goals (Baldwin 1971; Lawson 1983; van Bergeijk 1994; Nincic 2008). By 'replicable and operationalisable' it is meant that any typology of sanctions should be based on criteria that can be assessed and replicated across time and space so that comparisons become possible and knowledge can accumulate.

Placing sanctions in the foreign policy toolbox

Creating a definition of sanctions that would take the broader picture into consideration means that sanctions have to be placed in the foreign policy toolbox. Sanctioning is only one action of which foreign policy makers can avail themselves in their external relations. The other actions with third parties would be using violence, offering material gains and resorting to diplomacy. Their combined use can lead to the achievement of foreign policy objectives, while the individual contribution for each of the methods adopted can only increase, or decrease, the probability to achieve, fully or in part, a specific foreign policy goal. Table 3.1 introduces the overall argument of this study by attempting to answer this question.

This table has been created by integrating and developing the works of Baldwin, Art and Haas. In *Economic Statecraft,* Baldwin's goal is to define how a state can use economic levers to achieve political goals (1985); in 'To What Ends Military Power?', Art describes the different ways in which force can be used (1980); finally, in *International Conflicts*, Hass presents how conflicts can be articulated (1974). Here, the goal is to describe what foreign policy options are at the disposal of international actors.

The different policy instruments, divided into domains such as propaganda, diplomacy, economic statecraft and military statecraft, are defined as 'the area of policy instruments' (Baldwin 1985: 10–16). Policy instruments – 'tools', 'means' and 'levers' could be used as synonyms – are 'policy options available to decision makers in pursuing a given set of objectives' (Baldwin 1985: 12). An actor can be persuaded peacefully, by rewarding or sanctioning certain behaviours, and by physically forcing him into doing something. These are defined as the method of influencing another actor, which is: 'the way of influencing the target(s)' (Rummel 1963; Rummel 1966; Tanter 1966; Haas 1974). This can also be defined as the 'logic' or the 'mechanic' of sanctions.

Power relations can be either cooperative or non-cooperative. In both cases, the purpose of any action is defined as 'what a policy instrument is used for' or 'in what ways the target(s) is (are) influenced' (Art 1980). If the relation is cooperative, actor A can signal agreement with B, support him in achieving his goal, or cooperate with him in the achievement of his goal. If the relation is non-cooperative, A can signal disagreements with B, constrain him in achieving his goal, or coerce him to do something that he would not do otherwise. An exercise of power is intended to achieve a goal – 'aim', 'objective' and 'end' will be used

Table 3.1: A synoptic table of statecraft in foreign policy

Domains (Baldwin 1985)	Methods, Mode, Techniques (Haas 1974; Art 1980)	Tools, means, instruments, levers	Purpose (Art 1980) Scope (Lasswell and Kaplan 1950) Logic or mechanic		Ends, aims, objectives, goals	Targets (primary and secondary) (Baldwin 1999/2000)
			Cooperative	Non-cooperative		
Propaganda	Peaceful	Statements				
Diplomacy	Incentives	Diplomatic advantages Economic aids Etc.				
Economic statecraft	Sanctions	Financial Restrictions Travel Bans Arms Embargo Commodity Boycotts	To signal To support To cooperate	To signal To constrain To coerce	Milieu Possession Survival (Wolfer 1962)	Individuals Entities Domestic Audience States International organisations International Audiences
Military statecraft	Violence	Strategic bombing Invasion Etc.				

STATECRAFT

as synonyms[1] – and goals can be framed in different ways, for example by dividing them in the categories of survival, possession and milieu goals (Wolfer 1962). The target – 'who is to be influenced' – can vary. The primary target can be the actor that has been directly hit by sanctions, while the secondary target can be another actor that is supposed to change its costs/benefits calculation according to the imposition of sanctions upon the primary target, or also an audience, either domestic or international, that has to be signalled about something (Baldwin 1985; Baldwin 1999/2000).

To summarise, sanctions represent only one instrument in the foreign policy toolbox and they can achieve particular goals under specific circumstances. This research focuses on the purposes (logic or mechanic) of sanctions in non-cooperative relations, namely the use of restrictive measures to coerce, constrain or signal targets to create a classificatory typology of sanctions (Elman 2005: 297).

The three categories

Sanctioning is an exercise of power in foreign policy, and power has been described with three dimensions: winning conflicts, limiting alternatives and shaping normality (Berenskoetter and Williams 2007), which can be translated in coercing, constraining and signalling. There have been other attempts to formulate typologies on how sanctions influence targets, but these three aspects were not all present. For instance, dichotomous typologies were elaborated to maintain that sanctions can pursue substantive or symbolic goals (Doxey 1987: 10; Shambaugh 1999: 13) and expressive or instrumental motives (Galtung 1967: 412). Others have generated tripartite typologies of purposes, such as the one elaborated for air power to coerce, to deny or to punish, but adaptable to sanctions as well (Pape 1996: 1–12). However, these three forms of power, namely to coerce, constrain and signal are never included in one single typology.[2]

Sanctions are usually understood only through their coercive aspect, which implies that targets change their behaviour to avoid bearing the costs imposed by the sanctions, but this view presents three fundamental fallacies. First, it is taken for

---

1.   In 1971, Doxey talks about ultimate and intermediate goals: 'In the first place, the nature and circumstances of the crisis will determine specific final goals, while the tactical decision to use a certain form of coercion will establish intermediate goals. If, for instance, the final goals were the ending of hostilities between two states and the peaceful settlement of their dispute, and military measures were selected as appropriate means of coercion, then the intermediate goal would be to introduce an effective military presence into the area of hostilities, which would induce the delinquent state, or states, to abandon the use of force. On the other hand, if the ultimate goal of international enforcement were to prevent a threatened act of aggression, and economic weapons were selected as instruments of coercion, then the intermediate goal would be to deprive the would-be aggressor of the means of waging war, or to make it too costly for him to do so.' (Doxey 1971: 92)

2.   Albeit in different terms, the separation between coercing and constraining was already elaborated by George in 1971 (George 1971: xi) and later by others (Barber 1979; Pape 1992; Haass 1998), while the importance of signalling was clear to many (Kaempfer and Lowenberg 1992: 7; Cortright and Lopez 2000: 16; Schwebach 2000: 203; Martin and Laurenti 1997: 19).

granted that targets are always capable of complying with the demands attached to sanctions. Secondly, sanctions are always expected to have a material impact. Thirdly, the final objective of a sanction is to change the behaviour of targets. In fact, these conditions are rarely present together when sanctions are imposed. Senders may formulate requests that cannot be met by targets and sanctions do not always have a direct material impact on targets, namely they do not always bite. These two criteria are labelled 'request feasibility' (defined as the acceptability of the senders demand by the target), and 'direct material impact' (defined as the economic burden or the tangible discomfort directly imposed on targets by sanctions), and are used to distinguish the different episodes of sanctions. Finally, the primary objective of sanctions may not be the behavioural change of their target. A more functional typology is necessary to leap forward in the sanctions debate.

The most common definition of 'power' refers to the capacity of senders to make targets do what they would not do otherwise, but power is also the ability to limit the alternatives of targets and to send signals to certain constituencies. These three types of power in this investigation suggest that sanctions can coerce, constrain and signal as summarised in Table 3.2.

Table 3.2: Types of sanctions

Type	Logic	Possible positive outcome	Cases
Coercion	Impose a burden on targets to affect their cost/benefit calculation in order to do something	Behavioural change Creating a bargaining chip	UN on Libya EU on Belarus
Constraint	Impose a burden on targets to prevent the target from doing something	Stop targets Impose a burden on target	UN on Iraq EU on Zimbabwe
Signal	Signal the position of the sender without the imposition of a direct burden	Signal commitment Establish international standards Exercise diplomatic pressure Please audience Behavioural change under logics that different from cost imposed	UN on Rwanda EU on DRC

Coercion

This category of sanctions includes the cases of restrictive measures imposed in order to increase the probability of making a target behave in a way that it would not otherwise do. In other words, the sender intends to change the behaviour of the target and sanctions attach a cost on certain acts in order to affect the target's costs/benefits calculation. In this category, expected positive outcomes would be the actual behavioural change of the target, the greater probabilities for a behavioural change or the improvement of the bargaining position of the sender versus the target. Ideally, coercive sanctions aim at increasing the cost of all but one policy option available to targets.

The characteristics of a coercive sanction are high feasibility and high impact. First, working on the assumption that political actors enjoy total freedom of action until they endanger their own survival, the target should be able to acquiesce without encountering the risk of political suicide; otherwise it will always prefer to resist sanctions rather than to change behaviour. Consequently, senders have to make 'feasible' requests if they want to have them satisfied. Secondly, sanctions have to have a direct material impact on the target in order to affect its costs/benefits calculations. The impact has to be direct and there must be a material cost on the target if the mechanics of sanctions are to be coercive, which means that a target may change its behaviour in order to avoid the burden imposed by the measures taken by the sender.

Constraint

This category includes the cases of sanctions imposed in order to thwart a target in the pursuit of its policy. Whereas for a coercive sanction a target has to do something to meet the demand of the sender, for a constraint type of sanction the target is required not to do something. In this category, expected positive outcomes would be that of slowing down a target's implementation plans, increasing costs of actions or lowering the marginal utility that the target expects to gain from the achievement of a specific objective. Ideally, constraining sanctions impose a cost on one specific action that targets intend to undertake.

Similar to coercive sanctions, the measures under this category must have a direct impact on a target, but they usually make unfeasible requests. There must be a direct material impact in order to undermine what targets can or cannot do in. However, the voluntary behavioural change is not required on the side of targets when they cannot do what senders are demanding without endangering their existence. Targets cannot comply with the demands because compliance is incompatible with the political survival of the individuals or entities that have to make the decision or simply because there is no compatibility between the interest of senders and targets. This is not to say that senders do not know about this when they design sanctions, but it is to underline how reducing the list of possibilities from the target's menu of choice, which can include their capacity to survive at all, can be a legitimate objective in foreign policy that senders intend to pursue. To this extent, designing a demand in an unfeasible way could also be a political move to impose regime change or to simply deny certain actors their freedom to manoeuvre.

When looking at the most recent developments from comprehensive to smart sanctions, constraining sanctions are often used to fight groups or entities that are not willing to cooperate with the established norms of the international society. In other words, since the new threats of a post-cold war scenario are fought also with law enforcement techniques, this concept could be simplified by saying that targeted sanctions are to the international systems what penal codes are to states. Within domestic environments, laws that forbid murders or frauds are not useless because murders and frauds are committed. In fact, penal and civil laws limit the number of deviant cases and complicate the life of those who are willing to challenge the rules, but they cannot prevent all of them from acting. Similarly, targeted sanctions are not useless because terrorist attacks still occur or civil wars do not end right after the imposition of constraints on the actors; they could be useful and effective if they limit the capabilities of the target to carry out its acts.

Signal

This category includes the cases of restrictive measures imposed with the objective of sending a 'message' to one or more targets. Sending a message may contribute to the achievement of different goals, which includes but are not limited to the behavioural change of a target. However, the mechanic, namely how this behavioural change is brought about, would be different from a mechanic where the target changes its behaviour to avoid a material cost imposed by sanctions. Here, a target would change its behaviour to avoid reputational costs, to enhance its future gains, or to enjoy the benefit of multilateral diplomacy. These mechanisms would no need a direct material impact of sanctions to be triggered. Furthermore, a signalling sanction may use the primary target as a means to convey a message either to a domestic or an international audience. For instance, senders may want to please a domestic lobby about a specific crisis, or test how other international actors create a certain expectation on what senders will do in similar cases in the future.

While the two dimensions of feasibility and impact are important to distinguish between coercive and constraining sanctions, signalling sanctions have the only requirement not to have a material impact on targets. Therefore, regardless from the feasibility of the demand, this type of sanction differs in nature from the other types and should be analysed accordingly.

Signalling sanctions may have indirect material impacts, such as causing the loss of foreign direct investment in targeted countries, but as this would go beyond the direct control of senders, it cannot be considered as part of the mechanic of sanctions. Regardless of the specificities of each sanctions episode, the imposition of sanctions is expected to contribute to shape normality in what it is allowed and what it is forbidden in the international system.

Concepts in action

Once these three different concepts have been defined, how do we know them when we see them? This typology represents a leap forward in the existing literature as it can be replicated in other instances of sanctions. The typology is operationalised around basic assumptions about two factors that have been selected inductively.

The first factor is feasibility. If a sanction is feasible, then the target knows what to do and it can do it because the request does not endanger its existence. On the other hand, if the request cannot be accepted by the target, then the goal of sanctions cannot be its behavioural change. In this last case, the imposition of a constraint type of sanction is more likely. The feasibility of the demand is constituted by two dimensions: preciseness and practicality. Preciseness refers to whether the request has been articulated enough so that a target knows what to do to satisfy the will of the sender, and practicality means that the request can be met by the target without compromising its existence.

The demand is classified as precise if a sender asks a target to do one or more specific actions (e.g. Libya had to hand in two alleged terrorists for trial). If UN Security Council Resolutions or the European Council common positions include general normative benchmarks requesting adherence to moral values, then the demand will be classified as vague (e.g. a vague request would be one to improve the situation of human rights) as no specific requirement is set. The demand is classified as practical if the target can comply with it without endangering its existence (e.g. Kim Yong Il is able to comply without danger for his regime). On the contrary, if compliance means demise for the target, the demand will have a low practicality (e.g. Al-Qaida members are asked to stop their acts). Table 3.3 presents a general list of indicators used to determine the degree of feasibility.

The evaluation of practicality is strongly linked to the type of target that is sanctioned since not all international actors behave according to the same principles (Schneider and Post 2003). The framework differentiates between rational, ideological and criminal actors.[3] The first category encompasses actors that think and act strategically to increase their economic well-being (e.g. Uzbekistan, Libya); the second category regards those actors that reason in terms of costs/benefits, but they have built their legitimacy in opposition to the sender and deem it more important than the cost that they are shouldering for sanctions (e.g. Iran, Cuba); the third category involves actors that base their very existence in resisting sanctions: any costs that could be imposed upon them will not change their behaviour and compliance is not an option (e.g. Al-Qaida, National Union for the Total Independence of Angola – UNITA). This variable will be an important element to analyse the feasibility of the demands. Table 3.4 summarises the three categories.

Both preciseness and practicality are measured in a three point ordinal scale and are weighed as follows: low (1), medium (2), and high (3). Since the variable feasibility has two dimensions, high and low, the rates for the dimensions are mul-

---

3.   A similar typology has been used for the analysis of different types of terrorism, see (Hacker 1976).

tiplied and the classification in either high or low feasibility is defined as follows: if the combined score is less than five, then the feasibility is low; if the combined score is more than five, then the feasibility is high. Table 3.5 summarises this point.

Table 3.3: Feasibility of demand

		Kinds of evidence (the list is not exhaustive)
Preciseness	1: vague, the target does not know what to do	– the demands stated in official documents – the coherence of states after the approval of the official documents
	2: medium, the target has a partial knowledge of what to do	
	3: precise, the target knows what to do	
Practicality	1: little, the request cannot be met by the target	– regime change – domestic situation of targeted groups – whether there are demands at all
	2: medium, meeting the request may comport high danger for the target	
	3: high, the request can be met by the target	

Table 3.4: Taxonomy of explicit targets

	Goal	Costs/benefits	Sensitivity to costs
Rational	Well-being	Yes	High
Ideological	Legitimacy from confrontation	Reputational	Reputational
Criminal	Free ride within the system	No	Low

Table 3.5: Degrees of feasibility

		Practicality		
		1	2	3
Preciseness	1	Low	Low	Low
	2	Low	Low	High
	3	Low	High	High

The second factor is 'direct material impact'. It is important to note that the lack of material impact does not mean that senders lack the political will to effectively play a role in the crisis. For instance, light sanctions can be imposed with a concern linked to the impact on innocent civilians or to the intention to avoid the rally around the flag argument that can be used by the ruling elite likely to be targeted by sanctions. Instead, the implementation of sanctions may be made problematic by technical difficulties or lack of state capacity on the ground. These conditions would not reduce the importance of the role that sanctions can play in international affairs, but the quality of the contribution that sanctions can provide to each foreign policy crisis should be determined on a case-by-case basis.

The two dimensions for direct material impact are constituted by the cost of sanctions and the dependence on the resource denied to targets. Cost refers to the material burden that sanctions alone impose on targets directly. Dependence refers to the relative importance of the resources denied by sanctions to targets in relation to target activities. The cost is classified as high when the measures are implemented and monitored, and when there is a significant correlation between the action of the sender and what happens in the target. For instance, the UN embargo on Iraq, which saw the complete isolation of the country and the interruption of all trade, means a high cost on the target. If the trade structure or the level of discomfort created is reduced to a minimum, as could be considered for a travel ban to Europe, then the cost will be low.

Dependence is classified as high when the target needs specific resources to carry out its policies, such as the case of banning a crucial resource to the economy of a state (e.g. oil for Iraq, diamonds for Liberia, or travelling for the leaders of an independent region). Conversely, if targets do not need the resource denied to

Table 3.6: Direct material impact

		Kinds of evidence (the list is not exhaustive)
Cost	1: low, no cost imposed by sanctions	– degree of monitoring – degree of implementation – degree of international cooperation – sector's share of the economy
	2: medium, partial cost imposed by sanctions	
	3: high, significant cost imposed by sanctions	
Dependence	1: low, no dependency on the resource denied	– relevance of the resource denied – commodity share in the economy – domestic structure of economic benefits – rate of interdependence on the resource denied – short, middle or long term consequences
	2: medium, some dependency on the resource denied	
	3: high, high dependency on the resource denied	

them, as in the case of an arms embargo imposed on a heavily armed group that has multiple suppliers, then dependence is low. Table 3.6 presents a general list of indicators used to determine the degree of direct impact.

The combination of cost and dependence brings about the following classification, illustrated in Table 3.7, for the impact of the measure.

Table 3.7: Degrees of direct material impact

		Dependence		
		1	2	3
	1	Low	Low	Low
Cost	2	Low	Low	High
	3	Low	High	High

To summarise, the two dimensions – feasibility and direct impact – form the determinants for the creation of a taxonomy of sanctions, and Figure 3.1 illustrates the classificatory typology.

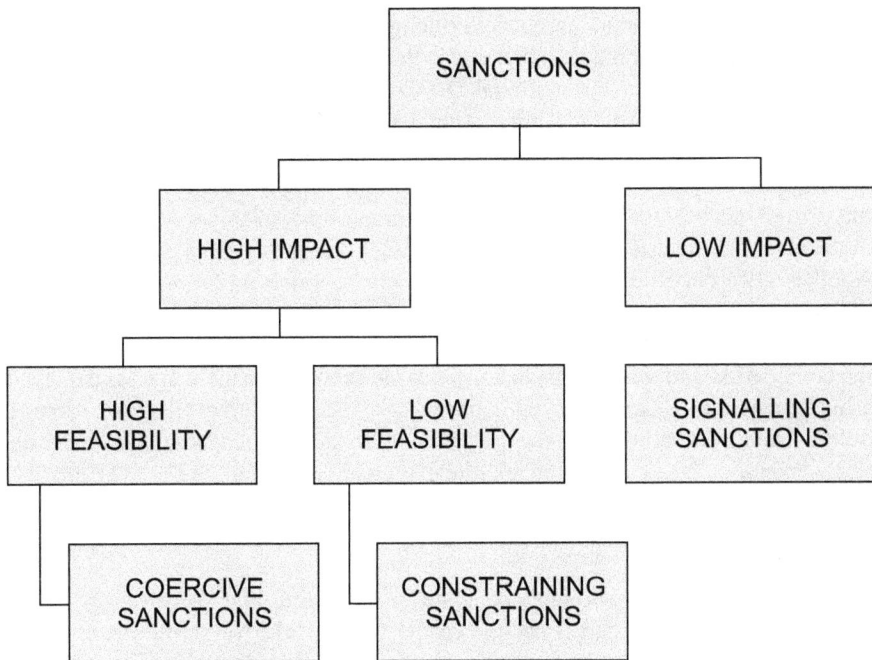

Figure 3.1: Taxonomy of sanctions

The environment: defining the independent variable

Sanctions are not imposed in a vacuum and the context in which they are adopted might influence the logic with which sanctions are expected to work. The 'system' of sanctions is defined as the attributes that distinguish one crisis from another and that can create the conditions for one logic to be dominant. The units are the international participants of the international system, which can play the role of senders, targets and audiences. Drawing from the main paradigms of international relations theories, the context of sanctions is characterised by the variables of threat, salience and complexity. These three variables encompass systemic elements of the context and represent an important component of the comprehensive framework.

Threat to sender

The variable 'threat' refers to the level of threat identified by the sender. In the anarchical international system, the realists hold that states pursue survival as their most important goal. Thereby, from a Clausewitzian point of view, if sanctions are the continuation of politics by other means, then the higher the level of threat against the sender, the higher will be the commitment of the sender to remove the threat by making sure that targets are no longer dangerous.

The threat to sender is a variable used in the International Crisis Behavior Project (ICB) at the Center for International Development and Conflict Management of the University of Maryland (International Crisis Behavior Project 2008). This variable has been adapted for the purposes of this study and differs slightly from the original definition. In the ICB project, this variable is called 'gravity of value threat' and has been defined as 'the most salient object of threat identified by any of the actors in the crisis'. Here, the relevant actor of the crisis is the sender alone. Another difference lies in the codification of the value threat. The ICB project defines seven levels of threat: economic, limited military damage, political, territorial, influence, grave damage and threat to existence. For the nature of the work, the codification adopted here is dichotomic. Threat will be high when senders have a high interest at stake identified as threat to existence, threat of grave damage, political and economic threat. By low level of threat, it is meant that the sender has a low economic interest at stake and the dispute does not put its survival at risk.

Creating the index

The indicators for this variable are 'issue', 'extension' and 'geostrategy'. Issue refers to the matter that motivates the sender to act or the triggering cause for the imposition of sanctions. The indicator has four possible categorisations[4]: (1) mi-

---

4.   Brecher and James had defined it in a six points scale as economic threat, limited military threat, political threat – threat of overthrow of regime, change of institutions, replacement of elite, intervention in domestic politics, subversion; territorial threat – threat of integration, annexation of part of a state's territory, separatism; threat to influence in the international system or regional

lieu, (2) economic, (3) political and (4) security threat. A milieu threat is a menace to norms and principles that do not have direct externalities for a sender's possession goals. For instance, human rights or democratic promotion may be included within this category. An economic threat is a menace to the trade of certain commodities that have a special relevance to senders as, for instance, the denial of oil, copper or timber supply may be the threat under which the sender might incur. A political threat is a menace to important pillars of international law, such as violations of non-proliferation treaties, mass violations of human rights or conflicts that have a spill-over effect on other neighbouring countries. Finally, a security threat is a direct menace to the safety of individual and properties of senders like, as for example, the terrorist threat, violations of borders with military means, or large conflicts that endanger the stability of the international order. Not all threats, however, are equal in importance: a security threat is considered the most serious of all, a political threat is less critical than a security threat, but more severe than an economic one, and an economic threat is more serious than a milieu threat. It is important to stress that milieu threat refers to those acts that do not imply economic or political consequences.[5]

The second indicator is the extension of the threat. The higher is the number of subsystem affected by the crisis or involved in the dispute, the more extended is the threat. There are five points in the scale for this indicator: (5) relevant to the global system, (4) relevant to the dominant system and more than one subsystem, (3) relevant to the dominant system and one subsystem, (2) relevant to more than one subsystem, and (1) relevant to one subsystem (Brecher and James 1986: 36). A threat relevant to the global system may be a terrorist threat, while a threat to a subsystem may refer to the situation in Haiti in the early 1990s that was relevant to the American subsystem mostly.

Adapted from Brecher and James, the last indicator is labelled as the 'geostrategy' and it refers to the geopolitical relevance for the senders of the areas where targets operate. This indicator is presented in a four point scale: (4) strong relevance, (3) modest relevance, (2) little relevance and (1) no relevance. Proximity and geopolitical importance are directly related to 'threat' as the higher they are, the higher should the level of danger be for senders. Proximity is deemed more important, therefore a close and strategically-located crisis would be rated as strongly relevant; a close crisis without strategic relevance would be deemed as modestly relevant; a strategically relevant, but distant crisis would have little relevance; and a distant crisis located in no strategic location would be considered with no relevance.[6]

---

subsystem – threat of declining power in the global system and/or regional subsystem, diplomatic isolation, cessation of patron aid; threat of grave damage – threat of large casualties in war, mass bombings; and threat to existence – threat to survival of population, of genocide, threat to existence of entity, of total annexation, colonial rule, occupation.

5. A milieu threat is different from a possession threat, see (Wolfer 1962).

6. Buzan and Waever talk about 'adjacency is potential for security because many threats travel more easily over short distances than over longer ones. The impact of geographical proximity on security interaction is strongest and more obvious in the military, political, societal, and

The weight of the dimensions is assigned inductively according to a ranking of importance among the indicators. The issue at stake is the most important value because a direct threat to security has the effect of a multiplier of strength in combats,[7] and it is followed by the geostrategic importance and extension of threat. In brief, the weights will be as following: issue = 3, geostrategy = 2 and extension = 1.

Salience

Salience is the second IV that attempts to depict 'the degree of importance attached to that issue by the actors involved' (Diehl 1992: 334). This concept has been widely adopted in the literature on conflicts and it is known as the 'issues-based approach to world politics' (Diehl 1992; O'Leary 1976; Mansbach and Vasquez 1981; Vasquez 1993; Hensel 2001). The salience of an issue can be correlated to the level of threat, but it refers to the importance of the crisis for reasons that are not directly linked to the survival of the sender. In other words, a salient crisis may not pose a threat to senders, and a threat may not be salient since salience is not measured in traditional security terms.

A salient crisis is characterised by a high level of media coverage and by the level of engagement of the sender in the crisis. This type of analysis is seldom carried out in the literature, but there is no question that this factor plays a role in influencing international events. As it is for threat and complexity, salience is a dichotomic variable. High salience is a crisis wherein the sender attaches a relevant value to it. Whereas this could coincide with a high threat to security, it can also imply that a crisis undermines or harms an important principle of the international system. For instance, the reaction to mass violations of human rights can raise salience and the expectations that the international community places on certain actors may contribute to it. On the other hand, the remoteness of certain conflicts may contribute to lower the attention and to blend the measures adopted to deal with crises.

Creating the index

The salience of a crisis is measured with two indicators: 'attention' and 'engagement'. The first indicator represents the level of attention that has been devoted to the crisis and is represented by a three-point scale: (3) high attention, (2) moderate attention and (1) little attention. The evidence for the attribution of this indicator comes from the intensity of news coverage of the target of sanctions in the two years preceding the imposition of the sanctions. The coverage of UN episodes was calculated by counting relevant articles in the *Financial Times* and *The New York Times*, while the coverage for EU episodes was evaluated by looking at the

---

environmental sectors' (Buzan and Waever 2003: 45).

7. See (O'Leary 1976; Keohane and Nye 1977; Mansbach and Vasquez 1981; Vasquez 1993; Diehl 1992; Brecher 1993).

F*inancial Times* and the *The Economist*. In both cases, the mere presence of the key targets in articles was deemed as sufficient to identify the interest of the international community. Indeed, the mere discussion or inclusion of the actor would not include the attention given only to the crisis, but it would also account for other areas that were affected by events occurring in or caused by the targeted actors.

The second indicator relates to the sender's level of engagement in the dispute. The assumption is that the higher is the commitment, the more salient is the issue for the sender. This indicator has to be treated carefully given that it could happen that the level of engagement is low because of the complexity of the crisis or the lack of agreement among the actors (the five permanent members (P5) of the Security Council in the case of the UN, the big states in the case of the EU). The indicator is measured on a three-point scale: (3) high engagement, (2) moderate engagement and (1) no engagement. The evidence for high engagement is military intervention and a large peacekeeping operation. The evidence for moderate engagement is small peacekeeping forces, other types of ground mission or an intense diplomatic activity by providing, for instance, good offices for negotiations. The lack of any above mentioned is classified as no engagement.

The weighted value of the indicators for salience considers the level of news coverage as the most important indicator and it is, therefore, more important to determine the final value of the salience of the issue. Thus, the weight will be attention = 2 and engagement = 1.

Complexity of the dispute

The final of the three variables that define context is the 'complexity of the dispute', which is an index that intends to picture the level of intractability of a crisis. The complexity of a dispute is a system variable that can have an explanatory power in foreign policy as interests can be incompatible; therefore, senders and targets enter into a zero-sum game, in which engagement is discouraged when the chances of winning are high and a tangible interest is at stake. Consequently, sanctions could be imposed to eliminate an enemy, to avoid the intervention in dangerous areas or to pursue some material advantage.

This variable draws from *Crises in World Politics* by Brecher and James, which has been used with adaptation several times in the literature (Brecher and James 1986; Brecher 1993; Colaresi and Thompson 2002; Ben-Yehuda and Mishali-Ram 2003). The original version was composed by six indicators: 'the number of actors, the extent of heterogeneity among them, the range of issues in dispute, its scope of geostrategic salience, the type of superpower/major power involvement, and the level of violence among the crisis adversaries' (Brecher and James 1986:32). This study reduced the indicators and adopted a dichotomic interpretation of this concept. High complexity refers to intractable conflicts characterised by the involvement of many parties, serious levels of violence and resistance to settlement; inversely, low complexity refers to crises with a limited number of actors, little or no violent clashes and marginal violations of international norms.

Creating the index

The indicators for 'complexity' have been specified as the 'number of actors' involved in the dispute, the 'level of violence', the 'number of issues' and the 'target's strength'.[8] The number of actors is directly proportional to the complexity of a dispute and it may vary. This indicator will consider the number of relevant actors actively involved in the dispute. The scale goes from 1 to 5 actors (where 5 defined as '5 or more').

The level of violence is an important indicator because of two reasons. First, a violent conflict is likely to occur if a history of conflict precedes it (Walter 2004; Wolfer 1962). Secondly, when a conflict escalates to open violence, the level of trust among the parties fades away and cooperation is more unlikely (Wallensteen 2007). Therefore, the higher the level of violence, the higher the complexity of the conflict. From Brecher (1986), 'a four-point scale ascends from no violence (1), to limited violence (2), [...] serious clashes short of war (3), to full-scale war (4)'.

The number of issues of a dispute affects its complexity: the more matters are at stake for the actors, the harder it is to find a solution to the dispute. Brecher (1986) says that there are three levels of issue: case, cluster and area. 'A case issue indicates the focus of a specific crisis, [...] a cluster issue refers to the common theme among related cases, [...] issue-area denotes generic substance, that is, a group of clusters of issues with a shared focus' (Brecher and James 1986: 39). The cluster can be of a security, political, economic, or cultural type. A crisis over a security issue alone indicates a high level of severity, and a multiple issue conflict has to be treated likewise. Therefore, 'five points on an issue scale have been generated: (5) three or more issues, (4) two issues, including [...] security, (3) a military-security issue alone, (2) two issues other than [...] security, and (1) one non-security issue' (Brecher and James 1986: 39).

The last indicator is a target's strength. The assumption is that the size of the target affects the complexity of the dispute. For instance, during the Cold War, the United States resorted several times to sanctions against the Soviet Union, but the strength of the target had an impact on the effectiveness of the measures. The kinds of evidence required are the economic strength (the GDP in case of states, qualitative analyses in case of individuals or entities) and the level of assistance that target enjoys. Target's strength is a three-point scale indicator: (3) strong target, (2) moderately strong target, and (1) weak target.

The level of violence is the most important indicator for the complexity of the issue. The strength of targets is also important, given that the stronger is the target, the lower is the leverage that senders have on them. Issues and number of actors have a lower rate of importance, but still relevant because the matter at stake determines the cost tolerance of the parties, while a high number of actors reduces the margins for agreements that can satisfy every actor of the crisis. Hence, the weights are set as follows: issue = 2, number of actors = 1, violence = 4, and target strength = 3.

---

8. Four out of five indicators come from Brecher and James (1986).

To summarise, Table 3.8 presents the three IVs and the indicators that have been used to measure them.

The three IVs are operationalised through the creation of indexes, which allow for the consideration of weighted multiple factors, thus cross-case comparisons become possible. The indexes are expressed in standardised values from 0 to 1 and they are codified as 'high' for values equal to or higher than 0.5, while they are 'low' for values lower than 0.5. The indicators for the variables have been selected inductively and are by no means definitive, so that eventual integration or alternative elements can be added in future studies. However, the current indexes represent a good indication of the trends of the studied phenomena.

The hypotheses of the research: a general overview

The theoretical framework formulated here should allow us to reason about the most likely logic of sanctions in relations to their context. There are two types of hypotheses that can be elaborated. The first type is more general and links the expectations of one specific outcome to each IV. The second type of expected association is more detailed and relates particular combinations of IVs to a more likely outcome.

In general terms, the variable threat should lead senders to reduce the level of danger by convincing the target to change behaviour or, alternatively, to limit the policy options of the target towards less dangerous conducts. The idea is that a high threat would motivate senders to focus on their more immediate interests defined in conventional terms (i.e. security) and to aim at removing the threat by changing the behaviour of targets. Thus, if threat is high, then it is more likely that senders adopt either coercive or constraining measures; contrarily, if threat is low, then it is more likely that senders impose signalling sanctions.

The variable salience refers to a specific pressure on senders to act, but with a fuzzy understanding of what the target has to do. The pressure can be societal, in which case the requests would be formulated not on specific issues that constitute a threat to the sender, but it would rather be based on normative stands that are difficult to implement and often incompatible with real world events. Alternatively, the pressures can also lead senders to compromise between the realist principle of non-intervention in case of low probability of success, and the need to satisfy the demands that originate from the lobbies or audiences by acting with the ambition to reduce tensions or conflict thresholds. The hypothesis is that the salience of an issue affects the actions of senders in a different way than threat does. Thereby, if salience is high, then senders are more likely to attempt either to modify the behaviour of the target or to react to violations of international norms with either coercing or constraining sanctions. On the contrary, if salience is low, then senders are more likely to impose sanctions that do not imply high costs to bear, namely signalling measures.

This leads to the final general expected association as when a crisis is complicated, then it is more difficult to require specific actions from targets, which would be more interested in how they can secure their survival. Thus, it would be more

Table 3.8: Independent variables

Independent variables	Definition	Levels	Indicators	Values	Weights
Threat (THREAT)	This variable identifies the level of threat identified by the sender in the crisis	High Low	issue extension geostrategy	$1 \geq x \geq 4$ $1 \geq x \geq 5$ $1 \geq x \geq 4$	3 1 2
Salience (SALIENCE)	The degree of importance that the sender attaches to a crisis	High Low	level of attention level of engagement	$1 \geq x \geq 3$ $1 \geq x \geq 3$	2 1
Complexity of the dispute (COMPLEXITY)	This variable identifies the complexity of the dispute either between senders and targets or among third actors that the sender would like to interact with	High Low	number of actors violence issue target strength	$1 \geq x \geq 5$ $1 \geq x \geq 4$ $1 \geq x \geq 5$ $1 \geq x \geq 3$	1 4 2 3

likely that senders attempt to stabilise the situations with general demands to all the parties to respect certain standards or, alternatively, to limit what specific actors of the crisis can do. Hence, if complexity is high, then senders are more likely to resort to constraining or signalling sanctions as they cannot modify the behaviour of targets (coercion) or they do not want to commit to a situation where they would have to pay a high cost (constrain). Contrarily, if complexity is low, then coercing or signalling sanctions become more likely. Thus, six hypotheses are formulated in Table 3.9.

The dichotomic operationalisation of the IVs determines eight different possible scenarios as presented in Table 3.10, but four specific hypotheses can be formulated as in Table 3.11.. The first one is that when threat and complexity are high, then sanctions are more likely to be of a constraining type (rows 1 and 2 in Table 3.10). The reasoning is simple: senders would like to change the behaviour of targets, but they cannot. Therefore, they attempt to limit the alternatives available to them. The second expected association emerges consequentially, namely that when threat is high but complexity is low, then coercive sanctions become more likely (rows 3 and 7 in Table 3.10). The third reasoning is that when threat and salience are low, then sanctions should be imposed with a signalling logic (rows 4 and 8 in Table 3.10). Senders do not have

Table 3.9: General hypotheses of the research

Independent variable	Intensity	Expected outcome
Threat	High	Coercing or constraining
	Low	Signalling
Salience	High	Coercing or constraining
	Low	Signalling
Complexity	High	Constraining or signalling
	Low	Coercing or signalling

to react to pressures either on normative or security principles and therefore their action is likely to be cost free. Finally, when threat is low but salience is high, then an action that implies the sustaining of costs is expected on the senders' side and sanctions are more likely to be of a constraining type (rows 5 and 6 in Table 3.10). The eight hypotheses will be tested as summarised in Table 3.10.

Table 3.10: Possible sanctions scenarios

N	Threat	Salience	Complexity	Sanction expected
1	High	High	High	Constraining
2	High	Low	High	Constraining
3	High	Low	Low	Coercing
4	Low	Low	Low	Signalling
5	Low	High	Low	Constraining
6	Low	High	High	Constraining
7	High	High	Low	Coercing
8	Low	Low	High	Signalling

Table 3.11: Specific hypotheses of the research

N	Threat	Salience	Complexity	Sanction expected
1	High	–	High	Constraining
2	High	–	Low	Coercing
3	Low	Low	–	Signal
4	Low	High	–	Constraining

Conclusion

In non-cooperative relations in international affairs, sanctions can be imposed to coerce, constrain or signal other actors. Sanctions are never used in isolation from other foreign policy tools and methods and looking at how they influence targets is a more functional way to distinguish among different episodes of sanctions. Indeed, it is an overall strategy – constructive engagement, selective engagement, critical dialogue, quiet diplomacy, isolation, etc. (Haass and O'Sullivan 2000; Tocci 2007) – that may have the objective to change the behaviour of the target, so the instruments that compose the strategy cannot determine the outcome alone.

Thinking about restrictive measures as instruments that only contribute to foreign policy outcomes seems also to provide a conceptualisation that is closer to real world events. An alternative way of approaching this analysis could be to categorise sanctions according to their form (e.g. arms embargoes, financial sanctions, etc.), but this would resemble more a purely descriptive typology rather than a conceptual framework useful to compare cases across time and space. The logic of sanctions, once again defined as 'how targets are influenced', can be recognised through the observation of whether there is a material impact on targets and whether the compliance with the requests made by the sender would undermine the survival of the target. Thus, senders can (a) impose sanctions to make a certain behaviour more costly to the target in order for it to modify its behaviour, (b) attempt to thwart its efforts towards a certain goal, and (c) signal disagreement or address specific concerns of either domestic or international audiences, or both.

The understanding of sanctions episodes is almost accomplished with the creation of the abovementioned taxonomy, but the introduction of contextual variables opens the door to explaining the variance among different types of sanctions: when do senders opt for constraining versus signalling? Why coercing instead of constraining? The three types of sanctions are imposed within an environment that offers opportunities and constraints to the use of restrictive measures. The context has been operationalised with three macro variables identified as threat to the sender, salience and complexity of the dispute. Sanctioning is a foreign policy method among many, and the best way to illustrate the point is to use a metaphor of the hammer for the carpenter. Indeed, as a hammer can be used to bed in nails but not to saw a plank, likewise sanctions can be used for specific purposes and their utility can be assessed only in relation to them. This metaphor can also be useful to include the system of sanctions in the picture. Indeed, it is the working environment that makes a specific use of the hammer more likely than others. The same is hypothesised for sanctions, as it is their system that could be conducive to specific types of sanctions.

These aspects do not undermine the utility of the tool in foreign policy, but they underline that restrictive measures can do specific things within larger strategies under a particular set of circumstances. This empirical investigation will evaluate whether the context and the purpose of sanctions are correlated in order to unveil that, regardless from the willingness of the sender, sanctions are restrained by the environment wherein they are imposed. Hence, the environment of a dispute seems to be crucial for understanding sanctions episodes and its inclusion in the framework appears to be a necessary step for explaining the purpose of international sanctions.

The empirical investigation begins with the following chapter that introduces the cases used to test the theoretical framework according to the main variables identified in this chapter. In other words, the following chapter will provide the first preliminary confirmation on the quality of the dataset and on whether sanctions differ from each other.

chapter four | the theoretical framework in practice

This chapter aims at testing the analytical value of the theoretical framework when applied to a database of sanctions. The analytical value of the theoretical framework would be ascertained by the capacity of distinguishing among sanctions episodes and by the ability of picturing the changing characters of the contexts of sanctions. Concepts valid across time and space are necessary instruments to compare and study the multiple cases of sanctions, but the literature has failed in this mission.

The concepts illustrated in Chapter 3 yield an added value to the study of sanctions and the picture that emerges from this chapter is extremely interesting. A very common assumption of sanctions is that they are imposed to change the behaviour of targets, but a descriptive look at the database tells us that sanctions are imposed with a coercive intent only ten times out of seventy, with twenty-two of the constraining type and thirty-eight of the signalling type. With regards to the IVs, it is noticeable to see that threat and salience are not perfectly correlated. A crisis that poses a high threat to a sender is not necessarily salient as senders undergo the sole pressure of a threat that may not have been perceived by the citizens. Indeed, threat is high on twenty-six occasions, salience is high on forty-five and complexity is high on thirty-five. The low frequency of threat also suggests that sanctions are used less as a last resort and more as a cheap foreign policy method.

This chapter is divided in three sections. The first introduces the database to the readers. The second part is a descriptive overview of cases classified according to the tripartite taxonomy of coercing, constraining and signalling to show that this classification captures important nuances within the real world. The third part illustrates the aggregate data for the IVs across the seventy episodes taken into consideration by this study.

The database

The conceptual framework is applied to a database of forty-three cases divided into seventy episodes of sanctions imposed by the United Nations and the European Union from the end of the Cold War to 2010. Cases taken from UN history count twenty-two and represent forty-one episodes. The cases from the experience of the EU are twenty-one and are divided into twenty-nine episodes. The database includes the entire population of sanction cases.[1]

The cases selected are foreign policy decisions, having been adopted under chapter VII of the UN Charter and under the Common Foreign and Security Policy

---

1. With the only exception of the EU terrorist list established by Common Position 931 of 27th December 2001.

(CFSP) of the EU. There are other foreign policy decisions that, under a more extensive interpretation, could be included in a study of sanctions. For instance, the EU can decide to suspend bilateral trade agreements with those countries who signed the Cotonou Agreement if they are responsible for violations of human rights in their own territories. Even so, such policy decisions would be contractual and not political. By contractual it is meant that a sanction is not imposed with a political goal under the discretion of a competent body, but is an automatic mechanism specified in international agreements. For instance, some have classified the EU sanctions under the Cotonou. I acknowledge the existence of other views in the literature (Jones 2007; Portela 2008), but I hold that the difference between political and contractual sanctions to be too important not to be accounted for.

The unit of analysis is a sanction episode, instead of a country or a case, because a sanctions regime can change throughout time. Thus each case will be split into multiple episodes if a structural change (e.g. the change of one dimension in defining the DV, or one or more indicators vary in the creation of the indexes for the IVs). Given this, then a different analysis should take place. For instance, the measures against the National Union for the Total Independence of Angola (UNITA, from the Portuguese *União Nacional para a Independência Total de Angola*) were not enforced in the early 1990s, but this changed towards the end of the decade. Another example is Iraq. The 1990 sanctions were different from the ones in 1991, and the 1991 sanctions were different from those of 2003. These differences have to be emphasised if an attempt is made to understand the importance of sanctions in foreign policy (Eriksson 2009; Cortright and Lopez 2000).

The timeframe of the analysis is limited from the end of the Cold War until 2010. The practice of sanctioning evolved substantially only in the past twenty years and the variance of the dependent variable is ensured. Going from the most typical case of economic embargo against Iraq, to the more targeted version of the measures on Iran and Uzbekistan, the database provides enough evidence to test the theoretical framework elaborated above without going further into the past. Additional studies would be of great use to the theoretical strength of the model, but the marginal utility of adding older instances of sanctions to the database of the present study is limited.

Applying the theoretical framework to the real world: the dependent variable

The factual observation of empirical cases has confirmed that sanctions are one among many tools in the foreign policy toolbox, so senders can resort to the same foreign policy method, but with at least three different logics. The aggregate data confirms that sanctions are used in foreign policy predominantly to signal, then to constrain and, finally, to coerce.

Sanctions are imposed predominantly with a signalling logic by both the UN (twenty-one times out of forty-one, equals 51 per cent of the times) and the EU (seventeen times out of twenty-nine, equals 59 per cent of the times). The second most frequent type is used to constrain targets in the international system for both the UN (fourteen times out of forty-one, equals 34 per cent of the times) and the EU (eight episodes 28 per cent of the total). Finally, coercive sanctions are seldom used by the UN (six times for a total of 15 per cent) and the EU (four times for a total of 14 per cent).

Only a minimal fraction of the sample seems to fit the criterion for coercive sanctions intended as sanctions imposed with the objective of changing the behaviour of the target. The UN and the EU resorted to coercive sanctions only in 14 per cent of the cases and this finding alone would undermine many empirical evaluations of sanctions. With 54 per cent of the episodes being of a signalling type and 32 per cent of a constraining type, the way sanctions are understood should profoundly change. Table 4.1 summarises this data.

Table 4.1: Frequencies of sanctions types

Type	Total	United Nations	European Union
Coercion	10 (14.29%)	6 (14.63%)	4 (13.79%)
Constraint	22 (31.43%)	14 (34.15%)	8 (27.59%)
Signal	38 (54.29%)	21 (51.22%)	17 (58.62%)
Total	70 (100%)	41 (100%)	29 (100%)

A quick look at the internal dimensions that constitute the types of sanctions shows a reality of sanctions that downgrade most of the analyses assuming that all sanctions are alike. For instance, the demand attached to sanctions is in almost 80 per cent of the cases (fifty-four out of seventy) classified as unfeasible. This fact could be interpreted in different ways, but the most likely one is in line with the argument by Drezner (1999) according to which sanctions are more likely to be imposed on enemies and actors with divergent interests and, often times, incompatible with each other.

The direct impact is also interesting as less than 50 per cent of the sanctions did have a direct impact on targets. While it was already known that some economic sanctions bite, others do not (Baldwin 1985); a systemic empirical evaluation is not commonly conducted on this aspect and sanctions are simply criticised of being ineffective. The lack of impact could be the product of a specific political will or, as investigated here, of specific systemic pressures that make senders more likely to resort to sanctions with a low direct impact as shown in Table 4.2, while in the detailed break-up for the indicators for feasibility and direct impact are available in Table 4.3.

Table 4.2: Frequency of dimensions for sanctions type

Dimension	Low	High	Total
Feasibility	54	16	70
Direct Impact	38	32	70

The distribution of indicators for dimensions of sanctions in Table 4.3 allows a few considerations on the demands of sanctions. The first one is that sanctions have precise requests in less than 30 per cent of the cases. This can surely be justified by the fact that senders, on purpose, intend to maintain the request vague. Making precise demands creates diplomatic wars of attritions in which either the target does exactly what the sender requires, which would correspond to a loss of face for targets, or the target does not do what the sender asks for, which would correspond to a loss of face for the sender. Ambiguity is broadly used in diplomacy and it does not constitute a surprise, but this evidence presents an important hurdle to the understanding of sanctions unless this aspect is included in the evaluation as it is done by this theoretical framework presented here.

Table 4.3: Distribution of indicators for dimensions of sanctions

Indicators	1 (high)	2 (medium)	3 (low)
Preciseness	20	40	10
Practicality	37	21	12
Material Impact	26	27	17
Dependence	18	25	27

A similar reasoning would follow the analysis of the dependence indicator in revealing that sanctions do not target resources crucial to the activities of targets in forty-three cases out of seventy, corresponding to 61 per cent of the episodes. There are four possible justifications for this. First, this could be a compromise between the pressure of doing something about a crisis and the one of making sure not to impose costly measures. Secondly, this could be a decision driven by the need of attracting the attention of a specific target towards the sender. Thirdly, senders may not be in the position of targeting crucial resources as targets can be either independent or enjoy a dominant position. Fourthly, senders know that certain regimes are able to redirect the costs of sanctions towards either innocent civilians or political opponents, so imposing costly sanctions could backfire. This is another important nuance that emerges from the adoption of this theoretical framework that is commonly disregarded. The description of the coercive cases of sanctions will emphasise this facet.

Coercive sanctions

The purpose of a coercive type of sanction is to attach a cost to a number of potential behaviours that a target can embark on in order to make a more specific behaviour more likely. The logic is to impose a cost that affects the costs/benefits calculation of a target by making one policy course more convenient. This means that the demand attached to a sanction identifies a specific behaviour required to ensure the lifting, assuming that such behaviour would not be incompatible with the political survival of the political actors who have to make the decision. There are ten cases in the database that fall in this category as summarised in Table 4.4. The UN sanctions on Libya and the EU measures on Belarus will be presented in the following chapters, while this chapter will focus on the UN on Iran and Eritrea, and the EU on Iran and the US.

Table 4.4: Episodes of coercive sanctions

Type	No.	Episodes	
		European Union	United Nations
Coercion	10	EU/Iran – 2010	UN/1267 – 1999 to 2001
			UN/Yugoslavia – 1994 to 1996
		EU/US – 1996 to present	UN/Eritrea – 2009 to present
		EU/Belarus – 2007 to present	UN/Libya – 1993 to 1999
		EU/Libya – 2004 to present	UN/Iran – 2006 to present
			UN/DPRK – 2009 to present

The labels are made of: sender/country where targets reside/year of imposition of sanctions/ year of lifting or 'present' for sanctions in force in December 2010.

UN/Iran – 2006 to present

Since the end of the World War II, Iran began its plan of developing nuclear power plants motivated by the need of maximising the profits from its oil sales. After the Islamic revolution in 1979, the level of attention of the international community increased further, but it was only in the past years that the crisis escalated. The Iranian plan to enrich uranium was revealed in 2003, but with the failure of several negotiations, the importance of this dispute has been tackled by the UN Security Council. The rearmament plans were declared a threat to international peace and security in 2006 when resolution 1737 froze the assets and prevented travel of certain individuals and blocked the export of commodities key to the nuclear program. Iran constitutes a threat not because of its intentions to produce energy with nuclear technology, but because of its lack of transparency with the inspectors of the International Atomic Energy Agency (IAEA) (Sagan 2006: 50). The number of targets increased from twenty-two to twenty-eight in 2007 (United Nations 2007c), and other 41 targets with resolution 1929 passed in 2010 (United Nations 2010a).

The UN sanctions against Iran have been defined as coercive because they make feasible demands and have an impact on the target. The current regime, as it inherited a long-term policy of Iran, would not be undermined by renouncing the nuclear program, and sanctions, especially the financial ones, do have an impact on the economy and the capacity of Iran to develop the nuclear programme (Alexander and Hoenig 2008; Khan 2010; Tarock 2006; Litwak 2008; Chubin 2010).

UN/Yugoslavia – 1994 to 1996

The conflicts in the Balkans in the early 1990s reached a level of unprecedented violence and brutality. After the end of the major conflict, the UN opened a negotiation with President Milosevic of Serbia in order to set the conditions to end the war and to disarm the groups operating in Bosnia, which were still undermining the peace process. The Security Council began to shift the target of sanctions gradually towards the Bosnian parties who did not comply with the agreements to settle the dispute, while it begin the gradual suspension of the measures on the Federal Republic of Yugoslavia with resolution 943 of 23rd September 1994. The suspension continued in parallel with the negotiations that led to the signing of the Dayton Agreement on 14th December 1995. Eventually, considering the successful implementation of the Dayton Accords, the sanctions – an arms embargo, a commodity boycott, a travel ban and financial restrictions – were first suspended with resolution 1022 of 22nd November 1995 and then terminated. The sanctions committee was then dissolved with resolution 1074 of 1st October 1996.

The feasibility of sanctions is rated high as the request of the international community was not incompatible with the presence of Milosevic in power, and there was an impact as the sanctions were implemented and enforced by UN personnel and by firm international monitoring (Brzoska and Lopez 2009; Berdal and Economides 2007; Bethlehem and Weller 1997; Dedring 2008).

EU/Libya – 2004 to present

Libya was sanctioned by the UN because of its lack of cooperation on the arrest of the two suspects of the Lockerbie bombing in 1988. When the suspects eventually arrived at the Tribunal set up in the Netherlands, sanctions were suspended in 1999 and lifted in 2003. The EU had also autonomous measures in force that were imposed on 27th January 1986, which were maintained in 1999 upon the suspension of the UN sanctions with common position 261 of 16th April 1999. The arms embargo and the travel ban were classified as signalling measures. Since 2004, however, the new episode of sanctions took a coercive form. In 2004, the Council of Ministers decided to protect EU companies from possible requests of damages or repayment from the implementation of the UN sanctions and passed common position 698 on 14th October 2004.

Sanctions are classified as coercive when the demand is clear and does not undermine the survival of the targets, while there is an automatic impact in case of a request of a reimbursement for the losses due to the UN measures (Niblock 2001; European Union 1999a; European Union 2004e).

EU/US – 1996 to present

In 1996, the US approved the Cuban Liberty and Democratic Solidarity Act (known as Helms-Burton Act) intended to strengthen the sanctions regime on Cuba by authorising the US Government to punish companies located anywhere in the world trading with Cuba. According to the World Trade Organisation (WTO), the extraterritorial application of this law violated the norms of international trade. The EU claimed that this law could have damaged its companies and passed joint action 668 on 22nd November 1996, to protect EU companies that were damaged by US regulations. An agreement was reached in early 1997 between the EU and the US, but the measure remains in force and a commission regulation has been passed in 2003 to modify former regulation. The mere fact that European companies could have retaliated against US acts may have prevented US actors using this possibility.

This is similar to the instance the EU adopted on Libya. Thus, the request is feasible as it does not endanger the survival of economic agents and political elites. There is a direct impact in case a lawsuit is attempted against European companies (Roy 1997; Lutterotti 2002). Although coercive measures have received most of the attention of the studies on sanctions so far, the twenty-two cases of constraint and the thirty-eight cases of signalling make up for 86 per cent of the population. These are now presented in the rest of the chapter.

Constraint sanctions

Sanctions are used most frequently to punish or to weaken targets in the international arena: intractable conflicts, rebel political leaders or terrorist organisations are the most common situations for this type of sanction. The logic of imposing such a sanction is to limit the alternatives available to targets. This type of sanction does not request targets to do something, but it only tries to reduce their degree of deviance. Using the words of Richard Barret, constraining sanctions aim at making the life of targets 'more difficult' (Barret 2008). Table 4.5 reports all the cases and this paragraph will provide a few examples selected randomly from the dataset.

UN/Haiti – 1993 to 1994

The democratically-elected Jean-Bertrand Aristide became president of Haiti in January 1990, but he was overthrown shortly thereafter by a military coup led by Raoul Cédras. After the attempt of the Organisation for American States (OAS) to negotiate and re-establish Aristide in power, the UN stepped in and threatened to impose sanctions if the military junta did not sit at the negotiating table. After their refusal, the Security Council decided to impose an arms and an oil embargo on 16th June 1993 with resolution 841 and negotiations started a few days later. Eventually, it ended with the Governors Island Agreement signed in the summer. This is classified as a signalling episode, but the lack of cooperation in implementing the agreement led to the re-imposition of sanctions with resolution 873 of 13th October 1993, which also included an aviation ban and stricter enforcement. A comprehensive embargo on export was imposed with resolution 917 of 6th May 1994 and a military mission was authorised in July.

While the compliance with the demand made to the military junta in the first episode entailed a possible coexistence with President Aristide, the second episode was characterised by the clearness of incompatibility between the military leaders and the return of Aristide. Therefore, the requests were unfeasible, while the

Table 4.5: Episodes of constraining sanctions

Type	No.	European Union	United Nations
			UN/Bosnian-Serbs – 1994 to 1996
			UN/Haiti – 1993 to 1994
			UN/Liberia – 2001 to 2003
		EU/Bosnia & Herzegovina – 2001 to 2006	UN/Cote d'Ivoire – 2004 to present
		EU/Milosevic – 2000 to present	UN/Iraq – 1991 to 2003
		EU/ICTY – 2001 to present	UN/Liberia – 2003 to present
Constraining	22	EU/Zimbabwe – 2002 to present	UN/Sierra Leone – 2000 to 2003
		EU/Transnistria – 2003 to 2010	UN/Cambodia – 1992 to 1993
		EU/Guinea – 2009 to present	UN/Unita – 1999 to 2002
		EU/Burma/Myanmar – 2007 to present	UN/Iraq – 1990 to 1991
		EU/FRY – 1998 to 2000	UN/Iraq – 2003 to present
			UN/1267 – 2002 to present
			UN/Somalia – 2008 to present
			UN/Yugoslavia – 1992 to 1994

impact, especially in the latter phase in the summer of 1994 when the military attack became imminent, weighed heavily on Haiti and the Haitians (Gibbons 1999; Malone 1997; Zaidi 1997).

UN/Iraq – 1991 to 2003

The Iraq case in the 1990s is among the clearest cases of constraint sanctions. In response to the invasion of Kuwait on 2nd August 1990, the UN Security Council initiated one of the most discussed sanctions regimes of its history with the imposition of a comprehensive embargo on Iraq (Cordesman and Hashim 1997; Arnove 2002; Alnasrawi 2001). After the military operation, the UN maintained the embargo to prevent Saddam from re-arming. Sanctions were imposed in 2001 with resolution 687 of 3rd April 1991, but the requests written in the official documents contrasted with the intention of the international community wanting Saddam out of power (United Nations 1991a). The sanctions regime was terminated in 2003 with resolution 1483 (United Nations 2003a), a resolution that commenced another sanctions regime that is supposed to sustain the transition towards stability of Iraq. The measures are still in force.

Given the external and the domestic distribution of power in Iraq, compliance was incompatible with an Iraq led by Saddam Hussein, especially given the contrasting political statements by the most influential members in the Security Council that underlined an existing incompatibility between declared and undeclared goals (United Nations 2008d; United Nations 2008e; Lopez and Cortright 2004). It was uncertain whether sanctions would have been lifted had Saddam stayed in power. Therefore, the demand is classified as unfeasible. One of the most criticised UN sanctions regimes had a visible direct material impact as sanctions were of a constraining type (Oette 2002; Bures and Lopez 2009; Alnasrawi 2001; Arnove 2002; Cordesman and Hashim 1997; Lopez and Cortright 2004).

UN/Cambodia – 1992 to 1993

The sanctions imposed against the Khmer Rouge in the early 1990s represent the first commitment in peace-building of the United Nations and also the first case of "smart" sanctions. After the human tragedy of the killing fields and the Vietnamese invasion, the end of the Cold War brought hopes for peace in the country. In 1990, the Security Council laid out a plan for the stabilisation of the country and a peacekeeping mission (United Nations Advance Mission in Cambodia – UNAMIC) was established as part of the Paris agreement signed in 1991 by the United National Front for an Independent, Neutral, Peaceful and Cooperative Cambodia (FUNCIN-PEC) with the Cambodian People's Party (CPP). However, the Party of Democratic Kampuchea (PDK) did not accept the terms of the agreement and was not among the signatories. The deployment the United Nations Transitional Authority in Cambodia (UNTAC) in March 1992 was assisted with the imposition of an oil embargo with resolution 792 of 30th November 1992. Elections were held in 1993 and the situation stabilised.

The request of the UN was clearly against the survival of the PDK, therefore the demand is classified as unfeasible. The presence of 21,000 UN troops ensured that the PDK was penalised by the denial of important resources for transport and industry, targeted in the area controlled by the PDK. These sanctions fall under the category of constraining (Brown and Zasloff 1998; Findlay 1995; Cortright and Lopez 2000: 135–146).

UN/Unita – 1999 to 2002

Angola has been afflicted by a traumatic civil war since 1975 and sanctions were imposed in 1993 with little impact registered. In 1999 and 2000, the arms embargo was complemented by a travel ban, a freeze of assets and a ban on the import of non-certified diamonds. The blatant violations of the embargo were monitored by an established monitoring mechanism with resolution 1237 of 7th May 1999 (United Nations 1993a; United Nations 1997a; United Nations 1998c). Angola has been the stage for one of the most devastating conflicts of the Cold War, where the US and the USSR backed UNITA and the Popular Movement for the Liberation of Angola (MPLA, from Portuguese *Movimento Popular de Libertação de Angola – Partido do Trabalho*) struggled over the government of the country. In 1992, a civil conflict erupted between the MPLA of dos Santos, which won the elections, and UNITA of Savimbi. The conflict (that sadly caused the death of 500,000 people) ended in 2002 with the murder of Jonas Savimbi.

The request made to UNITA was clearly impossible to satisfy as the Security Council asked it to give up the constitutive character of the organisation. Efficient

monitoring increased the impact of sanctions, which were then classified as constraining (Hare 2005; Conroy 2000; United Nations; Cortright and Lopez 2000).

UN/Somalia – 2008 to present

Somalia is probably the most typical of intractable conflicts. Affected by structural
instabilities since the early 1990s, the United Nations began to play an active role
with peacekeeping operations and peace-enforcement missions that became notorious with the Black Hawk Down incident. After sixteen years of a general arms
embargo imposed with resolution 733 of 23rd January 1992, the Security Council
passed resolution 1844 of 20th November 2008 imposing targeted sanctions via an
arms embargo, a travel ban and an assets freeze on individuals and entities engag-
ing in or providing support for acts that threaten the peace, security or stability of
Somalia, including acts that threaten the Djibouti Agreement of 18th August 2008
or the political process, or threaten the Transitional Federal Institutions (TFI) or
the African Union Mission in Somalia (AMISOM) by force; individuals or entities having acted in violation of the general and complete arms embargo; and individuals or entities obstructing the delivery of humanitarian assistance to Somalia,
or access to, or distribution of, humanitarian assistance in Somalia. In December
2010, there were nine individuals and entities subjected to these sanctions that
are monitored by the Sanctions Committee established pursuant resolution 751 of
24th April 1992.

Targets are required to halt their operations not to undermine the peace process even if such a request is unfeasible because of a lack of functional institutions
guaranteeing safety to the participants of the game. Furthermore, the dysfunc-
tional institutions allowed the activities of criminal organisations, which do not
comply with UN demands. Combined with the last round of measures, including
the ones on Eritrean actors, sanctions have made an impact on Somalian society (Berdal and Economides 2007; Crocker 2004; Boulden 2003; Berman 2000;
Dedring 2008; Murphy 2007; Katagiri 2010; Kasaija 2010; International Crisis
Group 2008b).

EU/ICTY – 2001 to present

This is one of the most convoluted episodes of sanctions. The International
Criminal Tribunal for the former Yugoslavia (ICTY) was created with resolutions
803 and 827 in 1993 to investigate crimes committed during the conflicts in the
ex-Yugoslavia. In order to support and sustain the functioning and the operation of
the Tribunal, the Council of Ministers decided to impose a travel ban on persons
who were thought to assist ICTY indictees to evade justice and freeze the assets of
the indictees themselves. In fact, these are two parallel regimes. The two regimes
have a prelude with common position 155 of 26th February 2001, when Milosevic
and his associates were banned from entering the EU alongside 'persons indicted
by the ICTY'. That led to the inclusion of a total of thirteen individuals (three of
them are ICTY indictees). The second regime was established with common posi-

tion 694 of 11th October 2004 targeting individuals such as Radovan Karadžić and in the blacklist in January 2011 of Ratko Mladić.

These sanctions are clearly of a constraining type. The demand is unfeasible, as it is unrealistic to expect people to give themselves up to an International Court, but there is an impact given that financial resources and travelling could be important assets for life while evading international police forces.

EU/Transnistria – 2003 to 2010

The Transnistrian conflict in Moldova is the closest secessionist case to the European Union. After the collapse of the Soviet Union, Moldova declared independence in 1991 and a conflict erupted in the eastern part of the country causing 1,500 casualties. Thereafter, Russian peacekeepers have been patrolling a buffer zone and Transnistria has made progress in creating a state institution. The EU became interested in the conflict with the eastern enlargement and the prospect for Moldova to be on the border of the EU. In 2003, a travel ban and an assets freeze were imposed on the Transnistrian leaders with the common position 139 of 27th February 2003 including seventeen people on its list. In 2004, further individuals were listed as a consequence of the attempt of the Transnistrian authorities to prevent the opening of Latin script schools in Transnistria. In 2008, a substantial change was introduced and sanctions were used to divide the internal society in Transnistria with the de-listing of the speaker of the Parliament. Sanctions were suspended in 2010 because of a request by the newly-elected government.

The sanctions from 2003 to 2010 are classified as constraining measures, since the Transnistrian leaders were considered unreliable negotiators. Indeed, any settlement would have undermined the position of power of the ruling elite. At the same time, the restrictive measures undermined the capacity to operate as they prevented Transnistrian leaders from acquiring the international legitimacy that is required to obtain independence (Herd 2005; Popescu 2005; Safonov 2009; Selari 2009; Vahl 2005a).

EU/Guinea – 2009 to present

On the 28th September 2009, demonstrations took place in the city of Conakry to protest against the decision of the military leader Captain Moussa Dadis Camara to run for president. Mr. Camara became president in 2008 with a military coup after the death of President Lansana Conte. According to the UN, 150 people died and 100 women were raped during the handling of the protests by the government authorities. On the 27th October 2009, the Council adopted common position 788, imposing an arms embargo and a visa ban in response to the violent crackdown by security forces on political demonstrators in Conakry on 28th September 2009. The concern was linked to the lack of stability in the country. Common position 788 listed forty-two people, but sanctions were strengthened only two months later with Council decision 1003 that listed seventy-one individuals and included a freeze of assets. Council decision 638 of 25th October 2010 confirmed the sanctions and renewed them for twelve months (European Union 2010d).

A request to restore peace and halt the fighting does not deal with the roots of conflict that cause the fighting. When violence is triggered, more is required than only a vague request to stop violence. For this reason, combined with the impact of the measures that can affect the costs/benefits calculation of the elite, sanctions are classified as constraining ones (European Union 2009c; European Union 2009d; European Union 2010c; European Union 2010f; International Crisis Group 2008b).

EU/Burma/Myanmar – 2007 to present

Sanctions on Burma/Myanmar represent the longest episode of autonomous restrictive measures imposed by the European Union. The crisis began in 1988, when a military junta – which called itself the State Law and Order Restoration Council (SLORC), later renamed State Peace and Development Council (SPDC), which came into power in order to fill the vacuum left by General Ne Win who was ousted by massive popular demonstrations. The army took control of the country with the objective of restoring order and establishing a multiparty system. In 1990, the National League for Democracy (NLD), led by Dan Aung San Suu Kyi, won the elections against the party backed by the junta, which refused to release power motivated by the fact the country needed constitutional reform to function in a pluralist democracy. An arms embargo was imposed in 1991, a travel ban in 1996, a freeze of assets in 2000 and a prohibition of lending in 2004. It was only in 2007 with common position 750 of 19th November that sanctions touched the banks and a number of precious minerals recognised to be the bases of the economic power of the military junta. Council decision 232 of 26th April 2010 listed over 1,200 companies and 400 people.

Sanctions are of a constraining type as the demand made by the EU is to restore the democratically-elected government and, since 2007, the measures have had an impact on their targets (Pedersen 2008; Eriksson 2004; Smith 2006; Smith 1999; House of Lords 2007a).

EU/Bosnia & Herzegovina – 2001 to 2006

This sanction regime is to be included in the larger picture of post-conflict reconstruction and stabilisation. The Dayton agreement was signed in 1995. While UN sanctions were lifted in 1996, the EU decided to maintain an arms embargo on the former republic of Yugoslavia with common position 184 of 26th February 1996. With the implementation of the Dayton agreements, the EU progressively lifted the embargo on Montenegro and Slovenia, leaving in place the arms embargo only on Bosnia and Herzegovina with common position 719 of 8 October 2001. Finally, the embargo was lifted with common position 29 of 23rd January 2006.

This sanctions regime is classified as constraining given its peculiar nature was limited to preventing the arming of actors. The closeness of Bosnia to the EU makes trading weapons illegally quite complicated. Unfeasible requests combined with impact makes this sanction of a constraining type (Paes 2009; European Union 2001b; European Union 2006b).

Signalling sanctions

The signalling type of sanctions is the most common one of the three logics. Signalling sanctions do not equal symbolic ones, which usually refer to poorly designed sanctions. This type of restrictive measure can be directed at targets that may be different from the explicit one. However, the distinguishing character of signalling sanctions is that they work without the imposition of a cost on targets, they may work according to different rules too. Whereas there is an element of signalling in every sanctions episode, there are cases of restrictive measures that are mainly designed to signal certain audiences or targets. A careful review of signalling cases will help us to define a list of strategies behind the imposition of signalling sanctions at the end of this research. Table 4.6 presents the complete list of sanctions. Only seven cases per sender are briefly presented below.

Table 4.6: Episodes of signalling sanctions

Type	No.	Episodes	
		European Union	United Nations
Signalling	38	EU/Belarus – 1998 to 1999	UN/Haiti – 1993 to 1993
		EU/Belarus – 2004 to 2007	UN/Sudan – 1996 to 1996
		EU/Comoros – 2008 to 2008	UN/Sierra Leone – 2003 to 2010
		EU/FYROM – 2001 to 009	UN/Libya – 1999 to 2003
		EU/Nigeria – 1993 to 1998	UN/Libya – 1992 to 1993
		EU/Uzbekistan – 2005 to 2009	UN/Ethiopia-Eritrea – 2000 to 2001
		EU/Transnistria – 2010 to present	UN/Liberia – 1992 to 2001
		EU/China – 1989 to present	UN/Sierra Leone – 1997 to 1998
		EU/FRY – 1996 to 1998	UN/Sierra Leone – 1998 to 2000
		EU/Nigeria – 1998 to 1999	UN/Hariri – 2005 to present
		EU/Afghanistan – 1996 to1999	UN/Somalia – 1992 to 2008
		EU/Burma/Myanmar – 1991 to 2007	UN/Unita – 1993 to 1999
		EU/DRC – 1993 to 2003	UN/DRC – 2003 to present
		EU/Sudan – 1994-2004	UN/Lebanon – 2006 to present
		EU/Sudan – 2004 to 2005	UN/Sudan – 2004 to 2005
		EU/Indonesia – 1999 to 2000	UN/Sudan – 2005-present
		EU/Libya – 1999 to 2004	UN/Yugoslavia – 1991 to 1992
			UN/Kosovo – 1998 to 2001
			UN/Rwanda – 1994 to 1995
			UN/Rwanda – 1995 to 2008
			UN/DPRK – 2006 to 2009

UN/Sierra Leone – 1997 to 1998

The civil war in Sierra Leone began in the early 1990s and the situation was strongly interconnected with the conflict in Liberia. The Revolutionary United Front (RUF), which was supported by Charles Taylor and led by Foday Sankoh, was involved in the illicit trade of arms and diamonds in the country. In 1992, Captain Strasser became president in a military coup that lasted until 1996, when he was ousted by another coup. General elections were held in the same year and they were won by Kabbah, who was declared president. The following year set the stage for a further military coup that removed Kabbah and installed General Koroma in power. This series of military coups and the source of instability that was destabilising the whole region led the Security Council to impose arms and oil embargoes on the country as well as a travel ban on the members of the military junta and their immediate families with resolution 1132 of 8th October 1997 (United Nations 1997b). The same document created a Sanctions Committee to monitor the implementation of the sanctions and asked for the return of Kabbah to power. After 10 months, a Nigeria-led Economic Community of West African States Monitoring Group (ECOMOG) mission re-established Kabbah in power militarily, but the fighting with RUF and with Sankoh did not end and the sanctions regime continued. It has been since adjusted to the mutated context with resolution 1156 of 16th March 1998 (United Nations 1998b).

The real source of power in Sierra Leone was the trade of diamonds, and this material was not targeted by the measures. The arms embargo among others had probably the highest impact as any military government requires military equipment to govern, but the impact of such a measure becomes visible only after a while. Overall, as there was no immediate impact, it is plausible to assume that the UN wanted to show its presence in Sierra Leone, and to justify its existence to the world audience (Olonisakin 2008; Malan 2002; Keen 2005; Kabia 2009; Ayissi and Poulton 2006).

UN/Liberia – 1992 to 2001

In 1980, Samuel Doe took power in a violent coup during which former President William Tolbert was killed. Doe's party, the National Democratic Party of Liberia (NDPL), won the elections in 1985 under heavy contestation of electoral frauds. In 1989, the National Patriotic Front of Liberia (NPFL) led by Charles Taylor launched a military campaign against Doe and entered Liberia from the Ivory Coast. ECOWAS intervened by establishing a Monitoring Observer Group peacekeeping mission (ECOMOG) that delayed Taylor's victory. As a result of the growing instabilities, President Doe was killed in September 1990. The civil war continued and the UN decided to impose an embargo on weapons and military equipment, with the exception of ECOWAS forces, on Liberia with resolution 788 of 19th November 1992 after several violations of a ceasefire in November 1990 and the failing Yamoussoukro Accords of October 1991 (United Nations 1992c). The UN established the United Nations Observer Mission in Liberia (UNOMIL) and carried out multiple diplomatic activities that resulted in the Cotonou agreement, the Akosombo and the Accra Agreements. Charles Taylor won the elections and Liberia remained under the same sanctions until 2001, when the conflict developed towards a different direction.

The arms embargo was a side measure if seen in the wider UN strategy. Indeed, the reports confirm that weapons continued to enter the country and other measures were not considered until 2001 (Boulden 2003; Déme 2005; Daniel *et al.* 2008).

UN/Hariri – 2005 to present

On 14th February 2005, the former Lebanese Prime Minister Rafic Hariri was killed along with other twenty-two people in Beirut. In order to help the Lebanese authorities to establish the truth, the UN Security Council established an International Independent Investigation Commission under resolution 1595 and imposed a travel ban and an assets freeze on the individuals indicated by the Committee as responsible for the bombing, with resolution 1636 of 31st October 2005 (United Nations 2005). The Commission issued eleven reports until 2008, after which the Security Council decided to create a Special Tribunal for Lebanon 'to prosecute persons responsible for the attack of 14th February 2005 resulting in the death of former Lebanese Prime Minister Rafic Hariri and in the death or injury of other persons'. In December 2010, no individuals were indicted, but the Tribunal is expected to issue the first name soon following heavy pressure to do so. Indeed, rumours indicate Hezbollah members as responsible for the attack, and Saad Hariri, the son of Rafic, who is now prime minister in Lebanon, it has been intimated by the leaders of Hezbollah, will reject the decisions of the Tribunal.

The indicting is taking longer than expected, and the naming of any responsible is undermined by the declared intention of Hezbollah to react violently if any of its members were to be indicated, thereby still no impact is recorded (Salem 2006; Safa 2006; International Crisis Group 2010b; El-Masri 2008).

UN/DRC – 2003 to present

The Democratic Republic of the Congo (DRC) has undergone a long period of instability since the early 1990s. After the genocide in Rwanda, the situation has worsened in Congo. Rwanda, Uganda and Burundi have supported rebel groups against the government of Kinshasa, and Angola, Zimbabwe and Namibia have become involved in the conflict, intervening in 1998. After a peace agreement signed in 2002, the foreign governments declared that they had pulled out from the DRC, but the conflict never ended. Riots and violence spread in Ituri, South and North Kivu provinces, so the UN Security Council imposed a wide range of sanctions (arms embargo in 2003 with resolution 1493 against individuals, entities and non-governmental groups operating in eastern DRC who were an obstacle to peace, travel restrictions and an assets freeze in 2004 on national individuals who were violating the sanctions and, in 2005, on foreign parties). Finally, seriously concerned about the rising use of child soldiers in the conflict, the Security Council imposed financial and visa sanctions on individuals and entities involved in child soldiering with resolution 1698 of 31st July 2006. A panel of experts was established in 2004, and in 2008 a partial lifting allowed the sale of weapons to governmental authorities. The UN is also present in the country with a peace-keeping operation, the United Nations Organisation Mission in the Democratic Republic of the Congo (MONUC).

However, these sanctions cannot receive full implementation given the precarious conditions that characterise the areas of conflict, so any logic with regards to sanctions would work without material considerations linked to sanctions (United Nations 2003b; United Nations 2010b; Kieh 2007; International Crisis Group 2010a; Furley and May 2006; Nest 2006).

UN/Sudan – 2004 to 2005

Sudan was torn by a civil war between the north and the south that started in 1983 and lasted for more than twenty years until a comprehensive peace agreement was signed in Nairobi in 2005. This agreement was the result of peace talks that began in 2003 between the north and the south, which basically focused on the autonomy of the south from the north and on the distribution of the revenues from the sale of oil from which parties in the western part of the country felt left out. This is one of the reasons that led the Sudan Liberation Army/Movement (SLA/M) and Justice and Equality Movement (JEM), based in Darfur, to embark on a military campaign to ensure that their voices were heard by the rest of the country. The Government reacted strongly to this new threat coming from Darfur and is accused of supporting a militia group, the Janjaweed, in putting down the protests. The Janjaweed became notorious for their actions. Sudan gained the reputation of hosting the first genocide in the twenty-first century. Almost 200,000 people died and two million were displaced since the beginning of the Janjaweed operations. According to Human Rights Watch, almost four million people in Darfur depend on humanitarian assistance to survive. In order to sustain the efforts of the African Union (AU) in the region and to contribute to the stabilisation of the area, the Security Council has imposed an arms embargo 'on all non-governmental entities and individuals, including the Janjaweed, operating the states of North Darfur, South Darfur, and West Darfur' with resolution 1556 of 30th July 2004 (United Nations 2004b).

The arms embargo was totally irrelevant on the capacity of Sudan to carry out military strikes because the embargo was limited to the actors operating in Darfur, a wording that is very difficult to implement (Ayers 2005; Sørbø 2010; Ekengard 2006; Farral 2007). In fact, sanctions have changed in 2005 and the international community increased the pressure on Bashir when the ICC issued an arrest warrant on him.

UN/Yugoslavia – 1991 to 1992

The break-up of Yugoslavia was among the worst human tragedies in Europe since the end of World Word II. The implosion of the country, which led to the creation of the term 'Balkanisation' to refer to a violent dissolution of a political community, is characterised by multiple layers of concurrent conflicts after the transition of authority due to the death of the leader of the country, Marshall Josip Tito, in 1980. The first frictions took place after Croatia and Slovenia gave course to their will to become independent. Armed conflict broke out first between the Yugoslav Army and the Croatian forces. The Slovenian declaration of independence of 25th June 1991 led to the ten-days war between the Slovenian and the Serbian forces. The Brioni Accord, setting the conditions for both the Croatian and Slovenian independence, was signed on 7th July 1991, and eventually implemented with the complete withdrawal of the Serbian forces in October 1991. Alarmed by the Yugoslav foreign minister on the acts of violence taking place in Yugoslavia, the Security Council imposed an arms embargo with resolution 713 of 25th September 1991 (United Nations 1991b), which was supported by the creation of a Sanctions Committee established with resolution 724 of 15th December 1991.

The arms embargo was not properly implemented and was not properly planned. Furthermore, the arms embargo was not accompanied by additional measures that could have been imposed on the conflict in Bosnia. The outset of the conflict in Bosnia led the Security Council to take the lead in the conflict and to impose a comprehensive embargo on Yugoslavia with resolution 757 in May 1992 (Berdal and Economides 2007; Bethlehem and Weller 1997; Brzoska and Lopez 2009; Carr and Callan 2002; Dedring 2008; Higgins 1993; Leurdijk and Venema 1996; Paes 2009).

UN/DPRK – 2006 to 2009

The quarrel between North Korea and the international community over the nuclear program of Pyongyang started in 1984 when a US spy satellite discovered a nuclear power plant in Yongbyon, about 100km north of the capital. Years of negotiations followed and North Korea became notorious as one of the rogue states of the international system, especially after it pulled out of the Non-Proliferation Treaty (NPT). States imposed different forms of sanctions on the DPRK, but the UN did not act until 2006 when Pyongyang escalated the level of tension. On 9th October, North Korea tested a long-range ballistic missile and brought the issue to the attention of the international community. That act was considered a challenge to the NPT and the international community responded. On 14th October 2006, the UN Security Council imposed an arms embargo, a travel ban, an assets freeze and a commodity boycott with resolution 1718 on people, groups or entities involved in the nuclear program of the DPRK (United Nations 2006a).

These measures could have had an impact, but no individuals were listed until 2009, therefore the material impact of multilateral sanctions was nil, but the international community was able to bond together a common position (Cha and Kang 2003; Cronin 2008; Eberstadt 2007; Jeffries 2010; Pritchard 2007; Rothman 2007).

EU/Belarus – 1998 to 1999

Lukashenko became President of Belarus in 1994. Since 1996, when he managed to change the constitution to favour his position, relations with the EU have become bitter. The first use of sanctions dates back to 1998, when the EU imposed a travel ban on Belarusian officials with common position 448 (European Union 1998b). The EU accused Belarus of violating the Vienna Convention for problems related to the renovation of the Drozdy (or Drazdy) compound, where western diplomats resided. EU officials feared that Belarus authorities intended to take over the compound. According to common position 448, about one hundred government members were denied the right to enter the Union. Furthermore, the EU froze its Technical Aid to the Commonwealth of Independent States (TACIS) Civil Society Development Programme, which was the last remaining major EU commitment to Belarus (Krivosheev 2003; Rudling 2008).

The travel ban was lifted in 1999 after an agreement was reached between the Government of Belarus and the European Union. Deprivation of travelling to Europe for some officials cannot be ranked among the reasons that led to an agreement (Bosse and Korosteleva-Polglase 2009; Dumasy 2003; Eriksson 2004; Jarabik and Silitski 2008; Lynch 2005; Rudling 2008).

EU/Comoros – 2008 to 2008

Comoros became independent from France in 1975, but the transition and post-transition phase has been characterised by turbulence. Since 1999, the Fomboni Accords have regulated the institutional balance between the three major islands. In 2007, when the three presidents were to be re-elected, the President of Anjouan refused to step down in order to run again and his forces clashed with the Union's sent to force him to step down. In November, the AU imposed a travel ban and an assets freeze on the island and the EU followed suit with a travel ban and an assets freeze on eight individuals with common position 187 on 3rd March 2008. After a few months, the African Union intervened militarily and the President of Anjouan was arrested. The EU lifted the sanctions with common position 611 of 24th July 2008 (European Union 2008b; European Union 2008c).

Given the short time in effect, the overlapping with the military action taken by the AU and the little importance of the resource denied to the targeted individuals, it is plausible to assume that sanctions served the AU as a justification of its actions, increasing its legitimacy more than changing the behaviour of the targets (Massey and Baker 2009; Svensson 2008).

EU/China – 1989 to present

In June 1989, large demonstrations of students took place in China asking for more rights and liberties. The Chinese authorities decided to put down the protests by force, which caused hundreds of casualties in Tiananmen Square and its surroundings. The international community strongly criticised the Government in Beijing for its decision and moved to sanction the massacre. With a Council Declaration on 27th June, the EU (then the European Community) called on its member states to prevent any arms sale to China. The arms embargo has been in effect since then (even though there was an intense discussion in 2004/2005 on what to do about it).

However, the embargo in force is among the weakest of EU legislations. There are three categories of products that can potentially be banned today: military equipment, non-lethal technologies and dual-use technologies. Only the first of the three was covered by the Madrid declaration and the Code of Conduct was not in force then. Hence, EU states have interpreted the arms embargo in different fashions. They made the embargo non-effective and merely symbolic. It would seem to serve the objective for the EU to talk with one voice, rather than coerce China into improving its human rights behaviour (Edmonds 2002; Hellstrom 2010; Kerr and Fei 2007; Kreutz 2004; Tang 2005).

EU/Sudan – 1994 to 2004

In 1983, the Second Sudanese Civil War broke out and lasted for almost twenty years up to 2005. The conflict erupted because the south, Sudan People's Liberation Movement (SPLM), accused the central government led by President Al Bashir of attempting to establish an Islamic state, despite the presence of a large Christian majority in the south. In 1990, the EU suspended development aid to Sudan while other actors, such as the Intergovernmental Authority on Drought and Development (IGADD) that was heavily funded by EU members, attempted several mediations. After the bombing of civilians in the province of Equatoria in February 1994, the EU imposed an arms embargo on military equipment with Council decision 165 of 15th March 1994. In 2003, the conflict in Darfur started and the Council confirmed the arms embargo in 2004 with common position 31, which determines a new episode of sanctions (European Union 1994).

This should be considered a signalling type for its lack of impact (Ali and Matthews 1999). There is no hope to affect or settle the conflict by stopping the sale of weapons to Sudan. On the contrary, the stronger side may be favoured. That is why this episode may be read through the lenses of EU identity formation.

EU/Nigeria – 1993 to 1998

After a turbulent decade in 1980, Nigeria entered an even more troublesome period in the early 1990s. After two rounds of elections annulled for fraud, the June 1993 presidential race was judged by international observers as the freest of the previous years in Nigeria. However, victory was disputed and the deadlock was broken by General Abacha, who was highly criticised by the international community, even if he was called into power. Both the US and the UK imposed sanctions and threatened to extend their tampering with the domestic life of Nigeria. From

June to November 1993, the EU also imposed a large variety of restrictive measures: it suspended military cooperation, imposed a visa ban on Nigerian officials, limited the movement of Nigerian diplomats and suspended the non-necessary visits of EU officials to Nigeria. Sanctions were revised after the case of the Ogoni nine in 1995 (European Union 1995), and were eventually lifted in 1998 when General Abacha suffered a stroke (European Union 1998a).

The measures were heavier than in other cases of sanctions, but the impact was still low for its lack of enforcement and because the main resource sensitive to Nigeria, namely oil, was not touched (King 1999; Osaghae 1998; Nmoma 1995; Falola 1999; Ayittey 1999; Agbu 1998).

EU/Afghanistan – 1996 to 1999

After the seizing of Kabul in 1996, the Taliban pushed the Northern National Alliance (NCA) parties to the North of the country and began the organisation of the political regime. Several human rights violations were reported and the strict application of Sharia Law triggered large protests in the country and raised concerns throughout the international community. Noticeably, the ban on women working raised much attention on the repressive regime installed by the Taliban. Only Pakistan, Saudi Arabia and the Arab Emirates recognised the new government led by the Taliban. The UN endeavour as peace-broker fell on deaf ears. An attempt to raise attention on the issue of Afghanistan was initiated and the UN Security Council passed resolution 1760 calling on all member states to stop selling weapons to the warring parties. The EU, particularly concerned with human rights and women's rights violations, followed suit and adopted common position 746 on 17th December 1996, which required all member states to impose an embargo on arms supplies to Afghanistan (European Union 1996).

The EU basically limited its external efforts towards Afghanistan with this measure and it was insufficient given the fact that the EU exports of weapons towards Afghanistan were negligible. Once again, this sanction seems more the result of the need to speak with one voice than truly improving the situation in Afghanistan (Anthony 2002; Kreutz 2005; Matinuddin 1999; Rashid 2001; Rashid 2000).

EU/FYROM – 2001 to 2009

The end of the wars in the Balkans and the stabilisation of the situation in Kosovo were sources of instabilities in neighbouring countries. In 2001, the EU began to think about sustaining the state building processes in its vicinity along with sustaining the FYROM. In 2001, the Council condemned 'all forms of terrorism in the Western Balkans region and remained committed to preventing such actions from undermining the democratic processes' and a travel ban was imposed on the individuals who were named as responsible for undermining the stabilisation process. Common position 542 was adopted on 16th July 2001 (European Union 2001a), but no names were included in the list. Names of up to twenty-one individuals were later added in 2005 (European Union 2005a) until the measures were not renewed in 2009.

This is a borderline measure, as it could have been classified as a constraining type only if financial sanctions had been imposed as well. The decision to limit the restrictive measures only to the travel ban reduced the impact of the measures and classified them as signalling ones (De Vries 2002; Paes 2009; Buchet de Neuilly 2003; Wouters and Naert 2001).

Describing the context: the three independent variables

The analysis of the context completes the description of the database. Threat, salience and complexity seems to offer an interesting view of the environmental setting of sanctions systems and the creation of indexes based on multiple weighted indicators allows to include many facets of composite realities. The three indexes are standardised, hence they are represented in a continuum from 0 to 1, where 0 is the minimum and 1 is the maximum.[2] Since all the cases are international crises, it is important to note that a 0 level for the variable does not signify absence for that variable, but only low intensity. For instance, a low level of complexity would correspond to a 0 value in the index of complexity. The same logic applies to salience and threat.

Threat to sender

The first IV shows the variation of the threat to the sender in the seventy different episodes of sanctions posed to the senders. The index of threat is based on three indicators: issue, extension and geostrategy.

Issue could have been assigned with values ranging from 1 to 4, and it is relevant to note that almost 40 per cent of the cases have received the value of 1 for this variable. Relevant cases like the UN sanctions in Sierra Leone in 2007 and Cambodia, and the EU restrictive measures on Nigeria and Burma/Myanmar have been assigned with a value of 1. The categories of 2, 3 and 4 have been filled respectively with thirteen (e.g. the UN sanctions on Yugoslavia in 1996 and the EU sanctions on the ICTY indictees), twenty-two (e.g. the UN sanctions on Iran, the EU case on Transnistria) and seven cases (e.g. the UN in Iraq and the EU in Kosovo).

The second indicator is the extension of the threat and it refers to the number of actors that are affected by it. Measured on a five-point scale, the dispersion for extension appears with a peak on the value 2: thirteen cases have received the evaluation of 1 (e.g. the UN sanctions on Liberia in 2003 and the EU measures on the Comoros), thirty-five of 2 (e.g. the UN sanctions on Sierra Leone in 2003 and the EU on Belarus in 2004), eight of 3 (e.g. the UN sanctions on Eritrea in 2009 and the EU sanctions on Belarus in 2007), eleven of 4 (e.g. the UN sanctions on

---

2.   A very simple equation has been used to standardise the indexes: $G = (D - Dmin)/(Dmax - Dmin)$, where G will be the index value for each observation, D is the specific value that will range from the lowest value to the highest.

Somalia in 2008 and the EU sanctions on the US in 1996) and the remnant three cases have been deemed to be a wide threat to the entire system (e.g. the UN sanctions on Iraq in 1990; no EU sanctions have been rated as such). In regards to this aspect, it is interesting to verify that the majority of the crises do not affect a large number of actors, and this consideration should have a place in explaining the role played by international organisations and the type of sanctions that are imposed.

The third indicator is geostrategy and this refers to the location and the distance of the target from the sender. Measured on a four-point scale, eight cases have been assigned with the lowest geostrategic importance (e.g. Ethiopia and Eritrea in 2001 for the UN and the Comoros for the EU), twenty-eight cases with little geostrategic relevance (e.g. the UN sanctions on Hariri's murderers, and the EU sanctions on Nigeria), twenty-four with moderate importance (e.g. the UN sanctions on Haiti in 1993/1994 and the EU sanctions on Transnistria), and ten with the highest importance (e.g. the UN sanctions on Iraq and the EU measures on the ICTY indictees). Table 4.7 summarises the data for each indicator of the variable threat.

Table 4.7: Distribution of indicators for threat

	1	2	3	4	5
Issue	28	12	22	7	–
Extension	13	35	8	11	3
Geostrategy	8	28	24	10	–

For instance, the case of Iraq in 1990 has been identified by this study as posing the highest threat to the sender, namely to the United Nations. The inviolability of national borders became the cornerstone of the international system since the Treaty of Westphalia, and military invasions have not been easily tolerated especially since the end of World War II. Moreover, the P5 were threatened by the fact that Saddam Hussein had gained control of the vast oil resource of Kuwait, which, combined with the Iraqi ones, were the largest known reserves in the world.

The lowest level of threat is posed by Rwanda, Ethiopia/Eritrea, Zimbabwe and the DRC, which sit in parts of Africa that do not represent strategic values to the P5 countries. Figure 4.1 summarises the standardised index of threat for the sample and the detailed results are in Appendix II.

Salience of the crisis

The salience of the issue at stake for the sender is the second IV and it is defined by two indicators: the level of attention and the level of engagement.

Level of attention is elaborated on a three-point scale: eighteen cases have been rated with 1 (e.g. the UN sanctions on Ethiopia/Eritrea and the EU sanctions on Sudan in 1994), fourteen cases with 2 (e.g. the UN sanctions on Libya in 1999, and the EU sanctions on the FYROM), and thirty-eight with 3 (e.g. the UN sanctions on Sudan in 2005 and the EU sanctions on Zimbabwe).

The level of engagement as well has been elaborated on a three-point scale, wherein sixteen cases have been attributed to the lowest point (e.g. the UN

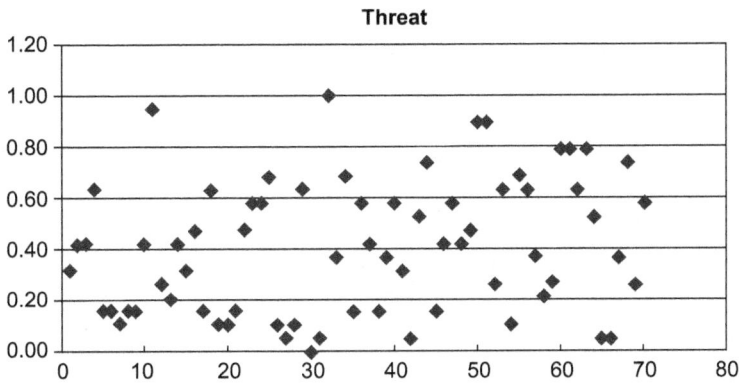

Figure 4.1: Indexes of threat

sanctions on Sierra Leone in 1997, and the EU sanctions on Burma/Myanmar in 1992), thirty-three cases to the middle value (e.g. the UN in Rwanda and the EU in Uzbekistan), and twenty-one cases to the highest value (e.g. the UN sanctions on Cambodia and the EU on Bosnia/Herzegovina). The following table summarises the frequency of the indicators of salience.

Table 4.8: Distribution of indicators for salience

	1	2	3
Attention	18	14	38
Engagement	16	33	21

The different values depict the reality of the seventy sanctions episodes considered and the variation among the cases. The crises in Iraq and Lebanon were among the most salient to the UN, while the crises of Yugoslavia and Belarus are among the most salient for the EU. Figure 4.2 summarises the finding related to the second IV which has been labelled salience, while the detailed coefficients are in Appendix III.

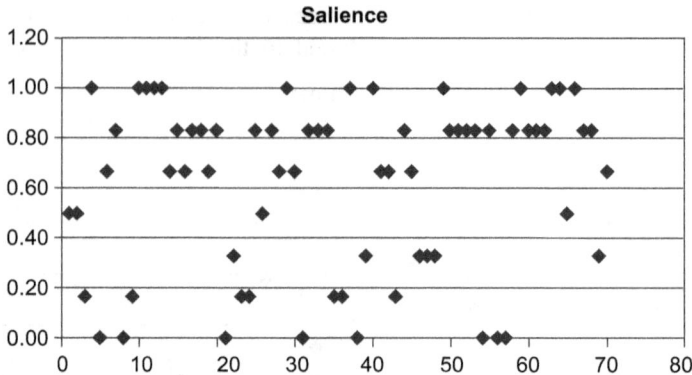

Figure 4.2: Indexes of salience

Complexity of the crisis

The complexity of the dispute is the last of the three IVs that characterised the context and is composed by four indicators: number of the actors, level of violence, number of issues, and target strength.

The number of the actors was rated on a five-point scale: five cases involved only one actor (e.g. the UN sanctions in Sierra Leone in 2003 and China for the EU), eleven cases involved two actors (e.g. the UN sanctions on the Taliban and the EU sanctions on the former Yugoslavia in 1996), twenty-four cases involved three actors (e.g. the UN sanctions on UNITA, and the EU sanctions on Guinea), twelve cases involved four actors (e.g. the UN on Al-Qaida in 2002 and the EU sanctions on Indonesia in 1992) and eighteen cases involved five or more actors (e.g. the UN sanctions on Sierra Leone in 1997, and the EU sanctions on Burma/Myanmar).

Violence refers to the level of violence reached by the actors in the dispute and it is presented with a four-point scale from 1 to 4, 1 being no violence and 4 open war. In this scale, twenty-two cases have received the rating of 1 (e.g. the situations in North Korea and Moldova), twenty-one episodes the rating of 2 (e.g. Cambodia and the Comoros), thirteen cases the rating of 3 (e.g. Ivory Coast and Sudan in 2004) and fourteen cases the rating of 4 (e.g. Somalia and Yugoslavia).

Issues is represented in a continuum from 1 to 5, being 1 where there is only one issue at stake that is not security related and 5 a multiple issues dispute with security relevance. A crisis on only one issue was encountered four times and were all EU cases (e.g. China and the EU), two issues fourteen times (e.g. Nigeria in 1993 and Libya in 1993), three issues fourteen times (e.g. the crises with the DPRK in 2009 and with Burma/Myanmar), four issues twenty times (e.g. the DRC and Sierra Leone) and five issues seventeen cases (e.g. the crises in Haiti and Yugoslavia).

Finally, the last indicator for the index of complexity pertains to target strength that has been operationalised with a three-point scale ranging from 1 (weak), to 3 (strong): out of seventy cases of the sample, eight have been classified as weak (e.g. Comoros and Haiti in 1993), thirty-nine has moderately strong (e.g. the Kmher Rouge in Cambodia and the regime in Uzbekistan), and 23 have been deemed strong (e.g. UNITA and Transnistria). Table 4.9 summarises the frequencies for the indicators of complexity.

Table 4.9: Distribution of indicators for complexity

	1	2	3	4	5
Actors	5	11	24	12	18
Violence	22	21	13	14	-
Issues	4	14	15	1209	17
Target strength	8	39	23	–	–

According to the analysis, the Somali crisis turned out to be the most complicated of all, followed by other crises such as the African conflicts in Ivory Coast, Angola, the DRC, and likewise the Afghani civil war during the rising of the Taliban. On the other side of the spectrum are crises like the EU/US confrontation over the extra-territorial imposition of US domestic law, the crises in North Korea, Belarus and Libya. It is interesting to notice how long-lasting crises, such as the one over the nuclear programme of Pyongyang are deemed less complex than others. This feature deserves further elaboration. One assumption of the study is that the length of a crisis does not necessarily mean that the crisis is complicated. In fact, the length of a crisis can be explained with other variables, such as threat or salience. Figure 4.3 presents the index value of salience for the 70 cases of the sample and Appendix IV summarises the coefficients.

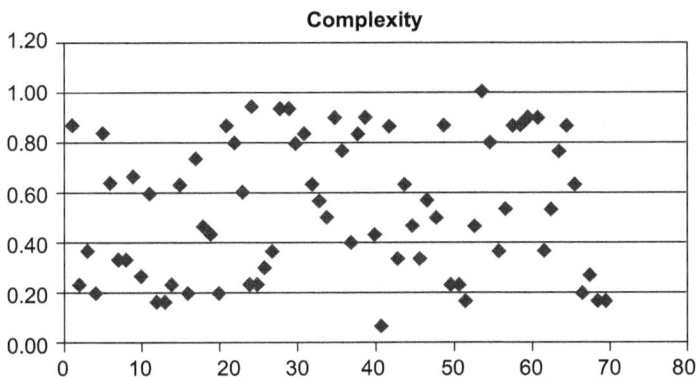

Figure 4.3: Index of complexity

Conclusion

Empirical analyses of sanctions rarely acknowledge that sanctions differ from one another; therefore, any systematic review is missing. This chapter demonstrates that sanctions differ from each other both by looking at their logic and at their context. The variance of the observable characteristics of sanctions emerges from the dimensions of feasibility and direct impact, which allow us to distinguish between coercive, constraining and signalling sanctions. The operationalisation of the systemic approach provides a view of the different contexts in which sanctions are imposed by looking at threat, salience and complexity. How does the context relate to the logic of the sanctions imposed? Chapter 5 provides a first answer to this question.

chapter five | a systemic explanation for sanctions

The aim of this book is to investigate whether systemic pressures that lead policy makers to resort to specific types of sanctions exist. The objective of this chapter is to verify whether the neorealist principle, according to which different actors behave similarly in similar contexts and similar actors behave differently in different contexts, is valid also in the sanctions field. This chapter presents the results of the empirical test with the database of seventy episodes of sanctions. Is it more likely to expect coercive sanctions for a higher or a lower level of threat? What happens if a threat is high, but a salience is low? And what if a crisis is complex? The hypothesis of this research is that the context, defined as the system of sanctions, provides constraints and opportunities for policy makers when they decide to resort to sanctions.

The results of the analysis show that there are consistent correlations between the IVs and type of sanctions. The first confirmation comes by looking at the individual IVs as, for instance, the level of threat is highly correlated with a direct impact on targets, and therefore with coercive or constraining measures. The results of the measurement of the combinations of IVs with the cs-QCA method are milder, but still positive. For instance, certain combinations confirm the hypothesis, such as the strong correlation for low salience and low threat with signalling sanctions. However, the combination of low threat and high salience does not lead to solid results. The theoretical framework is useful to explain 64 per cent of the sample, while the other 36 per cent will need further elaboration.

This chapter is divided in three parts: a summary of the hypotheses and a general overview of the associations found between individual IVs and type of sanctions; an exploration of the causal connections of combinations of IVs and the dependent variables; and a look at the ambivalent patterns that emerged from the empirical test. A short conclusion presents the main findings of the chapter and leads to the case studies in the remainder of the book.

A theory in the making 1.0: testing the general hypotheses

There were both general and specific hypotheses linked to the creation of a systemic approach to sanctions. General hypotheses refer to the expected association between individual IVs and a specific type of sanctions. The confirmation of these hypotheses should not surprise us, but it is relevant to discover how much of the DV can be explained. More specific hypotheses originate from the different influence on the type of sanctions of the eight possible combinations of the IVs. The results of the empirical test for the general hypotheses are presented in Table 5.1.

Table 5.1: General hypotheses of the research, the empirical test

Independent variable	Intensity	Expected outcome	Confirmation rate (%)
Threat	High	Coercing or constraining	84.62
	Low	Signalling	77.27
Salience	High	Coercing or Constraining	60.00
	Low	Signalling	80.00
Complexity	High	Constraining or Signalling	100.00
	Low	Coercing or signalling	79.41

In general terms, the results confirm the hypotheses even though the confirmation rate differs for each variable. For instance, there is a perfect match between high complexity and constraining or signalling. Contrarily, high salience correlates only to 60 per cent of episodes that take the form of coercing or constraining, while confirmation rates are around 80 per cent for low salience, low complexity, high and low threat. The detailed correlations are summarised in Table 5.2.

Table 5.2: Detailed associations between independent variables and logics

	Instances	Coercing	Constraining	Signalling
High threat	26	10 (38.46%)	12 (46.15%)	4 (15.38%)
Low threat	44	0	10 (22.73%)	34 (77.27%)
High salience	45	8 (17.78)	19 (42.22%)	18 (40%)
Low salience	25	2 (8%)	3 (12%)	20 (80%)
High complexity	36	0	15 (41.67%)	21 (58.33%)
Low complexity	34	10 (29.41%)	7 (20.59%)	17 (50%)

Some examples would help to illustrate this point. The first is that if a threat is high, then it is more likely to result in either coercive or constraining sanctions. The reasoning behind this hypothesis is that senders will be motivated to act and to impose sanctions with a direct impact in order to directly affect targets.

Cases of high threat include security-related crises, such as the ones about international terrorism or conflicts, for instance the 1267 committee and the sanctions that followed on the Taliban and Al-Qaida associates. The conflicts in former Yugoslavia or the Iraq invasion of Kuwait were ranked among high threats. Finally, the situation in Transnistria represents a direct concern to the EU. Transnistria has a relation to possible criminal networks for access to foreign markets and tensions can escalate in open conflicts such as the one that occurred in Georgia in 2008. Table 5.3 summarises the cases of high threat divided per type.

Contrarily, if the threat is low, then sanctions will be of a signalling type as senders would not be concerned about a short-term solution for the crisis. The interesting aspect is that there are no cases of coercive sanctions when threat is low.

Table 5.3: Episodes for high threat

Coercing

EU/Belarus – 2007 to present	UN/Libya – 1993 to 1999	UN/Yugoslavia – 1994 to 1996
EU/Iran 2010	UN/Iran – 2006 to present	UN/DPRK – 2009 to present
EU/US – 1996 to present	UN/Eritrea – 2009 to present	EU/Libya – 2004 to present
UN/1267– 1999 to 2001		

Constraining

EU/FRY – 1998-2000	UN/Iraq – 2003 to present	UN/Haiti – 1993 to 1994
EU/Transnistria – 2003 to 2010	UN/Liberia – 2001 to 2003	UN/Somalia – 2008 to present
UN/Unita – 1999 to 2002	UN/Sierra Leone – 2000 to 2003	UN/Yugoslavia – 1992 to 1994
UN/Iraq – 1990 to 1991	UN/1267 – 2002 to present	UN/Bosnian-Serbs – 1994 to 1996

Signalling

EU/Transnistria – 2010 to present	UN/Yugoslavia – 1991 to 1992	UN/Kosovo – 1998 to 2001
UN/Libya – 1992 to 1993		

Cases of low threat can be crises located far away from senders, such as Zimbabwe or Sudan for the EU, or Liberia or Cambodia for the UN. There are also cases that do not catch the attention of a wider public because of their fairly limited violations of human rights, such as the Hariri murder or the Comoros crisis. Table 5.4 lists the episodes for low threat.

Salience seems to have the least explanatory power of the three IVs as it correlates positively in 60 per cent of the cases of coercing and constraining. The need for senders to act and 'to do something' about the crisis could be a potential explanation for this variable. However, the high rate of signalling sanctions (40 per cent) offers mixed results and does not allow for strong generalisation. Episodes in the category of high salience are Libya and Iran for the UN, while the episodes of Burma/Myanmar since 2007 and Nigeria could be good examples for the EU. The other episodes are summed up in Table 5.5.

Low salience is associated in 80 per cent of the episodes with signalling sanctions and this scores as a strong correlation. Crises with low salience did not receive media attention for reasons that were not investigated in this research. We can, however, assume that a crisis can become relevant for a number of motives including the potential consequences on other countries, markets or particular trade routes. In other cases, which include minor human rights violations, crises – such as the EU in Transnistria or in Uzbekistan and the UN in Haiti or Sudan in 2004/2005 – did not attract a lot of attention. Table 5.6 summarises these results, while the detailed information with regard to the level of attention is in Appendix VI.

In complex situations, the identification of targets, the elaboration of precise demands, and the decisions of resorting to heavy sanctions are affected by the lack of information and by scarce expectations of playing a crucial role in changing the behaviour of targets. Thereby, if complexity is high, then constraining and signalling become more likely. This is confirmed by the 34 episodes classified as highly complex. Even in this case, coercive sanctions are not attempted when the crisis is complex. This recurrence is perfect to falsify the concept according to which sanctions are imposed to modify the behaviour of the target. Sanctions are imposed in a complex situation only to limit what targets otherwise would do, such as the cases of the UN in Haiti, Liberia and Ivory Coast since 2004 for the UN, the cases of the EU in Indonesia, the DRC and Afghanistan from 1996 to 1999 when sanctions were imposed on the Taliban. Alternatively, sanctions are used to send signals to targets and audiences. The full list is in Table 5.7.

Contrarily, low complexity allows for other sanctions as senders can either care about the crisis, then sanction would be coercive, or not care, then sanctions would be of a signalling type. Typical cases are the UN in Libya or Eritrea, while the EU engaged in Belarus in 1998 and 2004, Nigeria, Transnistria and Uzbekistan. Table 5.8 shows the comprehensive list of sanctions episodes for low complexity.

Table 5.4: Episodes for low threat

Coercing	No episode	Constraining
EU/Burma/Myanmar – 2007 to present	EU/ICTY – 2001 to present	UN/Liberia – 2003 to present
EU/Bosnia & Herzegovina – 2001 to 2006	EU/Zimbabwe – 2002 to present	UN/Cote d'Ivoire – 2004 to present
EU/Milosevic – 2000 to present	UN/Iraq – 1991 to 2003	UN/Cambodia – 1992 to 1993
EU/Guinea – 2009 to present		
Signalling		
EU/Afghanistan – 1996 to 1999	EU/Sudan – 1994 to 2004	UN/Hariri – 2005 to present
EU/Belarus – 1998 to 1999	EU/Sudan – 2004 to 2005	UN/Lebanon – 2006 to present
EU/Belarus – 2004 to 2007	EU/Uzbekistan – 2005 to 2009	UN/Libya – 1999 to 2003
EU/Burma/Myanmar – 1991 to 2007	UN/Unita – 1993 to 1999	UN/Somalia – 1992 to 2008
EU/China – 1989 to present	UN/DRC – 2003 to present	UN/Sudan – 1996 to 1996
EU/Comoros – 2008 to 2008	UN/Ethiopia-Eritrea – 2000 to 2001	UN/Sudan – 2004 to 2005
EU/DRC – 1993 to 2003	UN/Liberia – 1992 to 2001	UN/Sudan – 2005 to present
EU/FRY – 1996 to 1998	UN/Sierra Leone – 1997 to 1998	UN/Rwanda – 1994 to 1995
EU/FYROM – 2001 to 2009	UN/Sierra Leone – 1998 to 2000	UN/Rwanda – 1995 to 2008
EU/Indonesia – 1999 to 2000	UN/Sierra Leone – 2003 to 2010	UN/DPRK – 2006 to 2009
EU/Nigeria – 1993 to 1998	UN/Haiti – 1993 to 1993	EU/Libya – 1999 to 2004
EU/Nigeria – 1998 to 1999		

Table 5.5: Episodes for high salience

Coercing

EU/Belarus – 2007 to present	UN/Libya – 1993 to1999	UN/DPRK – 2009 to present
EU/Iran – 2010	UN/Iran – 2006 to present	EU/Libya – 2004 to present
EU/US – 1996 to present	UN/Yugoslavia – 1994 to 1996	

Constraining

EU/Burma/Myanmar – 2007 to present	UN/Unita – 1999 to 2002	UN/Cote d'Ivoire – 2004 to present
EU/FRY – 1998 to 2000	UN/Iraq – 1990 to 1991	UN/1267 – 2002 to present
EU/Bosnia & Herzegovina – 2001 to 2006	UN/Iraq – 1991 to 2003	UN/Cambodia – 1992 to 1993
EU/Milosevic – 2000 to present	UN/Iraq – 2003 to present	UN/Somalia – 2008 to present
EU/Guinea – 2009 to present	UN/Liberia – 2003 to present	UN/Yugoslavia – 1992 to 1994
EU/ICTY – 2001 to present	UN/Sierra Leone – 2000 to 2003	UN/Bosnian-Serbs – 1994 to 1996
EU/Zimbabwe – 2002 to present		

Signalling

EU/China – 1989 to present	UN/Unita – 1993 to 1999	UN/Sudan – 2004 to 2005
EU/FRY – 1996 to 1998	UN/DRC – 2003 to present	UN/Sudan 2005 to present
EU/FYROM – 2001 to 2009	UN/Sierra Leone – 2003 to 2010	UN/Yugoslavia – 1991 to 1992
EU/Indonesia – 1999 to 2000	UN/Lebanon – 2006 to present	UN/Kosovo – 1998 to 2001
EU/Nigeria – 1993 to 1998	UN/Libya – 1992 to 1993	UN/Rwanda – 1995 to 2008
EU/Nigeria – 1998 to 1999	UN/Libya – 1999 to 2003	UN/DPRK – 2006 to 2009

Table 5.6: Episodes for low salience

Coercing		
UN/1267 – 1999 to 2001	UN/Eritrea – 2009 to present	UN/Haiti – 1993 to 1994

Constraining		
EU/Transnistria – 2003 to 2010	UN/Liberia – 2001 to 2003	

Signalling		
EU/Afghanistan – 1996 to 1999	EU/Sudan – 2004 to 2005	UN/Haiti – 1993 to 1993
EU/Belarus – 1998 to 1999	EU/Transnistria – 2010 to present	UN/Hariri – 2005 to present
EU/Belarus – 2004 to 2007	EU/Uzbekistan – 2005 to 2009	UN/Somalia – 1992 to 2008
EU/Burma/Myanmar – 1991 to 2007	UN/Ethiopia-Eritrea – 2000 to 2001	UN/Sudan – 1996 to 1996
EU/Comoros – 2008 to 2008	UN/Liberia – 1992 to 2001	UN/Rwanda – 1994 to 1995
EU/DRC – 1993 to 2003	UN/Sierra Leone – 1997 to 1998	EU/Libya – 1999 to 2004
EU/Sudan – 1994 to 2004	UN/Sierra Leone – 1998 to 2000	

Table 5.7: Episodes for high complexity

Coercing		Signalling
No episode	Constraining	
EU/Burma/Myanmar – 2007 to present EU/FRY – 1998 to 2000 EU/Guinea – 2009 to present EU/Transnistria – 2003 to 2010 UN/Unita – 1999 to 2002	UN/Iraq – 1990 to 1991 UN/Iraq – 1991 to 2003 UN/Iraq – 2003 to present UN/Liberia – 2001 to 2003 UN/Cote d'Ivoire – 2004 to present	UN/1267 – 2002 to present UN/Haiti – 1993 to 1994 UN/Somalia – 2008 to present UN/Yugoslavia – 1992 to 1994 UN/Bosnian-Serbs – 1994 to 1996
EU/Afghanistan – 1996 to 1999	UN/DRC – 2003 to present	UN/Sudan – 1996 to 1996
EU/Burma/Myanmar – 1991 to 2007 EU/DRC – 1993 to 2003 EU/Indonesia – 1999 to 2000 EU/Sudan – 1994 to 2004 EU/Sudan – 2004 to 2005 UN/Unita – 1993 to 1999	UN/Ethiopia-Eritrea – 2000 to 2001 UN/Liberia – 1992 to 2001 UN/Sierra Leone – 1997 to 1998 UN/Sierra Leone – 1998 to 2000 UN/Lebanon – 2006 to present UN/Somalia – 1992 to 2008	UN/Sudan – 2004 to 2005 UN/Sudan – 2005 to present UN/Yugoslavia – 1991 to 1992 UN/Kosovo – 1998 to 2001 UN/Rwanda – 1994 to 1995 UN/Rwanda to 1995 to 2008

Table 5.8: Episodes for low complexity

Coercing

EU/Belarus – 2007 to present	UN/Libya – 1993 to 1999	UN/DPRK – 2009 to present
EU/Iran – 2010	UN/Iran – 2006 to present	EU/Libya – 2004 to present
EU/US – 1996 to present	UN/Eritrea – 2009 to present	
UN/1267 – 1999 to 2001	UN/Yugoslavia – 1994 to 1996	

Constraining

EU/Bosnia & Herzegovina 2001 to 2006	EU/Zimbabwe – 2002 to present	UN/Sierra Leone – 2000 to 2003
EU/Milosevic – 2000 to present	UN/Liberia – 2003 to present	UN/Cambodia – 1992 to 1993
EU/ICTY – 2001 to present		

Signalling

EU/Belarus – 1998 to 1999	EU/Nigeria – 1993 to 1998	UN/Hariri – 2005 to present
EU/Belarus – 2004 to 2007	EU/Nigeria – 1998 to 1999	UN/Libya – 1992 to 1993
EU/China – 1989 to present	EU/Transnistria – 2010 to present	UN/Libya – 1999 to 2003
EU/Comoros – 2008 to 2008	EU/Uzbekistan – 2005 to 2009	UN/DPRK – 2006 to 2009
EU/FRY – 1996 to 1998	UN/Sierra Leone – 2003 to 2010	EU/Libya – 1999 to 2004
EU/FYROM – 2001 to 2009	UN/Haiti – 1993 to 1993	

A theory in the making 2.0: testing the specific hypotheses

The real world is always more complex than formal models, that is why cs-QCA can contribute to reducing the gap between theory and practice by measuring the influence of interactive multiple IVs on a DV. In the exercise of this book, the context has been described by three main variables – threat, salience and complexity – deemed to have an explanatory power as postulated by the major theories of international relations. The empirical analysis of the seventy sanctions' episodes has led to the conclusion that the context is important to both understand and explain the logic of international sanctions. The three variables operationalised dichotomically create eight different scenarios that were considered in the study and a specific logic of sanctions was hypothesised for each of them. The first verification of these expected associations is presented in Table 5.9.

Table 5.9: Specific hypotheses of the research

N	Threat	Salience	Complexity	Expected sanction	Episodes	Test (%)
1	High	High	High	Constraining	8 out of 10	80
2	High	Low	High	Constraining	3 out of 3	100.00
3	High	Low	Low	Coercing	2 out of 3	66.67
4	Low	Low	Low	Signalling	7 out of 7	100.00
5	Low	High	Low	Constraining	8 out of 14	42.86
6	Low	High	High	Constraining	7 out of 11	36.36
7	High	High	Low	Coercing	8 out of 10	80
8	Low	Low	High	Signalling	12 out of 12	100.00

The theoretical framework is supported by the empirical analysis. If we consider the combination that presents a strong correlation between the context and the logic of sanctions, then the episodes explained are 45 (64 per cent of the sample). If we consider the episodes that confirmed the hypotheses, then the confirmation rate goes up to 71 per cent (51 episodes). Table 5.10 presents the frequency for the detailed results of the analysis. And the difference between positive and negative cases is evident.

A positive case is a case that was confirmed by the hypotheses. For instance, combination one was confirmed to be of a constraining type in eight cases out of ten. Here, we would have eight positive cases and two negative cases. This does not mean that the theory is wrong, but that the theory, as a simplification of the reality, could be further refined. The number of negative cases is low, but this does do not threaten the findings of the theory, according to which there are three dominant patterns for the relationship between system and sanctions types that have received empirical backing. A dominant pattern is a given combination of IVs that is strongly correlated with the type of sanction imposed. Contrarily, an ambivalent or ambiguous pattern is a given configuration of the system of sanctions that is not able to find solid empirical bases for the hypothesised link. The results are summarised in Table 5.11.

Table 5.10: Frequency of combinations

N	Threat	Salience	Complexity	Coercion	Constraint	Signal	Most likely	Total
1	High	High	High	0	8 (80%)	2 (20%)	Constraint	8 out of 10
2	High	Low	High	0	3 (100%)	0	Constraint	3 out of 3
3	High	Low	Low	2 (66.67%)	0	1 (33.33%)	Coercion	2 out of 3
4	Low	Low	Low	0	0	7 (100%)	Signal	7 out of 7
5	Low	High	Low	0	6 (42.86%)	8 (57.14%)	Signal	8 out of 14
6	Low	High	High	0	4 (36.36%)	7 (63.64%)	Signal	7 out of 11
7	High	High	Low	8 (80%)	1 (10%)	1 (10%)	Coercion	8 out of 10
8	Low	Low	High	0	0	12 (100%)	Signal	12 out of 12

Table 5.11: Recurrent combinations

N	Dominant pattern			Most likely		
	Threat	Salience	Complexity			
1	High	–	Low	Coercion	76.92%	10 out of 13
2	High	–	High	Constraint	84.62%	11 out of 13
3	Low	Low	–	Signal	100%	19 out of 19

Dominant Pattern N1: high threat and low complexity

The first combination refers to the contemporary presence of high threat and low complexity that correlates with coercive sanctions. High threat is alimented by a menacing policy implemented by targets, it is therefore in the interest of the sender to remove that immediate threat. A high threat tends to make policy actors responsible and, so to speak, more pragmatic. As a state with nuclear capabilities tends to be more rational, so an actor under threat tends to see the menace and prioritises its removal over other interests.

More realism translates into little interest for ethics and moral principles, so that the demands made by the senders would be related mainly to the behaviour that is deemed as dangerous. Moreover, since it is a questionable policy that has to be modified, the demand would regard only that behaviour and the target has to be able to comply. However, threat is necessary but insufficient to explain the outcome. The other variable in this case would be the low complexity that allows the sender to discern among targets, to elaborate clear demands and to exercise a relevant power over the appropriate target. In such cases, salience, which is mainly driven by serious violations in human rights that are more likely to lead to games of 'chicken', is not relevant insofar as the sender is threatened by the target's behaviour. According to the theoretical framework, in all these cases the senders are threatened by the crises or by the behaviour of targets and, since the dispute is not complex, their primary goal can be the one of changing the behaviour of targets. This configuration recurs thirteen times in the database as shown in Table 5.12: the UN sanctions on Iran and the Democratic People's Republic of Korea (DPRK) since 2009, the UN measures on Libya from 1993 to 1999, the EU restrictive measures on the US from 1996 to the present, and on Belarus from 2007 to the present. The episodes in italics (in Tables 5.12 and 5.13) are those that the theory seems unable to explain, but some considerations set out below prove the usefulness of the model.

The UN deems the rearmament program of Iran as threatening to the stability of the Middle East and as a menace to the non-proliferation regime. The achievement of 'the bomb' by Teheran might trigger an arms race, both in the area and in other parts of the world. At the same time, the crisis is perceived as non-complex because Iran has reasonably clear intents, the target is manifest and has an object over which a negotiation is possible. Therefore, the UN is trying to impose a cost on the behaviour of President Ahmadinejad and the Iranian elite in order to convince them to opt for alternative routes to nuclear capability.

The EU measures initiated against the US in 1996 meet the same principle. The principle of extra-territoriality that was violated by the Helms-Burton Act on Cuba and Libya represented a threat to EU companies and to the international trade regimes. The decision of the EU was motivated by the need of remedying an artificial modification of the market and re-establishing the *status-quo ante* in the passing of the Act. The threat was seen as high since an important international norm was questioned by the US administration that could not only have harmed the economy of the EU in the specific case of Cuba and Libya, but also in other

Table 5.12: Cases for high threat and low complexity

Pattern	Combinations	Episodes		N
1	3 & 7	UN/Libya – 1993 to1999	EU/US – 1996 to present	13
		UN/Eritrea – 2009 to present	UN/Iran – 2006 to present	
		UN/1267 – 1999 to 2001	UN/Yugoslavia – 1994 to 1996	
		EU/Libya – 2004 to present	*UN/Sierra Leone – 2000 to 2003*	
		UN/DPRK – 2009 to present	*UN/Libya – 1992 to 1993*	
		EU/Iran – 2010	*EU/Transnistria – 2010 to present*	
		EU/Belarus – 2007 to present		

Table 5.13: Cases for high threat and high complexity

Pattern	Combinations	Episodes		N
2	1 & 2	UN/Bosnian Serbs – 1994 to 1996	UN/Haiti – 1993 to 1994	13
		EU/FRY – 1998 to 2000	EU/Transnistria – 2003 to 2010	
		UN/Unita – 1999 to 2002	UN/Liberia – 2001 to 2003	
		UN/Iraq – 1990 to 1991	UN/Yugoslavia – 1992 to 1994	
		UN/1267 – 2002 to present	*UN/Yugoslavia – 1991 to 1992*	
		UN/Somalia – 2008 to present	*UN/Kosovo – 1998 to 2001*	
		UN/Iraq – 2003 to present		

contexts had the principle been accepted. Therefore, Brussels reacted specifically to counterbalance that policy. This aspect combined with the low level of complexity, given by the friendly relationship between the actors and the nature of the crisis, permitted the EU to identify the incompatibility and to advance a series of feasible demands that aimed at settling the incompatibility.

Finally, the UN sanctions on North Korea since 2009 represent another instance of this system configuration. The UN imposed sanctions in 2006 to discourage Pyongyang from pursuing its nuclear program. However, sanctions were light and they were part of a larger strategy that entailed the current political elite staying in power; therefore sanctions had a signalling function. In 2009, when North Korea tested a nuclear device, the Security Council tightened the screw and sanctions became more stringent, but compliance remained compatible with the current ruling elite. As a result, sanctions took a coercive form. Yet, why does the UN not ask for one of the most brutal contemporary dictators to leave power in exchange for lifting sanctions? The explanation is to be found in the very essence of the threat: Kim Yong-II has the military capability to strike Japan, other allies of the five permanent members of the Security Council, and represents a menace on the border of China (one of the P5). Therefore, the primary goal should be to change behaviour, not to seek for a regime change that could bring about unexpected consequences. Kim Yong-II could and should stay in power – retaining his privileges – and the brutality and the harshness forced on his people are not to be considered in the negotiation (as it would be and has been done in other negotiating contexts, such as the military junta in Burma/Myanmar).

The three cases that do not fit this explanation are the EU in Transnistria since 2010, the UN in Libya in 1992–1993 and the UN in Sierra Leone in 2000–2003. The first two cases can be explained with the dynamic of the negotiations. The EU in Transnistria attempted to break the stalemate in the negotiations between Chisinau and Tiraspol by removing one pretext for the leaders of Transnistria not to sit at the table to solve the conflict. Then there is the Libyan case in which the first phase of a string of episodes that followed the Lockerbie bombing could be viewed as the initial intention of the sender to avoid further measures by letting Tripoli know that the Council was going to act. Finally, the UN commitment in Sierra Leone would need further clarification, but it is plausible to state that in a post-conflict situation, the low constraining measures could be implemented in non-complex situations in a strategy of stabilisation and state building, where spoilers are fought by local authorities with the support of the Security Council.

Senders are more likely to act when they are threatened and since they are under threat, the primary goal remains one of changing the behaviour of the target. Low complexity suggests that they are capable of influencing someone's behaviour. A counterfactual discourse will strengthen this concept. Indeed, in the case of high complexity, sanctions are less likely to be of a coercive nature because it seems harder to distinguish among the actors and the lack of predictability of the system favours conservative behaviour. Furthermore, it appears to be easier to have low threat in combination with other logics of sanctions since senders generally opt for general or ambitious demands for two reasons. First, they do not run particular risk and targets of sanctions may be not the direct ones. Second, senders are not careful in designing the demands as there is not much to lose.

Dominant Pattern N2: high threat and high complexity

The second pattern is represented by high threat and high complexity that makes constraining sanctions more likely. The explanation can be simple: the sender is under threat and is prepared to shoulder the burden of enforcing the measure, but high complexity does not allow for specific measures; neither does it allow for the drafting of feasible demands. In other words, senders might not be able or willing to impose coercive sanctions because of either the nature of the target or the intricacy of the dispute, e.g. Somalia would be a case of high complexity in which chaos characterises the conflict and, therefore, even a high degree of intervention would have low chances of success. In this case, low threat would cause the sender to invest few resources in the dispute and, on the other hand, low complexity would encourage the sender to impose other types of sanctions.

When senders are under threat and the crisis is complex, then it is more likely they will impose constraining measures because the intention would be to remove the menace by changing the behaviour of targets. High complexity, however, makes the design and the implementation of the measures more difficult. This configuration recurs thirteen times in the database as shown in Table 5.13: the UN measures in Somalia and the UN sanctions on Iraq, and the EU restrictive measures on Moldova and the Former Republic of Yugoslavia (FRY) would fall into this category.

The UN sanctions on Liberia in 2001 or Iraq 1991 had the similar intention of undermining the targeted regime to its final removal. Talk about 'targeted regime', in reality refers to the ruling elite of a specific country, such as the cases of Saddam Hussein in Iraq and Charles Taylor in Liberia.

The UN case of sanctions on Iraq is composed of three episodes and two of them, which are of a constraining type, fit the combination of high threat and high complexity.[1] In the first case, from 1990 to 1991, an embargo was imposed to force the withdrawal of the Iraqi military troops from Kuwait, but the objective appeared to be the preparation for a military intervention to stop Saddam's plan to annex the invaded country. The level of threat was high, as the Iraqi move challenged the overall international architecture that was emerging after the Cold War, but the crisis was also complex as the fourth largest army in the world moved to war against another state. However, after the decision to invade was taken, Iraq also made steps to indicate that its presence was to be for the long term (e.g. water pipelines were installed to resupply the troops), so that the demand for full and unconditional withdrawal appeared to be too ambitious for sanctions alone. The

---

1. The case of the UN sanctions on Iraq from 1991 to 2003 was not deemed as threatening because issue was evaluated as low, given the reduced capacity of Iraq to maneuver in its foreign policy. This is in reality a border line case, but it would not change the validity of the framework as, even if threat is assessed as high, it would still be a case of constraining sanction as illustrated by the third combination.

explanation for constraining sanctions is to be found then in the need to undermine the capacity of Iraq to carry out its will, but the high complexity modified
the expected outcome from the imposition of sanctions. After the second phase
ended with the US invasion in 2003, the third phase was indicated as high threat
and high complexity. High threat was determined by the profound instability in the
region that was undermining the position of the US in the area. High complexity
was determined by the level of institutional disruption that there were vast parts
of the country out of control, used by the rebels to hide and plan their attacks and
disrupt stabilisation processes. The UN decided to impose sanctions to eliminate
the threat, but since the crisis was complex, the sanctions could only attempt to
limit the capacity of those who were committed against the Government. This
type of measure should be evaluated alongside other policy tools, as sanctions can
hardly build democracies, but they can help to create the appropriate conditions,
as seen in Iraq.

The EU decision in Transnistria represents another important example of how
restrictive measures can be used as components of 'policy mix' and how they
can serve specific purposes within a certain framework. Since the decision to accept Romania into the EU, Moldova reached the top of the political agenda in
Brussels because a stable and peaceful neighbourhood is among the priorities of
the EU as an international actor. The dispute between Moldova and Transnistria
has been a threat to the EU because Transnistria is used not only by Moldovan
authorities as a scapegoat to justify undemocratic practices and to explain poor
economic performances, but also by international criminal organisations and cor-
rupt businessmen that could have a negative impact on the EU market (e.g. import
of weapons, drugs, and also smuggling). The crisis is not only dangerous, but it
is also very complex due to the nature of the target and the support that it enjoys
(i.e. the Russian Federation). What can the EU do in this context? And more specifically, what can sanctions achieve under these circumstances? The answer from
this research is clear: sanctions are used to contribute to the overall policy goals
in solving the conflict between Moldova and Transnistria and to include Moldova
under the EU's sphere of influence. After this premise, constraining sanctions –
namely the measures that attempt to limit the capabilities of the target in achieving
their goals – are explained by the interest of the EU in solving the crisis and by
the incompatibility between the goal of the EU (united Moldova) and that of the
leaders in Transnistria (independence).

The last example for this combination is the EU policy towards Serbia during the Kosovo crisis. The interesting element here is also to notice that the EU
has imposed more rigorous sanctions than the UN, which is probably because of
the higher threat posed by the crises as not all the P5 were similarly endangered.
Complexity was highlighted by the commitment of the parties and by the use of
violence. The EU took on the defence of the Albanian minority and used sanctions
to limit what the Serbs were planning to do. Several sanctions – arms embargo,
travel ban, assets freeze, banning of investments, etc. – affected the functionality
of the Serbian institutions and limited what their intentions were, but Serbia's
commitment and the military operations made compliance by the ruling elite unlikely. The desire for regime change was proven by the indictment of Milosevic

immediately following the end of the crisis.

The negative cases here are the UN in Yugoslavia from 1991 to 1992 and in the Kosovo crisis in 1998. The latter could be justified by the parallel military operation of NATO that played a central role in the strategy, while the mixed threat perception of the members of the Security Council led to an imposition of sanctions to provide legitimacy for the intervention. Actually, Russia and China vividly complained about the operation as the military campaign was a violation of international law and, therefore, sanctions imposed by the Security Council did not have an impact. The case of the UN and the Balkan conflicts resembles the UN and Libya, where the Security Council decided to impose signalling sanctions to show an interest in the crisis, which escalated the following year.

The sender would not consider the implementation of coercive measures if it was not under threat because important resources would not be invested on a non-security-related subject. Furthermore, if the crisis was not complex, then the situation would be more predictable and targets could be easily distinguished.

Dominant Pattern N.3: low threat and low salience

The third dominant pattern that emerges from the empirical analysis refers to the high combination of low threat, low salience with signalling sanctions in nineteen out of seventy cases. This finding may suggest that when the sender is not threatened and the issue is not salient, then the imposition of sanctions may either aim at the behavioural change of the target through other mechanisms than the one envisioned by the so-called 'naïve' theory of sanctions (Galtung 1967) or aim at sending a message to other actors or audiences. If either threat or salience were high, then the sender would more probably impose either coercive or constraining sanctions depending on the other IVs.

Low threat and low salience, as above mentioned, do not stand for no threat and no salience, and since the DV is composed by cases of sanctions, all of them were of certain relevance. Nevertheless, the low level of both threat and salience do not motivate senders to adopt measures that would be costly to them as well. This does not rule out the possibility of imposing signalling sanctions to affect the costs/benefits analyses of targets, but this could take place through different mechanisms. Additionally, these types of sanctions can be executed to please or to pass an image to domestic and international audiences. As underlined many times above, signalling sanctions are not qualitatively inferior to the other types of sanctions. They are only different as they work according to different logics. This configuration recurs nineteen times in the database as shown in Table 5.14, cases such as the UN in Sierra Leone and Sudan, and the EU restrictive measures on Burma/Myanmar and China would fall in this category.

The international context seems to have influenced the UN decisions in Sierra Leone in the early phase of sanctioning, when the UN imposed sanctions without a real commitment to deal with the situation. The low level of threat and the low level of salience appear to explain the imposition of signalling sanctions, as there was neither a material nor a symbolic relevance connected to the resolution of the

Table 5.14: Cases for low threat and low salience

Pattern	Combinations	Episodes	N
3	4 & 8	EU/Belarus – 1998 to 1999 EU/Belarus – 2004 to 2007 EU/Comoros – 2008 to 2008 EU/Uzbekistan – 2005 to 2009 UN/Haiti – 1993 to 1993 UN/Hariri – 2005 to present EU/Libya – 1999 to 2004 UN/Sudan – 1996 to 1996 EU/Afghanistan – 1996 to 1999 EU/Burma/Myanmar – 1991 to 2007 EU/DRC – 1993 to 2003 EU/Sudan – 1994 to 2004 EU/Sudan – 2004 to 2005 UN/Ethiopia-Eritrea – 2000 to 2001 UN/Liberia – 1992 to 2001 UN/Sierra Leone – 1997 to 1998 UN/Sierra Leone – 1998 to 2000 UN/Somalia – 1992 to 2008 UN/Rwanda – 1994 to 1995	19

conflict. Sierra Leone did not represent a direct threat to the P5 so they did not have an interest in investing resources in a conflict that was not even salient from other points of view. Had the conflict been salient, then the UN would have participated heavily in the resolution of the conflict, condition that occurred in 2000 and that made Sierra Leone a model for UN peacekeeping missions. However, sanctions up to that point were used for reasons that differed from influencing the behaviour of targets through the imposition of a cost. That does not make signalling sanctions non-influential. Indeed, a more in-depth analysis of the case of Sierra Leone might show that signalling sanctions were either part of an incremental engagement with the actors, or the result of pressures from domestic constituencies in favour of a bigger role for the international community in the area. Thus, the 'must do something' approach could explain the desire to show involvement without really paying the price for it. Finally, the intention of the UN could have been also the one of communicating to other actors, either from the area or from other regions, that the UN is attentive to similar situations. While a pure realist approach assumes that expectations on what actors will do are formed by observing the past of those actors, the approach adopted in this research with the emphasis on signalling has a more nuanced process to structure expectations. What is the likelihood of one's behaviour on the international stage originates partly from his actions, and partly from the motivations for actions (which can also come from the resentment from not acting). Under this perspective, signalling sanctions can be both a predictor for stronger actions and the lack of commitment towards specific regions. For instance, the lack of action by the international community in the cases of Rwanda and Srebrenica was the main reason that the international community decided to act in Kosovo. Signalling sanctions can be interpreted as signs of attention from the international community, which 'could' translate into more invasive policies (as happened eventually in the case of Sierra Leone).

The UN action against Sudan in 1996 for its alleged support of international terrorism follows a similar path. The level of threat that Sudan posed in 1996 was deemed as low since only Egypt was directly involved in the crisis. Furthermore, the Sudanese government was at least in appearance complying to the demands of the international community as the links between Khartoum and international terrorist organisations was unclear. The signalling sanction is also justified by the low level of salience for the crises, both in 1996 and in 2004, and the model passes the empirical test because when the level of salience in regards to Darfur increased, the UN approach to the resolution of the crisis followed suit and the nature of the sanctions changed from signalling to constraining. The reasoning is by now clear: had the crisis been closer to the P5, the UN would have reacted in a different way.

Low threat and low salience describe the crisis between the EU and Burma/ Myanmar in 1990 to 2007. The misbehaviour of the military junta in Naypyidaw met the reaction of the EU and a series of sanctions have been in place since the late 1980s. Despite the apparent long-term interest in the Asian nation, whatever happens in Burma/Myanmar does not seem to alter the security or to harm the interest of the European Union. Furthermore, the remote location of the country and the unawareness of the situation in Burma/Myanmar in Europe may account

Table 5.15: Ambivalent patterns

Combination	Threat	Salience	Complexity	Coercing	Constraining	Signalling	Most likely
5	Low	High	Low	0	6 (42.86%)	8 (57.14%)	8 out of 14
6	Low	High	High	0	4 (36.36%)	7 (63.64%)	7 out of 11
5 & 6	Aggregate			0	10 (40%)	15 (60%)	15 out of 25

Table 5.16: Alternative data aggregation for low threat and low complexity

Combination	Threat	Salience	Complexity	Coercing	Constraining	Signalling	Most likely
4&5	Low	–	Low	0	6 (28.57%)	15 (71.43%)	15 out of 21

Table 5.17: Cases for low threat and high salience

Pattern	Combinations	Constraining (10)	Signalling (15)	Total
4	5 & 6	UN/Liberia – 2003 to present	UN/DPRK – 2006 to 2009	25
		UN/Cambodia – 1992 to 1993	UN/Sierra Leone – 2003 to 2010	
		UN/Iraq – 1991 to 2003	UN/Libya – 1999 to 2003	
		UN/Cote d'Ivoire – 2004 to present	UN/Unita – 1993 to 1999	
		EU/Bosnia & Herzegovina – 2001 to 2006	UN/DRC – 2003 to present	
		EU/Milosevic – 2000 to present	UN/Lebanon – 2006 to present	
		EU/ICTY – 2001 to present	UN/Sudan – 2004 to 2005	
		EU/Zimbabwe – 2002 to present	UN/Sudan – 2005 to present	
		EU/Guinea – 2009 to present	UN/Rwanda – 1995 to 2008	
		EU/Burma/Myanmar – 2007 to present	EU/FYROM – 2001 to 2009	
			EU/Indonesia – 1999 to 2000	
			EU/Nigeria – 1993 to 1998	
			EU/China – 1989 to present	
			EU/FRY – 1996 to 1998	
			EU/Nigeria – 1998 to 1999	

for the EU not adopting multiple tools or the fact that it is not tracking shipments of sensitive goods to the region. The explanation is that, since there is no threat and the issue is not salient, then Brussels could be trying to please its domestic lobbies, who are concerned with the disrespect of human rights in the country, or it could only use its foreign policy tool to exercise its role on the international stage.

Finally, another example of signalling sanctions is the EU arms embargo on China that was imposed after the events in Tiananmen Square in 1989. The threat to the EU members was minimal – and operates at a similar level today – while the salience probably reached its peak in the immediate aftermath of the event. Chinese practices with regard to human rights are generally overshadowed by the strong economic ties that link the EU and China. The embargo did not and could not have any material impact on any Chinese policy, starting with the handling of the student protests that culminated with the repression in Tiananmen Square. Once again, the absence of material impact does not make signalling sanctions a futile exercise of foreign policy. In this specific case, the most plausible hypothesis could be that the EU used the events in China to reaffirm a certain degree of unity among EU members on foreign policy matters and the matter did not pose any threat to EU interests. It was not salient enough to disrupt any specific interests. Public discussion over the possibility of lifting the embargo revealed that an important part of public opinion is in favour of banning the sale of arms to a government that does not respect the practice of basic human rights. This element could also explain why the embargo is still in place.

The counterfactual reasoning would bring the discourse back to the combinations presented above, as a high threat would create the conditions for the commitment of the sender and would result in coercive sanctions. On the other hand, high salience would still encourage dynamism from the sender, but it would more likely set the stage for constraining sanctions.

Thus, it appears that one type of sanction is correlated to certain contextual settings, so that these relationships are worth further investigation in order to explain these relations. More than relying on causal links, namely that the environmental characteristics directly influence the decisions of the sender, the context seems to create the structural conditions that confine senders to the adoption of one specific type of sanctions under certain conditions.

Ambivalent patterns

The dominant patterns explain 64 per cent of the episodes considered in this study, but what happened to the remnant 36 per cent? The hypotheses are not confirmed in twenty-five episodes of contextual configurations given by low threat and high salience, where the hypotheses suggested that sanctions were more likely to be of a constraining type; instead, the most frequent type was signalling.

If salience exercises a similar pressure created on the senders as the one created by high threat, then for high salience, senders should be committed to bear a cost for imposing sanctions. However, senders should be more likely to respond to salient crises either with general requests (e.g. improvement of human rights practices, steps towards democracy, etc.) or with absolute ones (e.g. regime change, etc.). This latter type of demand is possible because the sender is not threatened by the behaviour of the target – his priority is not to look for other behaviour on the target's side. Therefore, when senders are not under threat, but attribute a value to the issue at stake, then they are more likely to recur to the constraining type of sanctions than to other types. The explanation is based on the fact that when senders are not threatened, then the demands are less likely to be precise and more likely to be absolute and normative, therefore difficult to implement. High salience would further strengthen this argument, as senders have an incentive to act under the pressure of international watchdogs and they would impose costly sanctions even if under no threat.

This is a hypothesis based on a liberal interpretation of international relations, when costly acts can be undertaken also for normative goals and not only for material gains. If confirmed, then a combination of realism and liberal assumptions should be taken into consideration in studying sanctions. If it is falsified, realism should be the main paradigm. The pattern is constituted by the contextual configurations characterised by low threat and high salience and the associations with the dependent variable are summarised in Table 5.15.

The hypotheses are falsified as signalling is the most frequent type of sanctions counting for 60 per cent of the episodes, while constraining sanctions are imposed ten times out of twenty-five episodes. Even alternative data aggregation would not lead to better results as shown by Table 5.16.

This result allows us to reach two conclusions. First, when threat is low and salience is high, coercive sanctions are not likely to be imposed. Secondly, there is a measurable impact of complexity, as higher complexity corresponds to a slightly higher signalling rate. The configuration of low threat and high salience recurs twenty-five times in the database as shown in Table 5.17.

There are two types of cases that we can deal with in this part. First, there are the ten cases of constraining that fit the hypothesis, followed by fifteen episodes of signalling in search for further clarification. Among the ten cases there are the conflict stabilisation efforts of the UN in Liberia and the EU with the ICTY indictees, but also the crisis management of the UN in Iraq from 1991 to 2003 and of the EU in Zimbabwe since 2002.

Sanctions have been used to deal with the conflict in Liberia in its different phases and the last one falls within the category discussed here. This instance is of particular interest as several episodes could be interpreted as attempts of senders to sustain the creation of viable democracies. During the 1990s, Charles Taylor's presidency was terminated as a result of pressure from the international community and his forced departure opened a new phase in the conflict in 2003. With the support of the international community, Liberia was trying to recover from years of civil conflicts and administrative mismanagement and therefore the Security Council decided to impose certain sanctions to sustain the democratisation and stabilisation processes by freezing the assets and preventing travel by all individuals who intended upset the UN intentions. This type of 'absolute' request was possible mainly because the level of threat posed to the P5 was low, but the salience of the issue (e.g. the UN credibility in the area) could have been undermined by a failure in establishing functioning institutions. Once again, if the UN had been threatened, then the demand would have been feasible as the objective would have had been to alter behaviour. Similarly, the salience of the dispute created the conditions for the UN to impose constraining sanctions that aimed at limiting the capability of certain individuals to undermine the stabilisation process, and success should be evaluated accordingly.

The EU sanctions on the ICTY indictees would fall under the same category. Since the establishment of the Tribunal, the EU imposed sanctions to make sure that the people accused by the Tribunal were brought to trial. Under international pressure, the EU decided to show its commitment to stabilise the Balkans by contributing to the arrest of sought-after individuals with the imposition of sanctions that made the escape of these people more difficult.

The EU imposed comparable sanctions on Zimbabwe and Indonesia, where an analysis similar to the one done above for the UN in Liberia appears to be the most appropriate one. Indeed, the fall of the Suharto regime presented Indonesia with opportunities and challenges, and the EU decided to impose an arms embargo with the intent to favour the process of democratisation that was supported by the UN. The conflict in Indonesia was not directly threatening the EU, as for instance was the case of the war in the Balkans, so the high salience obtained by the conflict might explain the involvement of Brussels to support the action of the UN. Despite this apparent insignificance, Indonesia's stabilisation was salient to the EU and this would explain the EU's involvement in the issue. The relative importance of the country in East Asia, but also the dramatic events of Kosovo and East Timor, might have pushed the EU to contribute further to the success of the UN mission. Aside from the other efforts, the objective of the arms embargo was to create more suitable conditions (i.e. with fewer weapons) for a stable peace, and the salience would explain the imposition and the implementation of the restrictive measures. This case is relevant for two main reasons: on the one hand, it shows how actors decide according to values that differ from security reasons alone and, on the other hand, sanctions can (in fact, they do most of the time) play limited roles in a larger strategy.

Finally, the case of Iraq in 1991 should be further investigated as low threat leading to constraining sanctions. The Security Council was undermining the economic capacity of Iraq to limit its possible policy alternatives, but the regime was crippled by the war and there was little danger originating from Iraq to the P5. At the same time, the high salience can be motivated by the relevance obtained by the crisis on the international agenda, the crucial role of oil in the global economy and international terrorism. These three elements combined would explain why the Security Council decided to act with the imposition of tough sanctions, while the unfeasibility of the demands would find its explanation in the normative pressures coming from the international system.

The fifteen negative cases can also be represented according to the conflict phase. Indeed, it can be argued that signalling sanctions are imposed under these circumstances (low threat and high salience) in the last phase of conflicts, such as the UN in Libya and Rwanda, when the mere presence of international legitimacy is essential to sustain the newly-established local governments. Conversely, signalling sanctions can be imposed also at the beginning of a sanction string and this could follow a similar pattern identified in episodes of signalling for high threat. Indeed, high signalling could justify a first intervention to announce the commitment in order to create the expectation for further action. This could be the explanation for the UN measures on UNITA in 1999 or on Sudan since 2004. Signalling can also be important in crisis management to provide individual sanctioners with the global legitimacy required to resort to sanctions, as in the case of the UN on the DPRK in 2006. Finally, sanctions can be imposed with a signalling intent when high salience fuels the need for an actor to formulate an international identity, such as the two cases of the EU and China and Indonesia. Overall, while each individual episode of sanctions could have a unique explanation, the finding of this analysis is that salience does not have the same explanatory power that threat does.

Conclusion

A systemic middle range theory of sanctions took form in the empirical test run on seventy episodes of sanctions from the UN and the EU experiences imposed, or in force, since 1992. Different types of sanctions are correlated with combinations of the international system of sanctions that, by providing pressures and opportunities to policy makers, make the imposition of specific sanctions more likely.

Threat and complexity seem to retain a higher explanatory power *vis-à-vis* salience. The test on the combinations of variables led to the identification of three different dominant patterns that confirmed the hypotheses formulated in chapter three and repeated above:

1. High threat and low complexity are more likely to originate coercive sanctions.
2. High threat and high complexity are more likely to originate constraining sanctions.
3. Low threat and low complexity are more likely to originate signalling sanctions.

This finding confirms that sanctions are not all alike and that the analysis of the context is of a fundamental importance to understand the functioning of international sanctions. The taxonomy of sanctions purposes has revealed a strong capacity to interpret and to highlight the differences among sanctions episodes. The naïve conception of restrictive measures as a foreign policy tool that aims at changing the behaviour of the target is neither an efficient way to understand nor an analytical tool that encloses usable knowledge for policy makers. In fact, it could be a misleading approach that might have led to underestimating both utility and efficacy of sanctioning in international affairs, short of understanding how they work.

The empirical analysis showed twice that salience does not have the explanatory power that threat and complexity have since there is one ambivalent pattern – low threat and high salience – that does not offer solid data to formulate a causal connection between the context and the type of sanction hypothesised. Nevertheless, this theoretical framework is able to explain 57 per cent of the dataset for the hypotheses confirmed, namely forty cases out of seventy in total (it would be forty-five with the negative cases as well, which would take into consideration the entire cluster belonging to the configuration considered). Furthermore, this evidence could be further strengthened by adding the ten episodes that confirm the hypothesis also in the ambivalent pattern, which increase the explanation rate from 57 per cent to 71.43 per cent of the episodes.

The theory received a preliminary confirmation with a qualitative comparative analysis. The associations and the empirical verification elaborated so far are sound and they suffice to lay the solid foundations for a systemic theory of sanctions. There could still be a doubt in how the causal mechanism actually works and deeper analysis is needed. In order to strengthen this finding, the second part of the book adopts a typical case study approach to both improve the conceptualisations for coercing, constraining and signalling sanctions, and to corroborate the nexus between the logic of sanctions and the external environment wherein they are imposed.

chapter six | the united nations as global sender: the cases of libya, al-qaida/taliban and rwanda

This chapter aims at discovering how the comprehensive theoretical framework of sanctions performs in practice by looking at individual episodes in the UN experience. The objective is to verify how the context shapes the outcome of the model, namely the logic of sanctions. The case of the UN is a very relevant one because it is the only sanctioner with global legitimacy and has substantially increased its sanctioning trends since the end of the Cold War, demonstrating the growing importance of sanctions as a foreign policy method. The intergovernmental character of the United Nations is acknowledged, but it is still assumed to be a unitary actor for the purpose of this study.

This chapter focuses on three episodes of sanctions: the UN's coercive sanctions on Libya, the constraining sanctions on Al-Qaida/Taliban, and the signalling ones on Rwanda, and shows that the theoretical framework enhances our understanding of the problem. The case of Libya was selected because of its coercive aspect. The configuration of the context falls into a combination of high threat and low complexity making 'coercing' more likely than other types of sanctions. The case of the UN measures against Al-Qaida/Taliban is typical for constraining sanctions because there cannot be acceptable requests made to Al-Qaida members since their existence is justified in contraposition with those who are asking them to give up. The wide network of support enjoyed by Al-Qaida and its tactics complicate the resolution of the crisis. Combining this element with the high threat posed by Al-Qaida explains the constraining character of the measures. Finally, the signalling measures imposed on Rwanda are typical of a situation in which the senders are not directly threatened and the crisis did not catch a lot of attention in its initial phase. Here sanctions were directed at placating the rage of the international audience on the UN inaction to prevent the genocide, a condition that explains why sanctions were designed without care in regard to the impact they would have had on the ongoing genocide, assuming sanctions could have had any impact at all. The UN has adopted different sanctions in different contexts and the theoretical framework elaborated in this study is able to contribute to explaining and understanding those differences. Hence, future sanctioning policies could be designed, planned and evaluated accordingly.

This chapter is structured in three parts. The first part describes the sanctioning policy of the United Nations and displays the sanctions imposed since the end of the Cold War. The second part presents the analyses of the sanctions on Libya, Al-Qaida/Taliban and Rwanda. The third part concludes the chapter by emphasising the relationship between the external context and the purpose of the restrictive measures.

The sanctioning policy of the UN

The Security Council of the United Nations imposes sanctions under Chapter VII of the Charter, which deals with countries' 'action(s) with respect to threats to the peace, breaches of the peace, and acts of aggression'. As established under Article 41 of the Charter, the Security Council is authorised to impose 'measures not involving the use of armed force' that 'may include complete or partial interruption of economic relations and of rail, sea, air, postal, telegraphic, radio, and other means of communication, and the severance of diplomatic relations' (United Nations 1945).

The decision to impose sanctions originates from UN members that are usually seated on the Security Council and the information available to the UN is made available by its own members. The only previous consideration performed by the UN is over the potential impact of the measures on innocent civilians, an estimation that is carried out by the UN Office for the Coordination of Humanitarian Affairs (OCHA). Consequently, the Security Council also depends on member states when deciding the type of sanctions and targets, given that the information pertaining to the alleged misconduct is provided by national agencies (police, secret service, etc.). For all these tasks, the Security Council has to rely entirely on its members in order to identify who is to be sanctioned and how.

The Security Council plays a stronger role after the actual imposition, when it can decide to establish sanctions committees with the tasks of evaluating whether the target is complying with the demands, to assess the impact of the restrictive measures, to advise further restrictions and to report any violations. For instance, sanctions committees have been established in pursuant of resolution 1737 for Iran (United Nations 2006c), resolution 1718 for the DPRK, resolution 1291 for Sudan, resolution 1572 for Ivory Coast, resolution 1533 for the DRC, resolution 1521 for Liberia, resolution 1516 for counter-terrorism, and resolution 1267 for Al-Qaida/Taliban, associated individuals and entities. The sanctions committees are composed by the members of the Security Council, but the tasks represent a burden that is to be added to the long list of activities wherein they were already involved. Hence, sanctions committees may decide to set up auxiliary bodies that can assist them, the so-called 'Panel of Experts' (also 'Group of Experts', 'Monitoring Group', or 'Monitoring Team') that can be established to reinforce the monitoring activity of the committee or to carry out field research on both the impact and the enforcement of the measures. The size of the group is decided on a case-by-case basis according to their respective duties. For example, the sanctions committee on Al-Qaida and the Taliban has to control more than 300 targets, and it is composed of eight senior officials and four staff members. Other panels are sensibly smaller, such as the one on Sudan that is composed of only three people (United Nations 2007b).

The chosen panels are selected from a roster of experts, prepared and constantly updated by the Secretariat according to the experience and expertise of the candidates. Other panels of experts have been created in the cases of Somalia, Al-Qaida and the Taliban, the DRC, Ivory Coast and Sudan. This practice has been criticised because the UN should have a standing group to monitor the impact of sanctions (House of Lords 2007b) or a UN Sanctions Coordinator (Cortright and Lopez 2005; Cortright and Lopez 2002a: 201–224).

International sanctions were strongly criticised for imposing an unbearable toll on innocent bystanders after the embargoes on Iraq and Haiti in the 1990s did not lead to tangible results. The growing concerns contributed to the evolution of sanction practices, as described in chapter two – namely from comprehensive to targeted – had consequences as to how sanctions had to be designed. Targeted measures are accused of jeopardising their overall contribution to policy objectives as sanctions are more difficult to implement and easier to evade, so that the already low impact would decrease even further (Drezner 2003b; Tostensen and Bull 2002; Hufbauer et al. 2007: 141). Human rights became relevant also for listed individuals who claimed that fundamental rights were denied to them. The UN responded to these claims and began to apply exceptions and exemptions regarding the trade of specific goods, the granting of visas for health issues, while exemptions are common for travel bans (e.g. to attend international meetings or to receive health assistance in third countries).

Today, since the Security Council and the sanctions committees can decide arbitrarily to include whoever they deem useful in the lists of targets, the concerns over the unintended impact of sanctions has been joined by the unease towards the violations of the rights of black-listed individuals and entities (Biersteker and Eckert 2006). The growing criticisms against the United Nations and the interest of national and regional courts in reviewing decisions of the Security Council has led to the need of ensuring the rights of due process and giving an effective remedy to people that could have been wrongly listed as specified by the general guidelines for delisting requests. To this end, the Security Council passed resolution 1730 on 19th December 2006, stating its commitment 'to ensure that fair and clear procedures exist for placing individuals and entities on sanctions lists and for removing them, as well as for granting humanitarian exemptions', and:

> request[ing] the Secretary-General to establish, within the Secretariat (Security Council Subsidiary Organs Branch), a focal point to receive de-listing requests. Petitioners seeking to submit a request for de-listing can do so either through the focal point process outlined below or through their state of residence or citizenship.

(United Nations 2006b)

Basically, the Focal Point functions as an intermediary body between individuals and the governments that suggested the listing: it collects the requests for de-listing advanced by individuals and entities and it submits them to the member states that provided information about the petitioner for evaluation. If they do not answer within three months, the Focal Point submits the requests for de-listing to the competent committee. In January 2011, the focal point received fifty-eight requests from forty-one individuals and thirty-seven entities – and ten individuals and seventeen entities have been de-listed (UN SC Sanctions Committee, Focal Point Statistics).

The Focal Point was relieved from receiving requests from individuals that appear in the Consolidated List of the Security Council's Al-Qaida/Taliban Sanctions Committee (1267 Committee). Since June 2010, the Security Council appointed Kimberly Prost as Ombudsperson, created with resolution 1904 of 17th December 2009, and individuals and entities in the consolidated list direct their request to the Ombudsperson, while the Focal Point deals with other requests. In January 2011, Mrs Prost was working on six requests.

The database includes twenty-two cases of UN sanctions divided in forty-one episodes – six for coercing, fourteen for constraining and twenty-one for signalling – imposed since the end of the Cold War and listed in Table 6.1.

This chapter presents in-depth analyses of the cases of Libya, Al-Qaida/Taliban (1267 Committee) and Rwanda, which are typical episodes for the three logics of coercing, constraining and signalling.

Coercing Libya

The Security Council imposed sanctions on Libya as a result of the involvement of two Libyan citizens in the 1988 Pan Am 103 crash over Lockerbie, in Scotland, which caused the death of 270 people (United Nations 1992b; United Nations 1993c; Simons 2003). The case of the UN and Libya is divided into three different episodes. The first one begins with the imposition of sanctions in 1992 until 1993 and was of a signalling type. The second one lasts from 1993 to 1999, when sanctions were suspended. Finally, sanctions remained frozen until 2003, which has been classified again as another signalling episode of sanctions. The second episode, which is of a coercive form, is the one that is of interest here.

The investigation over the Lockerbie bombing led to the accusation of two Libyan citizens. The enquiry was more difficult than expected, but the link was made when the 772 UTA plane that crashed in Niger the year before was compared with the Lockerbie accident. Enough evidence was found according to the investigators, so that the US and the UK asked for the extradition of Abdelbaset Ali Mohmed al-Megrahi and Al Amin Khalifa Fhimah, two agents of the Libyan secret service, who were suspected for the bombing. Colonel Gaddafi refused to extradite the two suspects and conceded to hold the trial in Libya. Gaddafi and Libya had already been accused of supporting international terrorist organisations, and the lack of cooperation on the Lockerbie case did not improve the situation. The Security Council threatened and then imposed sanctions with resolution 748 of 31st March 1993, demanding both suspects to be handed over for trial in the US and that Tripoli halted its support to international terrorist organisations (United Nations 1992b). Resolution 748 imposed an arms embargo, a travel and an aviation ban, but the low level of implementation and the type of resource targeted contributed to the classification of the measures as signalling. The objective was to send a message of commitment to both Libya and the international community.

On 11th November 1993, the screw was tightened and sanctions began to work according to a coercive logic. Resolution 883 was adopted by the Security Council confirming the previous measures and imposing a freeze on assets and a com-

Table 6.1: UN sanctions episodes since the end of the Cold War classified per purpose

Coercing	Constraining	Signalling
UN/1267 – 1999 to 2001	UN/Unita – 1999 to 2002	UN/Unita – 1993 to 1999
UN/Libya – 1993 to 1999	UN/Iraq – 1990 to 1991	UN/DRC – 2003 to present
UN/Iran – 2006 to present	UN/Iraq – 1991 to 2003	UN/Ethiopia-Eritrea – 2000 to 2001
UN/Eritrea – 2009 to present	UN/Iraq – 2003 to present	UN/Liberia – 1992 to 2001
UN/Yugoslavia – 1994 to 1996	UN/Liberia – 2001 to 2003	UN/Sierra Leone – 1997 to 1998
UN/DPRK – 2009 to present	UN/Liberia – 2003 to present	UN/Sierra Leone – 1998 to 2000
	UN/Sierra Leone – 2000 to 2003	UN/Sierra Leone – 2003 to 2010
	UN/Cote d'Ivoire – 2004 to present	UN/Haiti – 1993 to 1993
	UN/1267 – 2002 to present	UN/Hariri – 2005 to present
	UN/Cambodia – 1992 to 1993	UN/Lebanon – 2006 to present
	UN/Haiti – 1993 to 1994	UN/Libya – 1992 to 1993
	UN/Somalia – 2008 to present	UN/Libya – 1999 to 2003
	UN/Yugoslavia – 1992 to 1994	UN/Somalia – 1992 to 2008
	UN/Bosnian-Serbs – 1994 to 1996	UN/Sudan – 1996 to 1996
		UN/Sudan – 2004 to 2005
		UN/Sudan – 2005 to present
		UN/Yugoslavia – 1991 to 1992
		UN/Kosovo – 1998 to 2001
		UN/Rwanda – 1994 to 1995
		UN/Rwanda – 1995 to 2008
		UN/DPRK – 2006 to 2009
6	14	21

modity boycott on equipment necessary for oil extraction (United Nations 1993c). Sanctions started to bite and to have a direct material impact.

The major disagreement between the UN and Libya over the Pan Am suspects was over the location of the trial, which is not considered a vital issue. The US and the UK asked for the extradition of the suspects, while Libya only conceded to hold the trial in Scotland under Scottish law (this concession came after the proposal of trying the suspects in Libya either with Libyan or foreign judges). According to the Montreal Convention of 1971, Libya was obliged to hold an investigation and to try the suspects of the bombing, but extradition was not mandatory in cases where there was no extradition treaty among the parties. On the other side, the UK and the US claimed that the Security Council represented the highest authority in the international system and its resolutions were international law.

The stalemate was broken in 1998 under changing conditions in the international system. Sanctions were not hurting only Libya, but the neighbouring countries were being affected as well. The intransigency showed by the US and the UK was not fully understood by African countries that threatened to stop their cooperation with the Security Council if a compromise was not reached. In order to avoid a diplomatic loss of face, the US and the UK proposed to try the suspects in the Netherlands with Scottish judges and Libya accepted this proposal. Resolution 1192 of 27th August 1998 established that sanctions were suspended upon the arrival of the two indictees in the Netherlands, which occurred in 1999. Here begins the third episode of the sanctions regime, as the Security Council kept the measures frozen until 2003, when resolution 1506 of 23rd September lifted all UN sanctions on Libya (Niblock 2001; Simons 2003; Cortright and Lopez 2000:107–121; McNamara 2007; O'Sullivan 2003:173–232; Vandewalle 2006).

The first verdict of the trial for the Lockerbie bombing was reached in 2001 with the condemnation of Mr al-Megrahi and the release of Mr Fhimah. After two appeals were rejected, al-Megrahi was released in 2009 on compassionate grounds for a severe medical condition.

The dependent variable: feasibility and direct impact

The second episode of the UN sanctions on Libya is classified as coercive. The measures did have an impact on the country. Therefore, the logic is to impose a direct toll in order to affect the costs/benefits calculation of targets. How is the calculation supposed to be affected? The intention seems one of imposing a cost on all possible policy options but the one desired by the sender. Thereby, if sanctions impose a cost and require a behaviour that does not endanger the survival of targets, then we are in the presence of coercive sanctions.

Sanctions had an impact and they target important resources for Libya. The measures were implemented overall as, for instance, the travel ban eliminated almost all flights to and from Libya (Cortright and Lopez 2000: 116). The foreign dependence of Libya for extraction technology (Vandewalle 2007: 179) and the low level of international support made Tripoli vulnerable to sanctions (Cortright and Lopez 2000: 116–117). Consequences were also reported at a social and economic level (Vandewalle 2007: 171–180; Niblock 2001: 60–92). The impact was also ensured by parallel sanctions in place, for example the ones imposed by the US since the mid-1980s (O'Sullivan 2003: 173–232). The resources targeted in the second episode were important and stronger sanctions would have closely approached a comprehensive embargo. In particular, the ban on spare parts for the oil extraction industry condemned Libya to lower production over time and a commercial ban that limited the availability of goods of any kind contributed to the domestic pressures on the regime.

The request was defined as feasible because the demand was moderately precise and highly practical. The demand was rated as 'moderately precise' by looking at resolution 731 of 21st January 1992, according to which 'the Libyan government must now comply without any further delay with paragraph 3 of resolution 731 (1992)' (handing over the two suspects and to cooperate with the investigation of the UTA 772 crash) and 'must commit itself definitely to cease all forms of terrorist actions and all assistance to terrorist groups and that it must promptly, by concrete actions, demonstrate its renunciation of terrorism' (United Nations 1992a). Thus, the demand was twofold: handing over the two suspects was simple and doable, while the other demand was broader insofar as it was harder to discern what exactly their support to terrorist organisations was (Simons 2003: 146–155). The practicality of the demand was high for two reasons: first, handing over two suspects did not endanger the regime; and, secondly, halting the support to terrorist organisations, albeit important both for domestic and international motivations, was not crucial to the regime since the 1980s (Niblock 2001: 85).

The independent variable: threat, salience and complexity

The systemic configuration of high threat and low complexity seems to increase the probability of having coercive sanctions, as it occurred in the second episode of the sanctions on Libya. Table 6.2 summarises the standardised coefficients that have been registered for the three episodes.

Table 6.2: String of episodes of UN sanctions on Libya

Episode	Threat	Salience	Complexity	Type of sanctions
UN/Libya – 1992 to 1993	0.89 (high)	0.83 (high)	0.23 (low)	Signalling
UN/Libya – 1993 to 1999	0.89 (high)	0.83 (high)	0.23 (low)	Coercing
UN/Libya – 1999 to 2003	0.26 (low)	0.83 (high)	0.17 (low)	Signalling

Since 1993 to 1999, threat is rated high with a coefficient of 0.89, salience is rated high with a coefficient of 0.83 and complexity is rated low with a coefficient of 0.23.

Threat was rated high: the Libyan involvement in supporting terrorist organisations in the 1970s and 1980s, culminating in its participation in the Pan Am and

UTA bombings in 1988 and 1989, relates the issue to security for the sender. The threat of terrorism was widespread and the Libyan support for many groups – from IRA to Abu Nidal, from the Red Brigade to the Basques – contributes to its broad extension. Geostrategically, Libya was an important actor because of its natural resources, mainly its oil and natural gas reserves consumed largely in Europe, and its closeness to the P5. Whereas the former has increased recently with the construction of the 'Greenstream' pipeline through Italy (Energy Information Administration 2007), the vicinity to Europe was crucial to boost the perception of danger from the Libyan dispute based on the historical record of Tripoli.

The crisis was salient as the level of attention and the level of engagement were high. A number of newspapers articles contributed to the high coefficient for salience. In the two years preceding the imposition of the second round of sanctions, the *Financial Times* published 318 articles on Libya (420 in the first episode and 343 in the third episode), and *The New York Times* 150 (122 in the first episode and 94 in the third one – see Appendix VI for the data of all the episodes). The level of engagement has been assessed as moderate, since there was a diplomatic effort on the part of the UN to broker a deal with Libya with the dispatching of the UN Special Envoy, Vasiliy Safronchuk (Simons 2003: 149).

The complexity indicators show that the dispute between the UN and Libya was not a complex one because of the low number of actors involved, the low level of violence and the low number of incompatibilities between the P5 and Libya. There are three main actors in the dispute: Libya, the UN (with the US and the UK more than others) and the Organisation for African Unity (OUA), which acquired importance when the risk of missed implementation was cast in the second half of the decade because of the rigidities of the UK and US position (Niblock 2001: 47). The actors were not involved in direct violence after the US bombing of Tripoli and Benghazi in 1986, in which Gaddafi's daughter was killed, and the number of issues was limited to the handing over of the two suspects for the Lockerbie case and the halting of the support to international terrorist organisations. Furthermore, Gaddafi had domestic troubles that led him to use sanctions as an explanation for his poorly-managed economy (Simons 2003: 176–179).

Finally, Libya is a moderately strong target for two reasons: first, its natural resources provide it with good bargaining leverage with those actors trading oil and gas with Tripoli, such as the European countries (Simons 2003: 58); and, secondly, the Libyan economy continued to operate in a similar way, but the price of sanctions was redirected to the population in order to alleviate the burden on the leadership (Simons 2003: 176–179; Niblock 2001: 64).

The theoretical model

UN sanctions imposed on Libya are a typical case of coercive sanctions because the objective was to attach a cost to certain behaviour of the Libyan leadership without endangering the stay in power of the ruling elite. Albeit Colonel Gaddafi had not enjoyed the admiration of western leaders for his foreign policy in the previous years, but the demands were not aiming at regime change in Libya.

The analysis of the context would explain the coercive measures because the UN was under threat and the dispute was not complex. Indeed, when threat is high, the primary interest of the sender is to remove the cause of the threat and the incentive to divert the focus of sanctions on other issues will be low. For instance, if there is a specific threat linked to the proliferation of nuclear technology, the objective will be to stop the proliferation only, without including other provisions in the demands, such as human rights, etc. In the case of Libya, the threat was high since the support to international terrorist organisations caused the death of innocent civilians in the west and the impunity of such an act could create further attacks. The strong response and the precise request were noted and this isolated Libya on the international stage. Eventually, Libya halted its support for international terrorist organisations. Hence, when threat is high, the demands are more likely to be precise and targets can voluntarily, albeit unpleasantly, meet them without endangering their existence.

High threat stands for high impact and feasible demands, but this second component is made possible by the low complexity of the crisis. Indeed, senders can make specific requests only under specific circumstances, for instance when there are clear behaviours that can clearly be identified as favourable. Also, targets have to be in the conditions of complying with specific demands, and this can happen only in contexts where they would not be endangered by compliance vis-à-vis other actors. For instance, Libya can comply with the requests of the Security Council, but in civil wars or intractable conflicts, the survival of the parties come before any request of the Security Council. The case of Libya is telling as the Security Council was able to formulate a precise and practical request specifically because the complexity was low. In other words, the low level of complexity made possible the formulation of precise demands, and the high level of threat created the conditions for the UN to impose sanctions that had an impact on the targets. Together, threat and complexity explain the imposition of coercive sanctions.

Constraining Al-Qaida and the Taliban

Al-Qaida gained notoriety with the wider public as a result of the 9/11 attacks, but the UN sanctions regime that was adapted to punish those responsible had been in place for two years already. In 1998, the US embassies in Tanzania and Kenya were targeted by terrorist attacks, causing hundreds of casualties. The Security Council decided to act and imposed sanctions on the Taliban because of their lack of cooperation with international authorities in securing to justice those responsible for the bombings. The first episode of sanctions began in 1999 with resolution 1267 of 15th October imposing financial and aviation restrictions on the members of the Taliban regime. A list of the targets was released and it was composed by all those individuals and entities that were accused of acting or supporting those responsible for the casualties in the two bombings (United Nations 1999). A cost was imposed and the request to hand in Usama Bin Laden does qualify as 'feasible' for the Taliban, making the first episode of sanctions a coercive type.

However, 9/11 changed everything. Al-Qaida and Usama bin Laden committed a horrendous crime that caused the death of 3,000 people and this act was to be pursued. With other foreign policy methods, which included also the Counter-Terrorism Committee (CTC)[1] and the 1540 Committee (also known as non-proliferation committee), the 1267 measures were adapted to the changed nature of the target. Al-Qaida members were associated with the Taliban through resolution 1390 of 16th January 2002. The same resolution imposed financial and travel restrictions, and an arms embargo on 'Usama bin Laden, members of the Al-Qaeda organisation and the Taliban and other individuals, groups, undertakings and entities associated with them' (United Nations 2002b). One day before, the aviation ban on Afghana Airlines was lifted with resolution 1388 (United Nations 2002a).

The list of the targets has been renewed with multiple resolutions. In 2008, the consolidated list includes: 142 individuals belonging to or associated with the Taliban, 228 individuals belonging to or associated with Al-Qaida, and 112 entities belonging to or associated with Al-Qaeda. On 1st December 2010, the individuals associated with the Taliban totalled 137, no entity and other group and undertaking associated with the Taliban; the individuals associated with Al-Qaida were 259 individuals, and the entities and other groups and undertakings associated with Al-Qaida were 92 entities. The most updated list at the time of writing was presented in 2011 and it included 137 individuals associated with the Taliban, 256 individuals associated with Al-Qaida and 92 entities and other groups and undertakings associated with Al-Qaida (United Nations 2011). The work of the committee was supported by a monitoring group in New York, by a Sanctions Enforcement Support Team since 2001, and by the Analytical Support and Sanctions Monitoring Team (the Monitoring Team) (United Nations 2004a), which was created in 2004 with resolution 1526 of 30th January 2004 in order to replace the five-person group of experts that was established in 2001 (United Nations 2001). The new body, which is composed of eight members, has also the task of formulating recommendations to make the sanctions regime more effective.

The dependent variable: feasibility and direct impact

This set of sanctions is only a small component of a much wider effort to fight terrorism. Sanctions only contribute to the UN strategy by undermining the operational capability of potential attackers. In other words, using the terms adopted in this research, sanctions attempt to constrain what Al-Qaida members can, or cannot, do.

The first step in our discourse is to classify sanctions by looking at their direct impact on events and by the resources targeted. There is definitely an impact on the events. Unfortunately, there are no solid statistics about the funding frozen since 2001, but there has been a steady improvement on the governance of financial transactions that have put the previously used method under control (i.e.

---

1. Even if Cortright and Lopez have cast doubts on the nature of the 1540 as a typical case for sanctions committees, see (Cortright *et al.* 2007).

Hawala) and have made financial institutions report on suspicious transactions (United Nations 2008a). In brief, it is plausible to say that financial transactions in favour of terrorist networks are more difficult today than they were in 2001. The same could be said for travelling. Obviously, these regimes have been criticised for their lack of impact, and part of this criticism is surely well founded. The problems related to the effective impact of the measures, which are linked to the lack of political will of important international actors to implement the measures,[2] do not undermine the effort of the implementation. For instance, states claim not to have the capacity to carry out the measures imposed by the Security Council (Biersteker *et al.* 2005; Cortright and Lopez 2007a), the identification of the individuals is still a murky process, the list of targets comprises mistakes (United Nations 2008a), and the changing nature of financing of Al-Qaida (Biersteker and Eckert 2008) makes enforcement harder. However, it is fair to argue that this is one of the most successful examples of international coordination causing the degree of impact sanctions to be high (Cortright and Lopez 2007b; Biersteker and Eckert 2008).

Feasibility is low due to the low level of preciseness and practicality. Since there is no request advanced by the Security Council to Al-Qaida, Taliban members and their associates, determining the preciseness or the practicality appears to be a difficult endeavour. The terrorists are outlaws and there can be no requests made to them aside from the one of halting all their activities.

The independent variable: threat, salience and complexity

This case represents the second dominant pattern identified in Chapter 5 of high threat, high complexity, and constraining sanctions. Table 6.3 presents the detailed coefficients for threat, salience and complexity for the two episodes.

Leaving aside the first episode of coercion, the second episode from 2002 to at least December 2010 is classified as a constraining type, and the analysis of the crisis make it a representative of the combination of high threat and high complexity.

Table 6.3: String of episodes of UN sanctions on Al-Qaida and Taliban

Episode	Threat	Salience	Complexity	Type of sanctions
UN/1267 – 1999 to 2001	0.53 (high)	0.17 (low)	0.33 (low)	Coercion
UN/1267 – 2002 to present	0.74 (high)	0.83 (high)	0.63 (high)	Constraint

---

2.   Interview with David Cortright, on April 2008.

Threat has a standardised index of 0.74 because both issue and extension are high, while the geostrategic relevance of the target plays a smaller role. Issue has a rate of four because the terrorist menace regards issues of security especially the safety of innocent civilians. Specifically after 9/11, counter-terrorism measures have climbed the world political agenda. The extension of the threat is wide, as the history of recent attacks shows (Jakarta, London, Madrid, Sharm el Sheik, New York, and others) (Global Terrorism Database 2008) and several subsystems are affected with particular emphasis on, for example, Central Asia and Afghanistan. Nevertheless, the assessment does not reach the maximum of the scale because countries judge the importance of the terrorist threat differently, as lamented by the monitoring group in one of their reports (United Nations 2007a; Bures 2010). The geostrategy index is low with a rate of two out of five because Al-Qaida and the Taliban, albeit their worldwide reach, do not enjoy either the benefit of being located in a specific area with rare resources or the structural vicinity to the P5 (even if the structure of Al-Qaida allows it to have cells inside many countries both in Europe and in the US, but with limited operative capacity). Another relevant aspect is that Al-Qaida is focusing its presence in two areas with worldwide atten-tion, namely Iraq and Afghanistan. Certainly, destabilising these two realities may have a multiplier effect in its struggle with the West.

The 1267 committee deals with a salient issue, index that has a standardised value of 0.83. The level of attention is moderate, since the data shows that the 1267 committee was discussed by 614 (84 in the previous episode) articles in the *Financial Times* and by 377 (125 in the previous episode) articles in *The New York Times* in the two years preceding the imposition of sanctions. The level of engagement for the 1267 committee has a slightly different definition previously mentioned in the sense that engagement here means the degree of interest and involvement of the international community to fight against the target. While no incentives and dialogue have been established publicly, the efforts of the inter-national community encompasses multiple actors – the Financial Action Task Force (FATF), the International Civil Aviation Organization (ICAO), the Office for Foreign Assets Control (OFAC), the World Border Organizations (WBO-Borderpol), the International Maritime Organizations, and others – and the level of integration in a certain field, namely the fight against the financing of terrorism, has produced effective international regimes in only a few years (Biersteker and Eckert 2008; Smith 2008).

Finally, complexity is rated as high with a standardised coefficient of 0.63 due to a high number of actors and, above all, a number of issues. The number of actors is rated as four out of five because Al-Qaida and the Taliban, the UN, NATO and a series of actors bordering both Afghanistan and Iraq have had mixed approaches towards the issue of terrorism.[3] The level of violence is currently low with a rating of two out of four because of the type of actions that are carried out by Al-Qaida, namely sporadic attacks against civilians, with the exceptions of the

---

3.   Namely Pakistan, Iran and Syria to mention only some.

Taliban operations in the southern part of Afghanistan (Riedel 2007). However, since targets of the 1267 are worldwide terrorists, it should be appropriate to focus on the level of violence that is related to it. The number of issues is high because of the various interpretations of Al-Qaida and the Taliban requests. Not intending to provide a full list of them, the requests vary from ideological clashes to territorial claims, from liberating the Arab peninsula of foreign occupation, to spreading Islamic values across the globe (Pape 2005: 27–36). Overall, it can be assumed that the issues at stake are concerned with security, economy, ideology and religion. Notwithstanding the variety of goals that can be attributed to Al-Qaida and the Taliban, they are considered criminal actors for the typology of actions that have been perpetrated and the recent illegal activities developed in order to sustain their operations, so not only are their objectives not subjected to negotiations or compromises, but criminal operations are undertaken to pursue them (Schneider and Post 2003). Finally, Al-Qaida and the Taliban are rated as moderately strong because of their small structure and their ability to adapt to different environmental conditions. Overall, targets enjoy the benefits granted them by the fact of being non-governmental actors able to operate across borders with extreme facility (Gunaratna 2002).

The theoretical model

The theoretical model elaborated here suggests that when a crisis is complex but threat is high, then constraining sanctions become the most likely outcome. The episode of UN sanctions on Al-Qaida and the Taliban since 2002 fits this instance.

Sanctions against Al-Qaida and the Taliban are of a constraint type. The international community is threatened by the actions of these international terrorists, but the nature of the target and the complexity of the situation allow only for sanctions that cannot change the costs/benefits calculation of targets to a point to change their behaviour. Al-Qaida and the Taliban are criminal actors committed to their own goals, which are fundamentally incompatible with the ones of the international community. Furthermore, it is in the very essence of this type of target to advance non-negotiable demands. However, sanctions can properly undermine the capabilities of Al-Qaida and associates by exercising that form of power defined as 'limiting the alternatives'.

The need to act and to bear a cost with the imposition of sanctions that aim at a certain weakness on the enemy's side is justified by the threat on the P5 posed by this type of terrorism. As noted previously, the fight against international terrorism has reached the top of the political agenda and many actors deem it as a serious threat to their peace and stability. The menace is real for many of them as proven by the long series of attacks carried out in several areas of the world. The reaction to highly perceived threat is to do as much as possible to limit them. To limit is the right wording because the high level of complexity of the crisis, due mainly to the nature of the target, does not allow aiming at other goals.

Signalling Rwanda

The crisis that is relevant to this investigation in Rwanda begins in 1990, when the Rwanda Patriotic Front (RPF), a Tutsi based group aiming at seizing power in the country, launched its campaign to take over Kigali. In fact, this was only the last move of a long standing confrontation between two ethnic groups in Rwanda known as the Tutsi and the Hutu, an ethnic separation created artificially during the time when Rwanda was a Belgian colony. The Tutsi were the minority of the Rwandans, but occupied the highest positions in power, while the Hutu were the majority, but they were relegated to lower positions. In the 1960s, the Hutu became dominant, took power and pushed the Tutsis out of the country. The attempt launched by the RPF in 1990 ended up as the Arusha Accord, signed in 1993, which established the pattern for a process of democratisation based on a power-sharing agreement between the two ethnicities. Unfortunately, this conflict was never really settled. Despite the arrival of the United Nations Assistance Mission for Rwanda (UNAMIR) established by resolution 872 of 5th October 1993 (United Nations 1993b), the Hutus were able to form and train the *Interhamwe*, private militias having as their main goal the elimination of the Tutsi population from Rwanda (Prunier 1995).

The spark that ignited the conflict occurred on 6th April 1994, when the President of Rwanda, Juvénal Habyarimana, and the President of Burundi, Cyprien Ntaryamira, died in a plane crash near the Kigali airport. The Hutus claimed that the RPF shot down the plane and began a campaign of killing against the Tutsis: 800,000 people died in only 100 days – one person every ten seconds. The targets of the *Interhamwe* and of the government forces were not the Tutsis solely, but also moderate Hutus that were not supportive of the ethnic cleansing (Jones 2001).

The international community reacted slowly, partly because of the lack of information in the early phase of the killings, and partly because of the low tolerance to casualties that western states were willing to tolerate in foreign missions after the deaths of eighteen US soldiers in the streets of Mogadishu in 1993. Nevertheless, the delay and the failure to act in Rwanda are now considered one of the greatest shames in UN history (Barnett 2002).

Despite the fact that UNAMIR was already deployed in the field for the implementation of the Arusha Accords, the UN Security Council decided to withdraw its troops instead of deploying a greater number of personnel, which would possibly have spared thousands of lives (Dallaire 2003). The size of UNAMIR varied throughout time, from its peak of 5,500 personnel reached right after the genocide to its lowest point during the outset of the massacre when UNAMIR was composed by only 267 people (United Nations 2008d), an extremely low number, which was unable to prevent or to stop the massive killings of the *Interhamwe*.

The Security Council resorted to sanctions and the case can be broken up in two episodes. The first one began with resolution 918 of 17th May 1994 imposing an arms embargo on Rwanda with the exception of UNAMIR and its predecessor, the United Nations Observer Mission Uganda-Rwanda (UNOMUR) (United Nations 1994). In this phase, sanctions were imposed with a signalling logic. The second episode of sanctions lasted for twelve years. It began with the imposition of resolution 997 of 9th June 1995, when the arms embargo was extended to the groups in neighbouring countries that intended to use or to bring arms into Rwanda (United Nations 1995b). The Government of Rwanda was exempted by the sanctions regime in 1996 under resolution 1011 of 1995, which terminated the measure dated 1st September 1996, but imposed the requirement on all states to give notice of their arms exports to Rwanda (United Nations 1995a). The episode ended with resolution 1823 of 10th July 2008, which cancelled the last measures in force and dissolved the sanctions committee (United Nations 2008c). This second episode is also classified as signalling, but the different degree of salience categorises it in the ambivalent pattern illustrated in Chapter 4 and will not be covered here.

The dependent variable: feasibility and direct impact

The first episode of UN sanctions imposed on Rwanda was of a signalling type. The fundamental factor is the lack of direct material impact that the measure was supposed to have, but it would be also useful to describe the demand attached to sanctions in order to emphasise a hypothesised connection with the complexity of the crisis.

The impact of the arms embargo on the events was nil for two reasons. First, the implementation of the embargo was difficult to obtain and it was not a priority for the UN forces on the ground. No checkpoints were established to enforce the measures, while implementation has been left entirely to the willingness of all states to cooperate with the sanctions committee. Neighbouring states were not involved and not properly informed on the matter; therefore, it is plausible to presume that weapons could have entered Rwanda easily (Melvern 2000). Enforcing an arms embargo in a densely populated country in the Great Lake Region is an enormous task even if it is attempted with massive personnel deployment. In the case of Rwanda, very limited resources were invested to this aim. Furthermore, the dependence of the Hutus on arms imports was minimal, since the genocide was mainly carried out with hand tools named *machetes* (Hatzfeld and Coverdale 2005). The monitoring was insufficient for the task since only a committee was established with a limited capacity (Vines 2003: 248; Cortright and Lopez 2000: 197). The final paragraph of the reports of the committee, which was not invested with great responsibilities and met very few times since its creation, is emblematic for the overall lack of enforcement:

> In the absence of a specific monitoring mechanism to ensure the effective implementation of the arms embargo, the Committee would like to recall its previous observation that it relies solely on the cooperation of States and organisations in a position to provide information on violations of the arms embargo.
>
> (United Nations 2008b)

Furthermore, the second shortcoming is the timing, as the embargo was imposed well into the perpetration of the genocide and little impact was expected to be reached with this measure. An arms embargo is purely a denial measure, but the halting of the genocide based on the extensive use of violence could not be achieved with measures that are, by nature, purely limitative of the capabilities of the actors. Other measures, such as financial or commodity boycotts, could have had a higher impact on the actors, but they were not imposed.

The criticisms for the lack of monitoring led to the creation of an International Commission of Inquiry (UNICOI) in 1995, and although the Commission did a good job in investigating and reporting the violations of the embargo, its activity did not bear fruit because of scarce resources and the lack of political considera-tion. Even if it was important for the monitoring and the implementation of other embargoes (Vines 2003: 248), the establishment of UNICOI was too late to affect the dynamics of the genocide (United Nations 1998a).

The lack of impact classifies this episode in the signalling category and the fea-sibility of the demands is not essential to determine the type of sanctions. However, it would be useful to establish the connection with the system of sanctions and, specifically, with the variable of complexity. Resolution 918 stated that it 'de-mands that all parties to the conflict immediately cease hostilities, agree to a cease-fire, and bring an end to the mindless violence and carnage engulfing Rwanda' (United Nations 1994), which sounds very general and simplistic for a conflict that has been ongoing for over thirty years. The actors should have stopped fighting, but there was no indication of who was guilty and why. The practicality is low as well, since the Great Lake region was afflicted by grave conflicts across space and time (Adelman and Suhrke 1999; Khadiagala 2006). Under a grave security threat, the possession – and sometimes the use of –weapons may be the only way to pre-serve one's own survival. Thereby, a feasible request to halt the violence should be accompanied by counter-balancing measures aiming at providing the parties with security, but this was not the case in Rwanda.

The independent variable: threat, salience and complexity

The context of the first episode of sanctions fits the third combination of low threat and low salience identified in the database. This configuration is present several times and it correlates with signalling sanctions, as in the episode investigated here of the UN on Rwanda from 1993 to 1994. Table 6.4 summarised the coefficient for threat, salience and complexity.

Table 6.4: String of episodes of UN sanctions on Rwanda

Episode	Threat	Salience	Complexity	Type of sanctions
UN/Rwanda – 1994 to 1995	0.05 (low)	0.17 (low)	0.87 (high)	Signalling
UN/Rwanda – 1995 to 2008	0.05 (low)	1.00 (high)	0.63 (high)	Signalling

The index of threat is the lowest of the database with a standardised coefficient of 0.05,[4] because of low values for issue, extension and geostrategy. The issue at stake regarded milieu objectives from the P5 and received the rating of one out of four. Rwanda and its domestic troubles did not pose a danger on either possession or vital objectives, since the P5 did not have commercial interests or were under the threat of political backlashes in case of inaction (Power 2002). Consequently, the extension of the threat did not go beyond the Great Lake Region while it was mainly Uganda and the DRC that were concerned with what was going on in Kigali, especially in regards to the fate of the masses of Hutus fleeing from Rwanda into their territories (Adelman and Suhrke 1999; Khadiagala 2006).

Salience as well was rated as low with a standardised coefficient of 0.17. The level of attention is low since the *Financial Times* published 119 articles (353 in the second episode) and *The New York Times* only 98 (compared to 466 in the two years preceding the beginning of the second episode). The motivation for the difference between the two episodes lies in the little that was known at the outset of the genocide. The information was fragmented and the newspapers did not devote attention to the problem. The level of engagement has received a rating of two out of three because of the deployment of UNAMIR from 1993 to 1996. Even if the role played by UNAMIR in the settling of the conflict and, especially, in the monitoring of the embargo is almost negligible, the level of engagement cannot be assessed with a rate of three because of the limited role and the restricted rules of engagement of the contingents. Furthermore, it is crucial to observe that the UN troops withdrew when they were needed the most and the peak of 5,500 personnel remained only for a few months from 1994 to 1995, when they were reduced to a contingent of less than 2,000 (Jones 2001).

Finally, the index of complexity reveals that the dispute in Rwanda was very thorny with an elevated standardised coefficient of 0.87 with number of actors, level of violence, and number of issues as main contributors to it. The number of actors has been established as four: the UN, the Hutu, the Tutsi and other relevant actors (namely France, China, South Africa and Zaire counted as one). The UN was involved with UNAMIR since 1993, while the Hutus and the Tutsis were active parts of the civil conflict that began after independence in 1960. In regard to France and China, the allegations are multiple and were known since the early stages of the genocide. *The Washington Post* published an editorial denouncing rocket launchers being used in Rwanda as coming from France and South Africa (Opinion Editorial 1994). The report of the committee in 1996 testifies to the allegations since it requested information from the governments of France, China, South Africa and Zaire over suspected violations of the embargo (United Nations 1996: 5–6). The level of violence has received the highest value since Rwanda's 1994 genocide and was the largest and the quickest mass killing since the end of the Cold War. Indeed, although other tragedies were larger in numbers of casualties, such casualties were spread throughout longer timeframes and were not the

---

4. A coefficient of zero does not mean 'no threat', but rather a low threat, as explained in Chapter 5.

result of planned mass exterminations. The number of issues as well has received the highest rate, five out of five, since the interest at stake for the competitors was that most precious thing, namely survival. The Tutsi were fighting to protect their very existence, while the Hutus were moved by the fear of being exploited and repressed once again by the Tutsi minority (Prunier 1995). Finally, the strength of the targets has been set as moderate because, on the one hand, both Tutsis and Hutus were non-governmental forces and lacked the economical resources to carry out large operations or to resist foreign pressure while, on the other hand, they were not vulnerable to sanctions for the very reason that they were not in-stitutionalised and enjoyed foreign support (Melvern 2000; Kroslak 2007). The Rwandan genocide was characterised by the extensive use of *machetes* by a very high number of people who had been targeted by a propaganda campaign against the Tutsi. The cost tolerance for the two sides was obviously very high.

The theoretical model

The first episode of the UN sanctions imposed on Rwanda can be explained by looking at the context in which the Security Council decided to act. The low level of threat and salience influenced the decision of the UN in resorting to sanctions with objectives that differ from influencing the targets through an alteration of their costs/benefits calculations based on material resources or on the costs im-posed by the sanction on itself. Why were they so?

The analysis of the context contributes to explaining the signalling purpose of the UN measures on Rwanda. The UN was not threatened by the events in Rwanda: no one was fleeing to the P5, no commercial interest was threatened, and little connections were ongoing between the P5 and the Rwandans (with excep-tions from France and Belgium). Therefore, the low impact determined by low enforcement is explained by the lack of interest in intervening. At the same time, the high level of complexity would explain why sanctions were designed to deny goods that were not crucial to the ongoing crisis. When a crisis is complex, little or no information is available to the sender, multiple actors interact with each other under limited structured frameworks and, therefore, the predictability of the actions is nullified. Furthermore, there is little that can be done to solve a deeply-rooted crisis such as the one that afflicted Rwanda for years since erupting in 1994. So, why did the UN impose sanctions if it was not under threat and they were not expected to have an impact? The answer is that sanctions were used in a wider strategy and did not have the objective of affecting the primary targets' calculations. An important clarification can be given at this point, as it could be asked why the UN deployed personnel if the crisis was not salient. There could be two different explanations. The first one is that salience may have increased over time to justify the deployment. The second is that the quality of the pressures may change from one episode to another, but the comparison and further verifica-tion of this evidence goes beyond the scope of this research. Given the conditions whereby sanctions provide only a limited contribution to the resolution of the crisis, they are imposed with the intent of signalling the actors of the international system, rather than to affect their primary targets.

The identification of audiences and possible targets of the signalling is outside of the scope of this research, but it is enough to argue that the main objective for a sender is to send a signal to an audience, and in this case there are two signals and two audiences. The first signal is that the UN is interested in the situation in Rwanda and that it is working for the resolution of the conflict. The second signal is directed to other possible perpetrators of similar acts and it consists of letting them know that the UN will react to such international misconducts. Further studies are required on this direction.

Conclusion

The conclusions reached in Chapter 5 are confirmed by the three episodes of sanctions presented here, which highlight the pressures and constraints that the system creates around senders when they decide to resort to sanctions. The fundamental premise is that the tripartite typology of sanctions performs well in clarifying the differences among sanctions episodes. UN sanctions imposed on Libya, Al-Qaida/Taliban and Rwanda are not only different from each other if we look at their form, namely whether arms embargoes or travel bans are imposed, but also the way they attempt to influence other actors, whether primary or secondary, distinguishes each from the other. The argument of this book is that there is a systemic explanation for this variance.

Coercing sanctions were imposed on Libya because of the level of threat on the sender was high and the complexity of the crisis was low. Colonel Gaddafi would not have seen his hold on power undermined with compliance and specific behaviour was demanded by the Security Council as the crisis posed a security threat on the P5. The theoretical model suggests that with different systemic conditions, the likelihood of seeing a coercive measure would have been different. For instance, for higher levels of complexity, it is likely that the UN would have imposed measures to limit the alternatives available to Tripoli. Alternatively, lower levels of threat would have led to either constraining or, more likely, signalling sanctions.

International terrorist organisations cannot be coerced, and in the moment they pose a threat to the P5, sanctions can only aim at making their life more complicated. The interests of Al-Qaida members and Taliban are fundamentally incompatible with the ones of the governments represented in the Security Council. Anyone could be targeted by the actions of terrorist organisations, therefore there is shared understanding that terrorism can be fought by undertaking a law enforcement approach. The international sanctions adopted by the UN go precisely in this direction. For lower level of threat, it would have been likely to have a signalling logic at work, while for lower level of complexity, coercion would have been the mechanism sought with the imposition of sanctions.

Finally, the arms embargo that was imposed on Rwanda in 1994 fulfilled mostly signalling expectations. There is little to be added to the fact that policy makers knew about the low level of impact on preventing the sale of rifles and artillery when the genocide was carried out mostly with *machetes*, especially considering that the embargo was imposed a few weeks after the beginning of the killings. Assuming that the main actors in Rwanda were the only targets, the way in which sanctions aimed at influencing their behaviour was not through the imposition of a direct cost on their actions. Counterfactually, the model implies that for a higher level of threat, sanctions would have been either of a coercive or constraining type, while for a higher level of salience, constraining sanctions could have been an alternative outcome.

Overall, the theoretical framework applied to sanctions episodes appears to yield explanatory power on the variation of sanctions purposes across time and space. The determinants of sanctions – threat, salience and complexity – may be able to guide policy makers in deciding and designing future sanctions according to what they would like and they can achieve in different situations. The results of historical narratives of the UN experience in Libya, against Al-Qaida/Taliban and Rwanda seem to confirm that there is a strong relationship between the way in which sanctions are supposed to influence targets and the contexts – or system – in which they are adopted. Chapter 7 looks for further evidence of this relationship.

chapter | the european union as a regional
seven | sanctioner: the cases of belarus,
        | transnistria and uzbekistan

The systemic theoretical framework has proved useful to analyse, understand and explain the sanctions of the United Nations. This chapter aims at verifying further whether the theoretical model has explanatory power over the logic of international sanctions. The experience of the European Union and the investigation of three more cases can provide further clarity on both the differences among sanctions episodes and on the explanation of the logic available to policy makers. The EU is an important sender in the international arena, and it has been selected for this study because it employs both comprehensive and targeted measures. Furthermore, it does act as a state in many respects, but it is still affected by those characters that are proper to an international organisation. Having acknowledged this status, the EU is assumed to be a unitary actor in this research.

The three episodes analysed for the EU are the restrictive measures on Belarus (since 2007), on the leadership of Transnistria from 2003 to 2010, and on Uzbekistan. These three cases have been selected because they are typical for each dominant combination that has been identified with the cs-QCA analysis adopted in Chapter 4. Sanctions against Belarus are coercive because they aim at making Lukashenka cooperate with the EU. The framework suggests that high threat and low complexity are systemic determinants for coercive sanctions. The measures imposed on the leaders of Transnistria attempt to constrain their capacity to cling to power and to pursue the independence of this rebel region of Moldova. Here, the model explains that the threat posed on the borders of the EU led the Council of Ministers to target a resource that is essential to reach independence, but the complexity of the crisis, given the Russian presence in the region and the substantial unwillingness to negotiate any compromise to break the deadlock, did not allow the formulation of requests that would be compatible with the survival of the current ruling class in Tiraspol. Finally, the measures on Uzbekistan are classified as signalling sanctions given their lack of impact. In this case, the context is useful to explain that, given the low threat and the low salience of the crisis, the EU decided not to bear the cost of imposing heavier measures. The analyses of the three cases add further evidence to the validity of the taxonomy of sanctions and to the capacity of the theoretical framework to explain why sanctions are constructed under a dominant driving logic.

This chapter is divided in three sections: the sanctioning decision-making process of the European Union and the database of EU restrictive measures; a description of the three cases from the EU experience since the end of the Cold War; and a summary of the objective of the chapter and conclusion that provides further verification of the hypotheses of the theoretical model presented earlier.

The sanctioning policy of the EU

The importance of the European Union as an international actor has grown substantially in the past decade and the development of a sanctioning policy is one of the contributory elements (de Vries and Hazelzet 2005).

The Treaty of the European Union (TEU) includes restrictive measures as one of the possible tools that can be employed to achieve the goals of its CFSP, thus it is the Council that imposes sanctions by the unanimous adoption of common positions. Moreover, the EU receives UN sanctions by passing specific legislation and can also suspend financial aid to the signatories of the Cotonou Agreement as established by article 96 (Cotonou Agreement 2000). The focus of this investigation is on the first type of sanctions that are decided by the Council of Ministers when it does not receive UN resolutions, also labelled as standing alone sanctions.

The growing importance of restrictive measures in the foreign policy toolbox is confirmed by the institutionalisation of their use with the approval of three important documents that aimed at improving the design, the implementation and the effectiveness of restrictive measures. On 8th December 2003, the Council approved the 'Guidelines on implementation and evaluation of restrictive measures (sanctions) in the framework of the EU Common Foreign and Security Policy' (hereafter 'the Guidelines'). This document, which was updated in December 2005, contains definitions and principles on how to design restrictive measures, important information in regards to the different types of restrictions that can be imposed and on how to measure their effectiveness (European Union 2005b). The main principles that inspire the adoption of sanctions are presented in the second relevant key document of the EU restrictive measures' policy. The document, which is named as 'Basic Principles on the Use of Restrictive Measures (Sanctions)' (hereafter 'Basic Principles'), was approved by the Council in June 2004 and it states that the EU should impose sanctions in accordance with the UN, but also autonomously whenever 'necessary' to meet the objectives of the EU. Finally, the third document is a living text on the implementation of restrictive measures that was passed initially in December 2004. The last version of 'The EU Best Practices for the effective implementation of restrictive measure' (hereafter 'the Best Practices') was approved in April 2008 and it contains the relevant information on how to identify the correct designated individuals or entities, and on the administrative modalities for freezing assets and banning products, including the procedure on how to grant exceptions and exemptions to the measures (European Union 2008d).

The policy-making process is similar to other external relations matters and it falls under article 29 (ex-article 15) of the Treaty of the European Union (TEU). The president or a member of the Council, assisted by the Council Secretariat or by the Commission, can make a proposal regarding the imposition of restrictive measures, but the Lisbon Treaty assigned this task to the High Representative of the Union for Foreign Affairs and Security Policy. The proposal is discussed by the geographical groups assigned to deal with the target and analyzed also by the Foreign Relations Counselors Working Group (RELEX) and the Political and Security Committee (PSC). Subsequently, it is the Committee of Permanent Representatives II (COREPER II) that has the responsibility of agreeing on a common position to be submitted to the Council for the final approval.

The implementation of the restrictive measures falls under the responsibilities of different actors. Whereas trade and financial sanctions have to be implemented with a Council regulation according to article 75 (preventing and combating terrorism), article 215 (measures of common foreign and security policy), and sometimes article 352, of the Lisbon Treaty, visa bans and arms embargoes have to be implemented by the adoption of national legislation. In other words, the former are dealt with by the EU, while the latter by member states. Arms embargoes are an exceptional case because of a provision on national security that has been part of the Treaties since 1957.[1] In cases of financial or economic restriction, the Commission has to elaborate a regulation on the matter that has to be approved by the Council. Before the entry into force of the Lisbon Treaty, there was a procedural difference when imposing sanctions on states or non-state entities, but it has been cancelled by the new Treaty. Thus, the decision can be approved with qualified majority voting (that are now called 'Council Implementing Decisions').

The general objectives for the imposition of sanctions are illustrated in article 21 of the TEU as any decisions on external relations. The document of the Basic Principles deals with this issue as well and it states that EU restrictive measures should be adopted in support of efforts to fight terrorism and the proliferation of mass destruction, to uphold respect for human rights, democracy, the rule of law and good governance (European Union 2004a). The Guidelines added an important element on this stating that 'the restrictive measures do not have an economic motivation' (European Union 2005).

Two EU bodies that are devoted to restrictive measures are: the Foreign Relations Counselors Working Group and the Restrictive Measures Team. The former has to monitor the effectiveness and the implementation of the restrictive measures and has to convene in ad hoc committees known as the Sanctions' Committee/RELEX to accomplish its duty. The Restrictive Measures Team, now moved to the European External Action Service, has a duty to assist the drafting of the regulations in financial and economic matters when sanctions are imposed. The activities of these two bodies are assisted by more generalist bodies, such the geographical subcommittees, the COREPER and the secretariat together with full-time officials on sanctions.

Member states are also involved in the policy-making of restrictive measures in determining the penalties for eventual violations, deciding on the exemptions and exceptions, providing information and making sure that private institutions follow the guidelines provided by the EU in implementing the sanctions (European Union 2007c). When states do not perform adequately in this field, the Commission can hold them accountable for their incapacity to fulfil EU decisions. States should be stimulated by the Commission to comply with the provisions of the treaty on the

---

1. Article 57 before, now article 296 of the TEU.

lack of implementation of EU restrictive measures, as provided by articles 259 and 260 of the Treaty on the Functioning of the European Union (TFEU).

European Union restrictive measures are bounded by the provisions of international treaties, UN regulations and, additionally, EU legislation. Therefore, EU sanctions contain several exemptions and exceptions that are necessary to protect the rights granted to individuals and entities by EU regulations. For instance, EU restrictive measures have also to respect the General Agreement on Tariffs and Trade (GATT) and WTO provisions, other than allowing listed individuals to receive healthcare treatments in the EU or to participate in international meetings held in European countries. Moreover, the individuals who have been listed have the right to appeal to the Court of First Instance of the European Court of Justice in Luxembourg and make their case for de-listing. This condition is granted with the intent of upholding the rights of due process and effective remedy. Exemptions are usually considered when restrictive measures are adopted considering the humanitarian needs and international obligations of targeted persons (European Union 2005: 9). The Best Practices specifies another instance when exemptions can be granted, namely the legal obligation of targeted individuals or entities to satisfy creditors (European Union 2008d: 22).

Albeit both exemptions and exceptions limit the evident violations of rights, many European citizens, who felt they had been abused when their assets were frozen or their travels prohibited arbitrarily, have challenged decisions in the EU Court. Initially, the Court tended to deny all the requests by claiming its lack of competence or authority, but this trend has slowly changed with the Court repealing certain decisions of the Council in the cases of Kadi and Al Barakaat (Yassin Abdullah Kadi and Al Barakaat International Foundation vs. Council of the European Union 2008) and Jose Maria Sison (Jose Maria Sison vs. Council of the European Union 2009). Alarmed by this trend, the Council reacted preventively in the case of the *People's Mojahedin Organisation of Iran (PMOI)* by de-listing the organisation before the Court could rule on the case (Runner 2009).

The database includes 21 cases divided into 29 episodes of autonomous restrictive measures adopted or in force from 1992 until 2010 under the CFSP umbrella. The list of episodes is presented in Table 7.1.

The data skewed towards signalling sanctions confirms the assumption that sanctions can be used for aims different than changing the behaviour of a target. This is also in line with the literature on the European Union as a normative power, thus more prone to the use of incentives and conditionalities rather than sanctions (Manners 2002; Manners 2006a; Manners 2006b; Tocci 2008).

The three episodes presented below represent the three dominant patterns identified in the empirical evaluation: the coercive measures on Belarus since 2007; the constraining approach towards Transnistrian leaders from 2003 to 2010; and the signalling ones on Uzbekistan.

Table 7.1: EU Sanctions episodes since the end of the Cold War classified per purpose

Coercion	Constraint	Signal
EU/Iran – 2010	EU/Bosnia & Herzegovina – 2001 to 2006	EU/Belarus – 1998 to 1999
EU/US – 1996 to present	EU/Milosevic – 2000 to present	EU/Belarus – 2004 to 2007
EU/Belarus – 2007 to present	EU/ICTY – 2001 to present	EU/Comoros – 2008 to 2008
EU/Libya – 2004 to present	EU/Zimbabwe – 2002 to present	EU/FYROM – 2001 to 2009
	EU/Transnistria – 2003 to 2010	EU/Nigeria – 1993 to 1998
	EU/Guinea – 2009 to present	EU/Uzbekistan– 2005 to 2009
	EU/Burma/Myanmar – 2007 to present	EU/Transnistria – 2010 to present
	EU/FRY – 1998 to 2000	EU/China – 1989 to present
		EU/FRY – 1996 to 1998
		EU/Nigeria – 1998 to 1999
		EU/Afghanistan – 1996 to 1999
		EU/Burma/Myanmar – 1991 to 2007
		EU/DRC – 1993 to 2003
		EU/Sudan – 1994 to 2004
		EU/Sudan – 2004 to 2005
		EU/Indonesia – 1999 to 2000
		EU/Libya – 1999 to 2004
4	8	17

Coercing Belarus

The European Union has clashed with Belarus many times since Lukashenka's rise to power in 1994. Such contrasts led the Council to resort to sanctions in three different occasions, which constitutes three different episodes. The one under scrutiny here is the third episode, which started in 2007, and it falls under the category of coercive measures.

The first episode of sanctions dates back to 1998, when the EU imposed a travel ban on Belarusian officials with common position 448 of 9th July (European Union 1998b). The EU accused Belarus of violating the Vienna Convention over problems related to the renovation of the Drozdy (or Drazdy) compound, where western diplomats resided. According to common position 448, about one hundred government members were denied the right to enter the Union. Furthermore, the EU froze also its TACIS Civil Society Development Programme, the last remaining major EU commitment to Belarus (Krivosheev 2003: 174). The travel ban was lifted in 1999 with Council decision 156 of 22nd February after an agreement was reached between the Government of Belarus and the European Union (European Union 1999b).

The prelude to the second episode occurred in 2002, when the members of the Advisory and Monitoring Group (AMG) were accused of violating their mandate, which led to their visas not being renewed. The EU reacted to this accusation and threatened the reimposition of the travel ban (Human Rights Watch 2003; Kreutz 2005: 37–38).

The crisis escalated again in 2004, after Lukashenka's victory in what international observes considered rigged elections. Subsequently, the EU decided to impose new restrictive measures on the leadership of Belarus, also linking the measures to the lack of investigation on the disappearance of four Belarusian officials in 1999 and 2000 for which the Pourgourides Report put the blame on government authorities (European Union 2004b). The Council imposed a travel ban on four people indicated by the Report as responsible for not carrying out the investigation with common position 661 of 24th September 2004 (European Union 2004d). The list of those on the travel ban was updated on 13th December with common position 848 (European Union 2004f) and on 18th May 2006 common position 362 froze the assets of the blacklisted individuals (European Union 2006c).

Lukashenka ignored the EU's concerns for his negative human rights records because of the country's ambition of forming the Union of Russia and Belarus, a process that was triggered in 1993 when the Belarusian Prime Minister Vyacheslav Kebich and the Russian Prime Minister Viktor Chernomyrdin established a monetary union (Ambrosio 2006: 412–414). The unconditional support from Russia, which had shouldered the cost of sustaining the Belarusian economy through the granting of special rates for oil and gas, allowed Lukashenka to stand firm against EU measures and find a substitute income. Lukashenka based his support on a skilful management of the rights of passage that Russia had to pay to ship its natural resources to Europe and on his anti-western and pro-Russian rhetoric (Zurawski vel Grajewski 2005).

However, the nature of sanctions shifted from signalling to coercive in 2007. Two mutated conditions contributed to this change. First, the energy crisis caused by the discordances with Russia revealed the vulnerabilities of the economic and social systems in Belarus to external shocks and strengthened the impact of EU measures. Secondly, the Council tuned the demands with a less confrontational approach towards Minsk so they became feasible.

It had been already towards the end of the second episode that the EU tailored the demands more precisely in order to guide the behaviour of Belarus. Common position 173 of 19th March 2007 sets the beginning of the episode with the renewal of the travel ban and the freeze of assets (European Union 2007a), but the improvement in the relations favoured a softening of the measures with common position 314 of 6th April 2009 (European Union 2009b), when the travel ban was suspended. Among the signs that indicate an enhancement of the relations are the opening of the EU delegation in Minsk in March 2008, the authorisation granted by the Government of Belarus to supervise the elections in 2008 and other policy moves that indicate a more collaborative stand from President Lukashenka.

Council decision 639 of 25th October 2010 confirmed the sanctions but suspended the travel ban until October 2011 (European Union 2010a). The goal is to influence the cost/benefit calculation of the leadership of Belarus towards human rights protection, rule of law and a more general pro-European foreign policy. Within this context, sanctions have the objective of creating an incentive to the ruling elite to collaborate with the EU. In early 2011, further sanctions were imposed by the EU after the rigged elections of December 2010 that may have changed the logic of sanctions, but this is outside of the scope of this research.

Travel bans and assets freeze were small elements of what seems to be a 'two-track' strategy towards Belarus. Although sanctions are trying to impose a cost on the leadership of the country, there are several assistance programs in place (TACIS, Cross-Border Cooperation – CBC, Humanitarian Aid department of the European Commission – ECHO, International Association for the promotion of cooperation with scientists from the independent states of the former Soviet Union – INTAS, etc.) that are in support of the Belarus population (EU-Belarus Relations; European Neighbourhood and Partnership Instrument, Belarus; Country Strategy Paper 2007–2013 2007). The presence of the EU through the Organisation for Security and Cooperation in Europe (OSCE) office in Minsk further shows a real commitment towards the country (What the European Union could bring to Belarus 2006).

The dependent variable: direct impact and feasibility

Restrictive measures by the EU against Belarus are classified as coercive because they have an impact and the requests can be met by the ruling elite without endangering their position in power. The travel ban and the freeze on assets directly affect the ruling elite in Belarus. The number of people involved ensures a widespread discomfort distributed among a cluster of interests that are found in the current regime. The travel ban can be annoying, but the financial restrictions, especially after the difficult relations with Russia, thwart the privileges of holding governmental positions in Belarus. There is not solid data on the amount of money frozen or on the financial transactions prevented, but it is plausible to state that the impact of these measures is substantial and is felt by the ruling elite, as also confirmed by the ongoing debate held in February 2011 over the possible reintroduction of sanctions (Rettman 2011). The deterioration of the relationships between Belarus and Russia represents a further element in favour of this interpretation of the sanction regime (Lindner 2007: 62–69; Rudling 2008: 68–69).

The demand is feasible because it is precise and practical. The EU's request to Belarus is to improve human rights practices, democracy and rule of law, to investigate the disappearances that occurred in 1999 and 2000, and to ensure that elections meet international standards (European Union 2004d). However, alongside the general expectation to respect democratic values, the rule of law and human rights, the EU demanded:

> the speedy release and rehabilitation of all political detainees, and in the light of reforms made to the Electoral Code to bring it into line with OSCE commitments and other international standards for democratic elections as recommended by the OSCE/ODIHR.
>
> (European Union 2006a)

Practicality is rated as the highest because the requests do not endanger the existence of the regime. Albeit free and fair elections would represent an important challenge, the support for Lukashenka appears to be large enough not to undermine his real possibility to win a democratic elections (Weir 2006; Rudling 2008: 71), and the assistance programs set up by the EU should be able to decrease the costs for compliance that the regime could bear (Lindner 2007).

The independent variable: threat, salience and complexity

This episode is typical for the first dominant pattern of high threat and low complexity. The context in the third episode of the EU sanctions on Belarus is characterised by high threat (standardised coefficient of 0.63) and low complexity (standardised coefficient of 0.20), and this configuration makes it more likely that sanctions are of a coercive type. Table 7.2 summarises the coefficient threat, salience and complexity.

Table 7.2: String of episodes of EU sanctions on Belarus

Episode	Threat	Salience	Complexity	Type of sanctions
EU/Belarus – 1998 to 1999	0.42 (low)	0.50 (low)	0.23 (low)	Signal
EU/Belarus – 2004 to 2007	0.42 (low)	0.17 (low)	0.37 (low)	Signal
EU/Belarus – 2007 to present	0.63 (high)	0.67 (high)	0.20 (low)	Coercion

The crisis with Belarus is rated as high because of the possible consequences that such policy behaviour in Minsk can have in the European Union, especially due to the geostrategic position enjoyed by the ex-soviet state. The issue of the dispute is rated as two out of four because Belarus controls the gas routes from Russia to the EU, even though the explicit dispute is on democratic promotion and rule of law that are considered milieu concerns. The extension of the threat is rated as three out of four, since there are many EU members that are directly affected by the contrasts with Belarus, in particular Germany, which was heavily affected by the energy crisis in the winter of 2006/2007 when the supply to the Druzhba pipeline was interrupted. Other countries such as the Czech Republic, Slovakia and Hungary were also affected (Rudling 2008; Energy Information Administration 2008). Consequently, geostrategy receives a high rating because of the role that Belarus has in the energy policy of relevant EU members, enhanced by its immediate proximity to EU borders.

The salience of the dispute between the EU and Belarus is rated as low. The level of attention in the third episode reached a medium value. In the two years preceding the imposition of sanctions, the *Financial Times* published 259 articles directly on Belarus or related to it (226 in the first episode and 142 in the second). In the same timeframe, *The Economist* published 68 articles (the articles were 53 for the first episode and 24 for the second). The level of engagement is moderate because of the level of diplomatic efforts and the incentives that have been laid out for Belarus. Furthermore, the level could be further increased by the presence of an OSCE office in Minsk, but the content of the mission is limited.

Finally, the complexity of the dispute is low because there is only one target that no longer enjoys the support of its primary ally. The number of actors is set at three, the EU, Belarus and Russia being the main participants of the dispute. The level of violence is rated as low (two out of five), since there is no major use of government-sponsored violence against the population or any extensive use of the military. The number of issues is limited to two, namely democratisation and rule of law, which are important for Lukashenka since compliance implies a strong change in his governing practices, but the current elite would still enjoy wide support. Given the contrasts between Belarus and the Russian Federation, the target is classified as weak since 2007. Putin's move appears to have left Belarus weak and isolated in the international scene. Russia is also working on the construction of a pipeline that would diminish Minsk's geostrategic value by shipping gas and oil to Europe through the Baltic Sea. Overall, this situation makes Belarus extremely vulnerable to EU actions and augments the relative value of the incentive package offered to Lukashenka.

The theoretical model

Coercion in this case is allowed by the permissive conditions of the 'system' of sanctions. The energy crisis increased the level of threat and motivated the EU to influence Belarus foreign policy. The higher level of threat corresponded to a higher pragmatism in the EU decisions, as demonstrated by the suspension and partial lifting of the measures when Belarus complied with some of the specific demands attached to the restrictive measures. The general provisions remained in place, but this would open an important development of this study as each sanction episode is composed by different components that can work according to different logic. This argument was anticipated in the previous chapter and it will not be covered here. The other permissive element for coercive sanctions is the low level of complexity. Lukashenka's administration had few alternatives other than talking to the European Union after Putin switched off the gas supply and decided to pay lower rights of passage to Belarus than turning west in search of support. This weaker position at the bargaining table was clear and the EU was then able to ask for tangible moves from the authorities in Minsk.

As happened before, a lower threat would not provide sufficient pressures to the EU to formulate precise demands and to impose sanctions implying a direct cost on targets. Hence, for lower level of threat there would be higher chances for sanctions to be of a signalling type. With higher level of complexity, sanctions would be more of a constraining type given that precise demands would not be possible, but sanctions are commonly used to affect the costs/benefits calculations of targets through a rational logic of pain imposition.

Constraining Transnistria

The restrictive measures of the EU on the leaders of Transnistria have been in place for almost eight years and they are divided in two episodes. The first of the two – a constraining type – is the one considered here.

Geographically speaking, the Transnistrian conflict in Moldova is the closest secessionist case to the European Union. After the collapse of the Soviet Union, Moldova declared independence in 1991 and a conflict erupted in the eastern part of the country causing 1,500 casualties. The region in question is known as Transnistria, which broke away from Moldova because of its desire to remain part of the Soviet bloc. The conflict was suspended thanks to the intervention of the Russian army and it has been frozen since 1994. Beyond the Russian peacekeepers, the five-sided format and the Joint Control Command (JCC) have been established to help settle the conflict. The five-sided format is composed by Russia, the Ukraine, OSCE, Moldova and Transnistrian envoys, and it is intended to negotiate a peace agreement between the parties. The JCC is a consensual decision-making body that comprises Russia, Moldova and Transnistria and has the task of supervising the buffer zone along the Nistru river (Dniester in Russian), where each of the members has the power of veto in any decision (Popescu 2004; Vahl 2005b; Borgen 2006; Botan 2009a; King 2000; Kolsto and Malgin 1998; Lynch 2000; Popescu 2005; Protsyk 2004/2005; Rodkiewicz 2008; Safonov 2009; Vahl 2005a; Vahl and Emerson 2004).

The conflict has remained low-key for a few years, but since 2002 the EU has increased its attention on Moldova because it was becoming clear that Romania would have entered the EU. Moldova would have then directly bordered EU territory making the crisis in Transnistria into the closest secessionist conflict to the EU.

With this in mind, the EU has turned to different items in its CSFP toolbox: incentives, diplomacy and sanctions. With regard to incentives, the EU has included Moldova in the European Neighbourhood Policy (ENP) and the Eastern Partnership (EP) framework and laid out trade preferences within the EU-Moldova Action Plan (Popescu 2005/2006; Neukirch 2004; Nantoi 2009; Botan 2009b; Crowther 2007; Giumelli 2010b; Herd 2005). Moreover, since 2005, the European Union Border Assistance Mission (EUBAM) has been established to improve border controls between Moldova and Ukraine (to date, there are over 200 people in EUBAM). A special representative was also appointed in 2005 to assist the parties towards a peaceful resolution of the conflict (European Union 2008e).

Despite diplomatic moves, the use of sanctions has been among the first actions of the EU towards the contended region. In 2003, Moldova and Transnistria started discussing the possibility of drafting a new constitution. The two sides encountered many problems in reaching an agreement, and the EU concluded that the Transnistrian leaders were the obstacle against resolving the impasse. As a response, the EU decided to impose a travel ban on 17 individuals with common position 139 of 27th February 2003 (European Union 2003).

This first sanctions episode is characterised by many different initiatives that modified the overall regime, without altering the determinants identified by the theoretical framework. The first of them took place in 2004, when the Transnistrian authorities were accused of obstructing the functioning of Latin script schools in the territory that they control. After the conflict in 1992, Transnistria decided to maintain its language based on Russian characters, meaning that schools taught predominantly using the Cyrillic alphabet. Nevertheless, a few schools resisted the pressures and decided to operate using the Latin alphabet (Neukirch 2006). At some point, the Transnistrian authorities decided to escalate pressure against these institutions and the EU intervened in the crisis. Once again, taking the side of the Moldovan authorities, the list of individuals targeted was extended to the Transnistrian authorities directly responsible for the events. Common position 622 of 26th August 2004 forbade the entry in the EU to ten additional individuals (European Union 2004c).

The measures were renewed every year, and after four years during which little had changed, the EU adopted a different approach regarding sanctions. The imposition of the travel ban on the ruling elite of Transnistria seemed to aim at changing the regime in Tiraspol, and common position 160 of 25th February 2008 represented an important confirmation of EU policy towards the conflict (European Union 2008a). While the entire ruling class had been targeted by the previous measures, the EU decided to narrow its focus and to favour one domestic constituency in the internal battle for the government of the rebellious region. This shift in policy aimed at creating internal contrasts in the elites supporting the regime. Six individuals were added to the list, but six were also removed, and among the latter was the speaker of the Supreme Soviet, Evgeny Shevchuc. Mr. Shevchuc was seen as the representative of medium and small businesses, which would benefit the most from joining the European market and it was hoped that his leadership would create more favourable conditions to the settlement of the conflict by bringing

Moldova into the EU. While the mechanism changed, the logic remained one of constraining the ruling party and the group that supported Igor Smirnov in power (Giumelli 2010a).

Common position 139 of 16th February 2009 renewed the measures for thirteen people who were responsible of thwarting the resolution of the conflict, while six were listed for the school incident (European Union 2009a). The year 2009 was tenser in Moldova with two rounds of early elections followed by harsh protests in April in which the Moldovan Parliament was set on fire and the presidential palace vandalised (Mungiu-Pippidi and Munteanu 2009; Bosse 2010; Senyuva 2010).

The July elections changed the Government in Moldova and, likewise, the EU decided to change its strategy towards the conflict. This fine and convoluted exercise of diplomacy marked the end of the first episode of constraining sanctions on Transnistria, leading thus to the second one that is classified as a signalling measure. Common decision 105 of 22nd February 2010 renewed the sanctions imposed in the previous year, but the Council suspended the measures with a view of furthering dialogue and favouring the reaching of an agreement between the two sides (European Union 2010b). In other words, sanctions are in place, but they are suspended as confirmed by Council decision 573 of 27th September 2010 (European Union 2010e). Given the lack of impact, this sanction is of a signalling type and will not be described any further.

The dependent variable: direct impact and feasibility

The measures imposed on the leaders of Transnistria are classified as constraining measures because of their high impact and low feasibility. High impact is given primarily by a specific consideration about the resource denied. While a travel ban may have little relevance when targeted at local authorities who do not depend on travelling to consolidate their power, travelling becomes a fundamental resource for leaders of a secessionist movement trying to gain international recognition and legitimacy. Without the possibility of travel to the EU, the Transnistrian ruling elite cannot obtain the necessary legitimacy to become independent. Attempts to travel were also blocked by international institutions, such as the visa denial by the UK embassy of blacklisted individuals and the refusal to permit Oleg Gudymo to enter Turkey for leisure (Giumelli 2011).

Low feasibility is determined by the fact that complying with the EU demand does not seem an option to the leadership in Tiraspol as it would trigger a political reshuffling in the government of the region. This is evident when looking at the precision of the demand, which cannot be deemed even as moderate when the Council requests a halt to obstructions, while the parties are immersed in full-time negotiations on a long list of shared competences. Simply said, there are several potential attitudes that could be considered as obstructionist, and with such wording the evaluation will be left to the political consideration of that specific moment, which is characterised by a hostile relation between the parties. The objective of the EU was to change the ruling class in Tiraspol, at first by banning the entire ruling elite and, later, by embarking on a strategy of *divide et adduc* (divide and influence) that would have undermined the power of President Smirnov and his group of pro-Russian supporters (Giumelli 2011). Compliance would possibly undermine the political survival of the ruling elite in Transnistria and it is likely that EU policy makers are aware of this. This confirms further, if needed, that the imposition of sanctions can sometimes be undertaken according to other political considerations.

The independent variable: threat, salience and complexity

The second episode of EU sanctions on Transnistria is one of the thirteen characterised by high threat and high complexity which corresponds to a constraining type of sanction. As illustrated by Table 7.3, the level of threat received a standardised coefficient of 0.58, while complexity received 0.60.

Table 7.3: String of episodes of EU sanctions on the leaders of Transnistria

Episode	Threat	Salience	Complexity	Type of sanctions
EU/Transnistria – 2003 to 2010	0.58 (high)	0.17 (low)	0.60 (high)	Constraining
EU/Transnistria – 2010 to present	0.58 (high)	0.17 (low)	0.23 (low)	Signalling

The systemic approach seems, once again, to provide an important analytical utility that enhances our understanding of sanctions. The variable of threat received an evaluation of three out of four since there are multiple concerns to the EU. First, the Transnistrian case is the stage for a direct military conflict with Russian soldiers. Secondly, the situation in Transnistria represents a challenge to the common market given the fact that Moldovan goods can enter the EU freely. The extension of the crisis affects the subsystem of the EU and its neighbours. Thirdly, the geostrategic value of Transnistria is relevant given its vicinity to the EU and, in addition to that, Transnistria hosts an important pipeline that delivers gas from Russia to Europe. Finally, Transnistria, commonly referred to as the 'black hole of Europe', serves as a hub for criminal organisations to carry out their activities in and out the EU.

Salience is low because this crisis did not receive attention in the press. The *Financial Times* published only 76 articles versus 126 of the second episode, while *The Economist* did not publish anything on both of the occasions. EU officials interviewed on the issue seemed pretty aware of the problems that an unresolved conflict can pose to the EU's neighbourhood stability, but it is likely that Moldova's small economy or its relative importance in the chessboard between Russia and the EU is thought to be low by the international community. The level of engagement also is not highest given that the presence is mostly in Chisinau (EU delegation) and in the Ukraine (EUBAM).

The complexity of the crisis in the first episode is high. The list of the actors in the field is long: Moldova, Transnistria, Russia and the EU, but there are also a series of lobbies in favour of keeping the status quo for economic and political reasons and, possibly, illegal practices. Thus, the number of actors is set to five. The level of violence is very low. After the initial conflict in 1992, only skirmishes took place between the parties, helped by the presence of the Russian peacekeeping force. The number of issues is fairly high including the evidence that this game could mean survival or demise for the ruling elite in Transnistria. Aside from that, a number of economic factors are at stake in the case of Transnistria. Local economic agents profit from the situation as well as international actors. Italian, Spanish and German companies invested in Transnistria, but the grey areas in which companies operate in the region (the import of chicken per capita is many times the one of Germany) undermines the functioning of the market in the EU. Finally, the strength of the target is moderate. If it is true that Transnistria is a small economic entity, the support of a large part of the Russian elite compensates for the weak assets of the rebel region.

The theoretical model

Sanctions are of a constraining type because the crisis threatens the security of the EU, which makes it willing to accept a cost to remove the threat. This case of sanctions represents an interesting example since high impact does not require senders to bear a high material cost. Nevertheless, the overall approach of the EU towards the crisis in Transnistria unveils the importance of threat and complexity as explanatory variables for the logic adopted. High complexity prevents the EU from making precise demands to the Transnistrian leaders and crystallises a circumstance under which the two entities have incompatible needs. In other words, a complex situation creates a zero-sum game, and sanctions can take on the role of undermining the capabilities of the adversary even though more is also needed to change, forcefully, the behaviour of the actors involved in the game.

Lower threat leads to signalling or constraining measures according to the level of salience since the EU could have imposed different sanctions or could have avoided their implementation. On the other hand, lower complexity could lead to precise and feasible requests that limit the behaviour of the Transnistrian leaders according to a rational logic: economic pain versus political gain.

One last word is due to justify the decrease of threat between the first and the second episode of sanctions. Aside from the fact that the second episode is an exceptional event under which sanctions are imposed but suspended, the lower level of threat originates from the different consideration of the issue at stake that composes the variable. Indeed, there seem to be different evaluations of what a part of the ruling elite wants for the future of Transnistria. While there was a strong view among some that being part of Russia was the most likely scenario, a large part of the business community views the EU as a good opportunity. This alone makes cooperation with Moldova more likely and the crises less complex.

Signalling Uzbekistan

On 13th May 2005, a large crowd gathered in Andijan to protest against the arrest of twenty-two local businessmen and to manifest their discontent with the authoritarian practices of the central government led by President Islom Karimov. Andijan is the fourth largest city of Uzbekistan and it is at the centre of the Fergana Valley, known to be a fertile and dynamic part of the country as well as to host the activity of radical Islamic organisations, who are accused of undermining the stability of the national secular institutions. The rally was eventually dispersed by the Uzbek police forces under unclear circumstances. Human rights groups lamented severe violations of fundamental rights and denounced government violence, while Karimov claimed that the police responded to a foreign-inspired revolt against the stability of Uzbekistan. Even the outcome of the riots is unclear: NGOs claimed that over 1,000 people were killed, while the local authorities affirmed that the casualties were less than 200 and were mostly terrorists (International Crisis Group 2005; Akiner 2005; Human Rights Watch 2006).

Immediately after the events, the UN criticised Karimov's disproportionate use of force, calling for an independent investigation on the events (Donovan 2005) and the Council of the European Union followed suit (Lobiakas 2005). The OSCE, the US and the UK governments joined the call for an independent investigation that President Karimov rejected on the argument that what happened in Andijan was an internal affair (Burnashev and Chernykh 2007: 72; Alikov 2005).

The relations between the West and Uzbekistan experienced a *bell époque* after 9/11, but after 2004 they became bitter. The war on terror was fully supported by the Government of Islam Karimov, so that both the US and the EU made important efforts to avoid any interference with the domestic practices of Uzbekistan not to alter the susceptibility of their central Asian ally. Independent since 1991, Uzbekistan is the most populous country in central Asia with over 26 million inhabitants. Decidedly under the Russian sphere of influence, even after the fall of the Berlin Wall, and ruled continuously by Mr Karimov since its conception, Uzbekistan enjoyed a relative period of stability that was interrupted by the Tashkent bombing in 1999, in which sixteen people were killed in an attempt to assassinate President Karimov, and in 2004 with a series of attacks in Tashkent and Bukhara (Radio Free Europe 2004).

The Government accused the Islamic Movement of Uzbekistan (IMU) and Hizb ut-Tahrir for the attacks and of religious terrorism. This looming threat on the stability of the Uzbek institutions was used to support the slow pace of democratisation under the excuse that quicker reforms could undermine the stability of the country. With a tacit understanding of this approach as well as the shared common threat of radical Islam, the US and the EU benefited from the alliance with Uzbekistan in the war on terror because of its strategic location as a bordering state with Afghanistan. However, Uzbek interests were in direct contrast with those of Western countries and the lowest point was reached with the events in Andijan.

The deaths in Andijan were the pretext to formalise diverging interests. Uzbekistan feared the menace of radical Islam and was concerned about the spread of the coloured revolutions that had occurred before in Georgia, the Ukraine and Kyrgyzstan, while the West was not willing to tolerate further similar actions. The EU condemned 'the excessive, disproportionate and indiscriminate use of force by the Uzbek security forces' on 23rd May 2005 (European Union 2005b) and threatened to impose sanctions if a proper investigation of the facts did not take place. On 13th June (Council of the European Union 2005:15), the Government of Uzbekistan responded by establishing an internal investigation into the events, but this was not enough to fulfil the UN's request for an international investigation (United Nations, E.a.S. 2006). The Council, therefore, decided to impose an arms embargo on equipment that could have been used for internal repression together with a travel ban on those member officials who were allegedly responsible for the repression with common position 792 of 14th November 2005 (European Union 2005b). The twelve sanctioned individuals were part of the local and the military units directly responsible for the events.

Initially, sanctions were imposed for twelve months, and renewed in similar forms in 2006 with common position 787 of 13th November, which had the objective of 'bringing about, through dialogue, compliance by Uzbekistan with the principles of respect for human rights, rule of law and fundamental freedoms' (European Union 2006). Relations between Uzbekistan and the EU improved in 2007 to the point that the Council decided to suspend the travel ban with common position 734 of 13th November, while keeping the arms embargo in place (European Union 2007b). The travel ban was then lifted with common position 843 of 10th November 2008, and the arms embargo was not renewed in October 2009 by the Council.[2] The theoretical framework is valid here to identify the constant logic even if the form of sanctions is changing.

The EU has taken a wider approach on Uzbekistan by restoring suspended programs after two years and by maintaining the cooperation that remains ongoing with the Government in Tashkent, which includes projects worth €32.8 million (European Union 2008h; European Union 2008h; Castle 2006; International Crisis Group 2006; Traynor 2007; Soares 2007).

The dependent variable: direct impact and feasibility

The low level of impact is decisive to classify the sanctions as signalling measures, but a quick look at feasibility would allow us to reach some conclusions on the solidity of the theoretical framework as well.

The impact is considered low because of the minimum direct effect that the measures had on Uzbekistan. The types of resources denied were not structural to the normal functioning of the institutions. The direct effects were not negligible as it was never registered that the ban from entering the EU was particularly damaging to the reputation of the blacklisted individuals or to Uzbekistan. Additionally,

2. While a common position was not needed to lift the sanctions that expired naturally, a Council regulation (1227/2009) was necessary to lift the arms embargo.

Uzbekistan is among the world's major exporters of weapons and the prohibition of export could have caused material costs on Uzbekistan affecting their costs/ benefits calculations (European Union 2008g; European Union 2008h). In other words, the forms of sanctions adopted seem to have been tailored so as not to have a direct material impact on the central Asian country.

Having already identified the signalling logic at work, an analysis of the low feasibility of the demands is briefly discussed. The two demands cannot be rated as highly precise: the first requires the carrying out of an independent investigation, which could be conducted in different ways, and the second refers to a general statement on the improvement of human rights. Practicality cannot be rated as high, since the Uzbek Government would appear weak before radical Islamic groups, but it cannot receive the lowest evaluation either, since an international investigation could have taken place with the ruling elite (Naumkin 2006; International Crisis Group 2008a). Carrying out the investigation would also run the risk of vanquishing part of the credibility as an ally of Russia. Consequently, compliance with UN and EU demands would widen the gap between Moscow and Tashkent, with a move in the opposite direction of Karimov's foreign policy goals (Naumkin 2006; Trenin 2006; Fumagalli 2007).

The independent variable: threat, salience and complexity

The EU sanctions against Uzbekistan are a case of signalling restrictive measures and this can be explained by looking at the context that is characterised by a low level of threat (0.11) and a low level of salience (0.50).

Table 7.4: String of episodes of EU sanctions on Uzbekistan

Episode	Threat	Salience	Complexity	Type of sanctions
EU/Uzbekistan – 2005 to 2009	0.11 (low)	0.50 (low)	0.30 (low)	Signalling

Threat is rated as low with a standardised coefficient of 0.11. Issue has a value of one out of a four-point scale because what triggered the dispute was a disagreement on human rights issues. The extension of threat is likewise low because the Andijan killings and the poor human rights records of Uzbekistan do not seem to affect the other actors in the area. Finally, geostrategy has received a higher rate because Uzbekistan is on a route of natural resources from Russia and, despite the distance, represents an asset to Germany as a supplier of natural gas (European Union: 5–6; Matveeva 2006).

Salience has a standardised coefficient of 0.50. The level of attention is moderate as the *Financial Times* has published 187 articles and *The Economist* 42. The level of engagement is moderate because of the variety of tools adopted. On the one hand, the EU has offered a package of incentives to guide the Government in Tashkent to better human rights practices, and on the other hand, the EU personnel presence in the country, albeit minimal, ensures the interest of Brussels in the development of the situation (Europa House 2010).

The complexity of the dispute is rated as low with a standardised coefficient of 0.30, a value among the lowest of the ranking. The number of actors is counted as three: the Government in Tashkent, the EU and the opposition groups in the country.[3] The level of violence is moderately low, since it is the Uzbek Government that has used force against the demonstrators in Andijan and against members of the opposition, but the use of violence is unidirectional and there are no other actors involved. The number of issues is low because the dispute between the EU and Uzbekistan is over the respect of human rights in the country. Whereas other issues could be at stake, restrictive measures are linked mainly to the events in Andijan, while there does not seem to be an intention to undermine the stability of Uzbekistan. Finally, the target's strength is rated as moderate because, despite the support of Moscow, the current regime has not been able to implement a series of structural reforms that the country needs (Naumkin 2006).

The theoretical model

The EU sanctions on Uzbekistan are an important empirical test for the theoretical model that has been examined in this study. Whereas it would seem hard to explain the rationality of the restrictive measures imposed by the Council on the Government led by Islom Karimov by simply looking at the rational argument, the tripartite conceptualisation of sanctions combined with the analysis of the contextual variables contributes to explain their adoption. The EU adopted a complex strategy towards Belarus that has changed overtime. The arms embargo and the travel ban imposed with a signalling logic can be understood and explained only if we place them into their context.

Signalling sanctions are more likely to occur when the level of threat and salience are low as discovered in Chapter 4 with the third dominant pattern identified in the database. Indeed, it is plausible to maintain that the EU has imposed signalling restrictive measures because it was not threatened by the deteriorating situation of human rights practices in Tashkent and because the issue was not at the centre of attention. Another explanation is that it was not relevant to the overall foreign policy approach of the EU. If anything, the divisions among EU members are further proof of everything but that of a looming menace posed by Karimov's government. The low level of salience confirms that also the attention of the audiences was not focused on this issue and, therefore, it would be natural for the EU to impose low impact restrictive measures.

The counterfactual test of the theoretical framework would lead us to think that in case of higher threat, we would have seen more precise demands and measures with high impact. The former would be justified by the need of the sender to ensure that a specific policy is not implemented by the target and the latter by the necessity to impose a sanction with material consequences so as to affect the costs/

---

3. Russia is not considered as an active participant in the dispute.

benefits calculations of the target. Conversely, for higher salience, the expectations would be higher to have constraining sanctions, as the sender would be under pressure from public opinion and would be more inclined to impose sanctions with a direct impact and to formulate unfeasible demands.

Conclusion

The analysis of the EU experience showed the utility of the theoretical framework in also analysing regional organisations. This chapter completes the empirical part of this study proving that threat, salience and complexity can contribute to answering many open questions in the sanctions debate.

The EU resorted to coercive sanctions in order to bring Belarus in line with behaviours that would not destabilise its immediate neighbourhood and endanger the gas supply from Russia. Sanctions began to work according to a coercive logic in 2007, when the vulnerability of Belarus increased and the threat perception of the EU was shaken by the energy crisis of the winter. The explanation for the imposition of this type of measure *vis-à-vis* the other two types is to be sought in the context of the dispute: the EU attaches an important value to the event in Minsk and the relative low complexity of the problem – also boosted by the deterioration of the relationship with Moscow– suggesting that sanctions motivated a behavioural change.

The conflict between Moldova and Transnistria is of a different nature than that of Belarus for two reasons: the EU decided to take part in the crisis by adopting the side of Chisinau as its own; and the leaders of Transnistria had tied everything they had to their position of power in the separatist region. Whether referring to the ruling elite or discussing the business community, the actors that matter are strongly motivated to continue their activities. Initially, the EU could not do anything else but impose constraining sanctions in order to undermine the capacity of the leaders in Transnistria to obtain their objective. This is explained by the high complexity of the crisis, as illustrated above, which also highlights that few alternatives are available under similar circumstances, and by the fact that the conflict in Transnistria is a destabilising factor in the area.

Finally, the case of Uzbekistan is a typical example of a signalling sanction. This is explained (or rather allowed) by the low level of threat posed by Tashkent on EU members and the low level of salience gained from the crisis between the EU (or the West) and the central Asian state. The EU imposed sanctions to signal to both Uzbek's neighbours and its own international audience in order to consolidate its role as a global actor.

The analysis of EU sanctions has substantiated the validity of the theoretical framework. The three case studies of the EU restrictive measures on Belarus, Transnistria and Uzbekistan confirmed that not all sanctions are imposed with the same logic and that the logic that inspires the imposition of the sanction varies according to context. The conclusions of this research emphasise once again the theoretical and policy relevance of the framework created and tested within this wide-reaching investigation of international sanctions.

chapter eight | conclusions

The focus of this work was on the logic of international sanctions and on how the context influences the selection of this logic. What we have learned is that not all sanctions are equal. There are observable characteristics that distinguish one case from another and identify the way in which restrictive measures influence their targets. The range of choices that policy makers can pick from is made up of three options (coercive, constraining and signalling type of sanctions), but these are available only in theory. In practice, this 'menu' of logics changes according to several factors and this book focused on the systemic element that alters such choices.

By verifying how the context of sanctions (defined also as the 'system' of sanctions) affects the logic with which sanctions are imposed, this book intends to contribute to a more accurate understanding of this complex foreign policy tool. The seventy episodes of sanctions taken from the UN and the EU experience after the Cold War supported this analysis with empirical evidence and with anecdotal examples that clarified the concepts used. The results confirm that the context of sanctions provides senders with constraints and opportunities when deciding to resort to international sanctions. Simply speaking, the menu of logics available to policy makers changes according to the context in which they are called to decide.

This final chapter presents both the theoretical and policy implications of this book in four sections. The first part summarises the results of the empirical test by presenting the hypotheses that were confirmed and those that were falsified. The second part elaborates on the theoretical contributions expounded, in particular focusing on the definition of the success of international sanctions. The third part applies the usable knowledge that stems from the application of the theoretical framework to real world cases. Finally, I indicate ways in which this research can be expanded, complemented and further developed.

A systemic explanation of the logic of sanctions

The centrality of sanctions in international relations is reinforced by the numerous studies that have covered this topic in the past decades. However, little effort has been put into a broader analysis of the sanctions phenomenon, particularly when it comes to understanding the actual relationship between the type of sanction and its context.

This book argues that the type of sanction depends on certain configurations of the system. As sanctions are not imposed in a vacuum, the context is able to explain most of the logic variance according to which sanctions are supposed to work. The theoretical framework tested on a database of seventy episodes taken from the UN and the EU experience indicates that the context seems to explain the logic of sanctions in over 64 per cent of the episodes. There exist three dominant patterns that are explained by the framework and one ambiguous configuration that will need further investigation.

According to Kenneth Waltz, a context creates the structural conditions for an event to occur, it does not necessarily determine it (Waltz 1996). The context of a theory of sanctions 'can describe the range of likely outcomes of the actions and interactions of' actors 'within a given system and show how the range of expectations varies as systems change'. The theoretical framework adopted here is a macro-analysis of the system and it does not intend to explain the behaviour of single units by looking at their motivations. Rather it looks at 'what pressures are exerted and what possibilities are posed by systems of different structure'. This systemic approach makes the outcomes more predictable, as a theory of sanctions aims at explaining only certain aspects of complex relations such as the ones that characterise sanctions episodes.

Three IVs and one dependent variable compose this theoretical model. The independent variables – threat, salience and complexity – characterise the context, or the system, of sanctions. The dependent variable – how sanctions aim at influencing their targets – can be of three types: coercion, constraint and signal. Six general hypotheses and eight more specific ones were formulated from this framework.

The general hypotheses focuses on the relations between individual IVs and the type of sanctions imposed. The IVs are operationalised dichotomically, therefore six associations were founded as reproduced in Table 8.1.

Table 8.1: General hypotheses of the research

Independent variable	Intensity	Expected outcome	Confirmation rate (%)
Threat	High	Coercing or constraining	84.62
	Low	Signalling	77.27
Salience	High	Coercing or constraining	60.00
	Low	Signalling	80.00
Complexity	High	Constraining or signalling	100.00
	Low	Coercing or signalling	79.41

There are strong correlations between contextual factors and sanctions types, especially for high complexity, high threat and low salience. Taking into consideration the possible configurations of the three IVs, the analysis of the framework confirms that the logic of sanctions is affected by their environment. There are eight possible system configurations and the result of the empirical investigation is summarised in Table 8.2.

The eight configurations can be simplified to four by combining pairs of IVs. Three configurations are the recurrent patterns expected according to the hypotheses of the theoretical framework and are summarised in Table 8.3.

Table 8.2: Specific hypotheses of the research

Comb.	Threat	Salience	Complexity	Sanction	Episodes	Test
1	High	High	High	Constraining	8 out of 10	77.78
2	High	Low	High	Constraining	3 out of 3	100.00
3	High	Low	Low	Coercing	2 out of 3	66.67
4	Low	Low	Low	Signalling	7 out of 7	100.00
5	Low	High	Low	Constraining	8 out of 14	42.86
6	Low	High	High	Constraining	7 out of 11	36.36
7	High	High	Low	Coercing	8 out of 10	72.73
8	Low	Low	High	Signalling	12 out of 12	100.00

Table 8.3: Dominant patterns

Combination	Threat	Salience	Complexity		Most likely	
3 & 7	High	–	Low	Coercion	76.92%	10 out of 13
1 & 2	High	–	High	Constraint	84.62%	11 out of 13
4 & 8	Low	Low	–	Signal	100%	19 out of 19

When threat is high and complexity is low, sanctions of a coercive type are more likely. This configuration of the system occurred thirteen times and in ten of them the sanctions were of a coercion type. The second dominant pattern is for high threat and high complexity, which was associated to constraining sanctions in eleven episodes out of thirteen. Finally, sanctions were of a signalling type in all the nineteen episodes of low threat and low complexity.

These three dominant patterns represent 64 per cent of the sample, while the other 36 per cent would need further investigation. The ambiguous pattern consists of low threat and high salience, which recurs twenty-five times in the dataset as presented in Table 8.4.

Table 8.4: Alternative pattern for low threat and low complexity

Combination	Threat	Salience	Comp-lexity	Coer-cing	Constrain-ing	Signal-ling	Most likely
5 & 6	Low	High	–	0	10 (40%)	15 (60%)	15 out of 25

The ambiguous pattern consists in the weak correlation between low threat, high salience and signalling sanctions, which recurs in 60 per cent of the episodes, over 40 per cent of constraining sanctions. However, the relevant finding is that low threat and high salience never correlate with a coercive type of sanction, and this proves that threat and salience do not influence the behaviour of actors in the same way.

This is only the first of several conclusions that can be drawn from this empirical test. The understanding of sanctions changes substantially if they are evaluated in relation to their context. Contrarily to what is often assumed, what sanctions can achieve is directly related to when and under what circumstances they operate. Context does not enter the picture when sanctions are studied and evaluated; sanctions would influence their targets only through the imposition of a material cost. The investigation in this study demonstrates that the analysis of the context is mandatory for understanding sanctions as the logic adopted is its direct consequence. The inclusion of the context combined with a more elaborated definition of how sanctions are supposed to influence targets enhance our knowledge and understanding of what sanctions can achieve and under what circumstances.

The books findings can be generalised and applied to international organisations and states alike. The cases of the UN and the EU were chosen specifically because they are international organisations. The UN is a global institution and its actions are characterised fully by its nature. The Security Council reaches decisions after long negotiations and bargaining processes that often lack of transparency and clear logic. At the same time, the UN is the only international organisation that enjoys global legitimacy and can, therefore, embark on several actions that would not be permitted to other actors. Contrarily, the EU is a regional organisation with supranational tendencies. On the one hand, the EU is affected by a murky decision-making process that is typical of inter-governmental forums, but, on the other hand, it yields a power that resembles closely that of nation-states. Despite their differences, the UN and the EU are assumed to be unitary actors. Although this is a strong assumption to make for international organisations, it is appropriate in order to also extend the results of this investigation to nation-states, which are closer to the assumption.

Discussing how sanctions influence targets, rather than thinking about sanctions as driven by policy objectives, provides a greater understanding of their utility. We now know what sanctions can achieve, which allows us to measure success by different criteria. Finally, a policy perspective is also favoured by a systemic approach as lessons can be drawn from what sanctions can and cannot achieve in different contexts.

Additional findings: evaluating the effectiveness of sanctions

The success of a sanction should be evaluated according to three criteria. First, the effectiveness of any foreign policy tool depends on its comparative utility, namely if other foreign policy tools would have led to better results *ceteris paribus*. Secondly, sanctions do not achieve foreign policy goals but rather contribute to wider strategies, which are designed to achieve foreign policy goals. Thirdly, sanctions contribute to wider strategies not by pursuing limited policy objectives, but by coercing, constraining and signalling targets.

The first criterion draws from David Baldwin's argument of the logic of choice, elsewhere defined as the 'comparative utility of sanctions' (Baldwin 1999). Baldwin says that each foreign policy tool is effective or ineffective according to its alternatives: what could have achieved better results *instead* of the adoption of sanctions? The counter-terrorist measures adopted since the end of 2001 should not be evaluated according to the fact that terrorist attacks continue to happen, but they should be evaluated according to the number of terrorist attacks that happened compared to the number of attacks that *would have* happened had sanctions not been in place. A proper analysis of the context allows one to have a clearer view of what are the alternative courses of action under certain conditions.

The second criterion was illustrated in Chapter 2 and it points at the fact that a sanction is only one foreign policy tool that alone cannot determine the achievement of foreign policy objectives. Instead, a sanction is one element in a larger foreign policy strategy and it can only contribute to achieve specific foreign policy objectives.

The third criterion covers the three logics of sanctions. Coercing, constraining and signalling present clearly how sanctions can influence the target and success will have to depend on whether the effects of sanctions fulfil the expectations created by the logic of sanctions. A coercing sanction aims at changing the behaviour of a target by reducing the costs/benefits calculations of one policy decision compared with all the others. The target has to do something in order to satisfy the demand of the sender and the logic behind it is to increase the material costs of all the alternative policies to the action that is intended to be prevented. Hence, a sanction in this category would be successful if the target's costs/benefits calculation is tilted towards the sender's demand. Sanctions could be successful even if targets do not change behaviour.

A constraining type of sanction aims at limiting the alternatives available to targets and, therefore, success will consist in limiting the policy options of targets. Whereas coercing aims at meeting the demand of a sender, a constraining type of sanction does not aim at forcing a target to comply with its demands. Consequently, the logic of the sanction is to attach a cost to a specific target policy, while leaving other alternatives untouched. The extreme example of this type of sanction regards the imposition of sanctions as a means to increase the costs of political survival for individuals, non-state entities, ruling elites or entire regimes. A successful constraining sanction would increase the costs of a behaviour that the target intends to undertake. A constraining type of sanction may be used when a target is too strong to be coerced, when it does not intend to negotiate about its goals or does not represent a legitimate actor of the system, e.g. a terrorist organisation.

Finally, signalling sanctions intend to send signals to targets without imposing any direct material cost on them. There are diverse reasons behind the decision of imposing a signalling sanction. First, a signalling sanction may be imposed with the intent of censoring certain behaviour in order to uphold international norms or standards. The logic is to draw the line between what can be done and what is considered unacceptable to the sender. Secondly, signalling sanctions can be imposed as an international statement to please domestic groups on specific issues. This case is well presented by the 'must do something' formula, which refers to those cases in which grave infringements of international law need to be addressed, regardless of the expected outcomes from those actions. Thirdly, signalling sanctions may also be useful to meet international expectations on given matters. As illustrated by Mercer, the reputation of an international actor is not only measured on its past, but on the expectations that actors have on the possible course of actions of others (Mercer 1996). For instance, the imposition of restrictive measures should follow even if a behavioural change is not expected because this would deter other actors, who may be more vulnerable to certain types of sanctions, not to reiterate banned misconducts. Finally, sanctions could simply aim at achieving an agreement among domestic actors to condemn certain policies. Especially in regards to international organisations (but it would also be true for states), the decision to impose a restrictive measure could be successful to the extent that senders are able to reach agreements on foreign policy issues. In other words, the purpose of sanctions would be to send a signal of unity and to shape the identity of the actor that is imposing the measure. In the case of the UN, a signalling sanction may serve a member state the purpose of achieving international legitimacy.

Generally speaking, this type of sanction would be successful if the message is delivered to the target(s) and the behavioural change is not central to the assessment. The success of a signalling type is the most complicated one to capture empirically because it relies on the analysis of non-events (i.e. in the case of deterrence) and can, therefore, only be presumed. Similarly, a signalling sanction is a double-edged sword as it can be perceived as a sender's lack of commitment or as the incapacity to adopt other instruments. Where the aim is to appease domestic opinion, a sanction is successful if a sender's domestic constituencies are satisfied with it. However, if domestic constituencies dislike the measures, for instance by blaming the sender for lack of more decisive action, then the sanction is unsuccessful.

The evaluation of success that originates from the theoretical framework elaborated in this book does not rely on whether targets change their behaviours after the imposition of sanctions, but it depends on a more complex understanding of how sanctions influence actors on the international stage.

Policy recommendations

This study's theoretical framework produces usable knowledge for policy makers. 'Usable knowledge' is not to be taken as a specific set of guidelines, but rather as a general principle that can guide the policy-making process. Such general principle has to be complemented by the judgement of policy makers (George and Bennett 2005: 276).

The numerous variables used to construct the framework indicate a series of causal links that should inspire the three phases of sanctioning, namely designing, implementing and monitoring. The first phase regards the creation of sanctions as when senders decide what objectives to pursue and which foreign policy instruments are more appropriate for the job. These two tasks must take into consideration the type of targets and the context in which sanctions have to operate, both elements that are important components of the framework.

Targets are essential in understanding what sanctions can achieve. Terrorist organisations or military rulers are not as willing as democratic leaders to negotiate their objectives. It is also more likely that terrorist organisations will pursue goals that are incompatible with the ones of senders. What sanctions are capable of achieving will be then decided by the type of target, but this is not the sole element, as what targets can achieve is determined also by the context. Political actors can be accommodating under a safe institutional framework, but during a civil conflict the parties tend to secure their position and survival versus other parties. When senders get involved in civil conflicts as mediators, negotiators or direct participants, the menu of logics available in regards to the imposition of sanctions is limited. Improving the designing phase is essential to elaborate feasible or unfeasible demands, which is a determinant for coercing and constraining measures.

Sanctions should be designed by focusing on whether a target should be coerced, constrained or signalled. This starting point would be strongly dependent on the crisis in which senders and targets are interacting, but the clarity of intent would avoid potential contradictions among the different elements of a sanction or among different policy instruments in the same strategy. Probably, one of the elements on which the 'pessimists' base their argument is that sanctions were not used with explicit goals and, therefore, the design was not coherent with what was intended. Good strategic planning means imposing sanctions alongside a set of other tools and imposing sanctions with a specific logic in mind would allow senders to invest the appropriate resources without wasting energy in implementing half-hearted measures.

For instance, if the behaviour of a target endangers a sender, then the latter should try to convince the former to change its behaviour, not only through sanctions, but also by encouraging compliance. Proper resources should be dedicated to improve the capacity to carry out certain policies because if a measure cannot be enforced, then sanctions should be used with other tools to attain any coercive ambitions. To this extent, senders should run pre-assessment analyses to ascertain what are the causes that make targets behave in a certain way and to take them into account in drafting the requests. If the intent of the UN is to coerce an actor to do something, then the request should not be too burdensome, otherwise the target will not comply and might even become more resistant to the measures.

What can be achieved derives from the contextual configurations. The framework presented in this study includes the eventuality wherein certain misconducts have to be censured, but lack of enforceability undercuts what sanctions can achieve. In such case, a sender should not emphasise the role of sanctions because they cannot be equally important under different circumstances. This does not undermine the overall utility of sanctions in foreign policy, but it underscores that sanctions can be more or less useful according to the crisis. Thus, policy objectives can be reached only by a careful adoption of a policy mix as foreign policy tools are capable of reinforcing each other. In the case of sanctions, the use of incentive is particularly recommended when a threat is posed on senders, in order to support and to make a specific behaviour more convenient for targets.

The second phase of sanctioning is the implementation of the measures and, again, this is linked to the understanding of what a sender is capable of imposing, what type of costs the actors are willing to take on and the degree of executive capacity available to the sender. The imposition of sanctions is decided by political bodies, which are seldom aware of the operational capacities of their administrative branches. This is an essential aspect that also overlaps with the first phase, namely that senders should impose what they can implement. Limits to the implementation of sanctions can come from domestic agents that may not be willing to cooperate with the sanctions regime as it would not be in their economic interest, and in the institutional capacity to prevent and block, for example unauthorised transactions or travelling. This was common for sanctions imposed in West Africa in the 1990s, where the Security Council prevented trading and travelling across unpatrolled borders. In such a case, it would have been better to design demands that did not need this degree of implementation. Improving the capacity to implement sanctions would allow the Security Council to adjust the variable of direct impact so as to decide whether to impose coercing, constraining or signalling sanctions.

Recent developments of sanctioning practices – from comprehensive to targeted measures – have increased the technical knowledge and the capacities required for good implementation to the point that many actors, even if willing to cooperate, are not capable of enforcing sanctions. This capability/expectation gap undermines many sanctioning regimes and decreases their overall utility. The United Nations should invest more resources in developing guidelines for implementation and the enforcement capacity of the actors involved, starting with regional organisations in sensitive areas. Targeted measures need high capabilities to be properly implemented and the UN should work towards the construction of international regimes, as it did in the fields of international money laundering or terrorist financing. Similar objectives can be reached for arms embargoes and travel bans. Having greater capacities to implement and enforce sanctions would substantially improve the current UN practices. The connection is straightforward: if restrictive measures can be properly implemented, then they are more likely to have an impact on the calculations of targets.

Given the interdisciplinary character of international sanctions, senders need to make an effort to coordinate and integrate the administrative aspect of the sanctions process. This is a shortcoming that must be faced by the UN and the EU. Even if both organisations are international actors limited by the disagreements of their members, improvements are possible by rationalising and facilitating the communication among the different bodies involved in sanctions episodes. The Security Council should be aware of what can, or cannot, be enforced beforehand by being constantly in touch with the UN's Sanctions Branch of the Department of Political Affairs. Consequently, the Security Council should take the lead in encouraging international initiatives aimed at developing the capacities of states to enforce targeted measures. Another recommendation goes to the EU, where desk officers in collaboration with regional delegations could work on pre-assessment evaluations of what form of sanction can be imposed on what target.

The third phase looks at the monitoring of sanctions. Senders need to develop this capacity, especially for coercing and constraining sanctions. In such cases, targets have to be affected in their positions of privilege or in their capacity to operate. Sanctions, especially the targeted ones, are extremely easy to evade, which means that there must be an institutional capacity devoted to avoiding this. Currently, there are administrative units at the UN and at the EU that coordinate sanction monitoring, but a policy recommendation is to involve international police organisations, such as Interpol, with the creation of a dedicated office that would take up the investigative task of the more technical measures. This is a fundamental step towards guaranteeing target compliance.

An alternative to the involvement of Interpol could be to strengthen the Sanction Branch at the UN, given its current alarming inability to influence the sanctioning process. Aside from the lack of funding and the shortage of personnel, the dramatic problem is the absence of investigative power of the Sanctions Branch. Presently, the committee of experts can only verbally condemn targets. Despite these structural problems, the UN's monitoring committees are an important tool and their activities should have stronger consequences. An occasional practice that should be consolidated is the imposition of sanctions on actors that violate existing sanctions regimes. The reports of the investigative teams of the Security Council were used to justify the imposition of sanctions in West Africa on Charles Taylor and on actors in Eritrea because of their violations of the sanctions on Sierra Leone and Somalia. However, these teams do not have the mandate to force state authorities to cooperate and meet their requests and I believe that strengthening the powers of such a relevant instrument could lead to greater cooperation among UN members and lower levels of defiance. Penalties – such as the suspension of aid or limited participation to the activity of UN Agencies, etc. – should be considered not only for the actors who violate sanctions regime, but also for UN members who do not cooperate with UN bodies.

Likewise, the EU should monitor measures imposed by the Council of Ministers. The most striking element of the EU sanctioning policy is the absolute lack of monitoring mechanisms to evaluate the impact of targeted measures and to investigate possible violations. The EU has imposed many autonomous sanctions in the last two decades, but it does not seem to be interested in evaluating how they have been implemented or what impact they have had, in order to improve its procedures and mechanisms. The Restrictive Measures Team at the Commission , and eventually at the European External Action Servce (EEAS), should be strengthened in this respect and member states should be made accountable for the information that they are able to gather and share with the EU.

A final policy recommendation focuses on information sharing. Proper implementation can occur only if the bodies that have to implement the measures know what happens in the field. This shortcoming is particularly evident in the EU sanctioning experience, where information sharing among the EU, member states and private actors is almost non-existent. States are supposed to communicate violations or attempted violations of sanctioning regimes to the EU, but little is done in this regard. Private institutions as well are required to notify when blacklisted individuals' bank accounts are frozen, but only partial activity is recorded and at a national level, not with the EU. The only area where something has been done is on arms embargoes. From the viewpoint of this study's theoretical framework, the EU should improve the most basic mechanisms for implementing targeted sanctions by increasing its investments in foreign policy. The degree of monitoring and a prompt information-sharing mechanism would permit a switch between low and high direct impact and to change the sanction regime from signalling to constraining and coercing.

These are only a few political recommendations gathered during this study. Overall, the underlining message of this research is that sanctions must be acknowledged as a single tool among the many available to policy makers. Integrated approaches, capacity building, realist expectations – among others – should remind politicians and theorists alike that their analyses of international sanctions must take into consideration the context, type of sanction and other tools adopted.

Looking forwards: new sanctions studies

In the twenty-first century, sanctions are likely to become comparatively more appealing than other foreign policy tools. The increasing costs of military intervention, peacekeeping operations and the nature of new international threats present the most favourable conditions for enhancing the effectiveness of targeted sanctions, as will a better knowledge of this instrument. This book contributes to fill this gap, but much is still to be done and this research provides the basis for further studies in the field of sanctions.

The principal challenge in developing the theoretical framework presented in this book is to include intervening variables to investigate further the episodes in which the context is defined by low threat and high salience. The contradictory findings do not allow strong explanations for the logic of sanctions in such episodes. A list of possible intervening variables that could strengthen the validity of the model includes a more elaborated typology of targets, a different conceptualisation of salience, and a classification of crises according to wider categories.

Further studies should concentrate on the development and expansion of the theoretical framework in micro–micro, macro–micro and micro–macro analyses. One possible line of research is to investigate further the micro correlations among the indicators of the variables. The variations of the indicators that compose the IVs and the DV could be linked by causal mechanisms. One suggestion for a macro–micro investigation is to examine the link between high salience and low feasibility. Finally, one micro–macro line of research could be based on the analysis of the relationships between micro factors (e.g. the number of actors in a crisis, the level of violence or the geostrategic importance of targets) and macro events such as the purpose of sanctions.

Since part of the objective for the theoretical framework is to set new criteria to ascertain the effectiveness of sanctions, the natural continuation for this research is to measure the success of international sanctions as a foreign policy method using the theoretical framework elaborated in this study. The assessment, however, should not be done in black and white terms, but instead it would be appropriate to adopt a fuzzy logic to evaluate whether sanctions have been effective in specific contexts. In other words, the success of sanctions should be assessed according to the purpose of achievements and the widespread attempt to measure sanctions in a success/failure dichotomy should eventually be overridden.

A fuzzy set logic can be adopted, not only to measure success, but it can also be applied to the overall theoretical framework in order to establish more precise connections between IVs and the DV. The crispy set logic adopted in this framework was chosen due to its focus on theory development, but once the connections are proven in present/absent terms, more specific measurements can be carried out for the variables considered. The indexes for the independent variable are ready to be analysed with fuzzy logic; the only missing element is the fuzzy operationalisation of the DV.

This theoretical framework should be applied also to both state and non-state entities in order to test the proposed hypotheses. Whereas this study focuses on international organisations only, empirical verification for the theoretical model could be added by looking at countries such as the United States, Russia or China. Since the United States is the actor *par excellence* in international sanctions, the application of this theoretical framework to it would provide further insight on international sanctions. To the same extent, the cases of Russia and China would contribute to the debate and help to enlarge the empirical validity of some of the hypotheses verified. The assumption to be tested would be that international organisations and nation-states follow the same rules when it comes to sanctions.

Other less studied international organisations that act as senders could be studied in future works: the AU, the Southern African Development Community (SADC), the Organization of American States (OAS), the Economic Community of West African States (ECOWAS) and the Association of South East Asian Nations (ASEAN). The adoption of more cases would both serve the purposes of strengthening, or falsifying, the hypotheses and contribute to the accumulation of knowledge of this crucial method of statecraft in foreign policy.

The deployment of troops by the major powers in many countries, such as with two current conflicts in Afghanistan and Iraq, and the already over-stretched resources dedicated to sustain the efforts of several peacekeeping forces around the world make sanctions, in comparison, a cheap and efficient way of exercising a presence in the international arena. The nature of the threat combined with the legal challenges arising from the imposition of targeted sanctions could pave the way for a more comprehensive adoption of international sanctions in the future.

Amongst the different types of sanctions, the case concerning signalling sanctions is particularly interesting as they are inspired by multiple motivations and they may hide several internal causal mechanisms not based on material consequences. This is more relevant if it is assumed that signalling sanctions can aim at changing the behaviour of targets although they would do it according to logics that differ from altering the cost/benefit analysis of targets in realist terms.

International targeted sanctions seem to be the product of a change in the nature of the international system and further investigations should aim at investigating this link. There are a number of changes in the international system that contribute to the establishment of a norm with regard to international individual responsibility, namely that individuals become accountable for their action before the international community. Targeted sanctions are one aspect of this changing nature of the international system, as individuals were liable personally for their actions only within the state in which they operated. Other signs are the creation of the Responsibility to Protect Principle (R2P) and the International Criminal Court, which is supposed to try individuals who committed crimes against humanity when their own states are unwilling or incapable of doing so.

In addition, the restraint in using sanctions because of their humanitarian consequences has faded away with the creation of smart sanctions, which has opened a new horizon for sanctions enthusiasts since financial and travel bans affect directly the lives of the 'bad guys'. Whereas dictators could have claimed to be penalised by international sanctions even if they were able to redirect the damage caused by the measures either on their political opponents or on common citizens, targeted sanctions can be avoided but they are more difficult to redirect, thus cutting back on the humanitarian toll associated with sanctions.

Another reason for the rise of targeted sanctions is their cost effectiveness. Despite all the claims maintaining that smart sanctions are as expensive as comprehensive ones, targeted sanctions are limited to very specific sectors or to limited groups of individuals. This statement is valid for sanctioned countries such as Liberia (Charles Taylor supporters), Angola (military spare parts for UNITA) and Moldova (travelling for the leaders of Transnistria). More information is needed on the effects of targeted sanctions within targeted societies (a notable exception is Eriksson 2007).

Targeted sanctions can also contribute to the establishment of new norms and new regimes that are created as a consequence of the ever-evolving character of the international system. The international financial regime that has been created since 9/11 to both fight money laundering and to tackle the dangers raised by terrorist activities is due, at least in part, to its growing importance in the international order. One organisation created in 1989 that is becoming essential in targeted financial sanctions is the FATF (Biersteker and Eckert 2008).

Wars, civil conflicts, human rights violations and international terrorism are likely to remain at the top of the world's political agenda for years to come. In order to fight against these sources of instability, international actors have to employ effectively all the foreign policy tools at their disposal and targeted sanctions are likely to play an ever-growing role in foreign policy.

This book contributes to enhancing the knowledge of sanctions through unveiling and clarifying the utility of restrictive measures in the international system and in foreign policy. The reputation of sanctions is generally affected by the low rate of effectiveness associated to them. This fact analysed blindly often leads to the conclusion that sanctions are not useful in foreign policy. Contrarily, this book has argued that sanctions can be very useful as long as they are used properly. This means that it must be clear what sanctions can achieve and under what conditions, and this investigation clearly solves these problems. This research helps to unveil the constraints that bind senders to impose certain types of sanctions, contributing to explaining and understanding the functioning and the utility of international sanctions. Further discussion towards a more comprehensive theoretical framework is needed in order to better grasp both the potential and the flaws of this powerful foreign policy element. This book sets this process on the right track.

| references

Adelman, H. and Suhrke, A. (eds) (1999) *The Path of a Genocide: The Rwanda Crisis from Uganda to Zaire*, New Brunswick, NJ: Transactions Publishers.

Agbu, O. (1998) 'Political Opposition and Democratic Transitions in Nigeria, 1985–96', in A. O. Olukoshi (ed.) *The Politics of Opposition in Contemporary Africa*, Uppsala: The Nordic Africa Institute.

Akiner, S. (2005) *Violence in Andijan, 13 May 2005: An Independent Assessment*, Silk Road Paper, Washington, DC, Uppsala: Central Asia-Caucasus Institute & Silk Road Studies Program.

Alexander, Y. and Hoenig, M. (2008) *The New Iranian Leadership: Ahmadinejad, Terrorism, Nuclear Ambition, and the Middle East*, Westport, CT: Praeger Security International.

Ali, M. M. and Iqbal, S. H. (2000) 'Sanctions and childhood mortality in Iraq', *Lancet,* (355): 1851–7.

Ali, T. M. and Matthews, R. O. (1999) 'Civil War and Failed Peace Efforts in Sudan,' in T. M. Ali and R.O. Matthews (eds) *Civil Wars in Africa*, Montreal: McGill-Queen's University Press.

Alikov, A. (2005) 'Uzbekistan: uncivil clashes', *Transitions Online*, 24.

Alnasrawi, A. (2001) 'Iraq: economic sanctions and consequences, 1990–2000', *Third World Quarterly*, 2: 205–18.

Ambrosio, T. (2006) 'The political success of Russia-Belarus Relations: insulating Minsk from a Color Revolution', *Demokratizatsiya: The Journal of Post-Soviet Democratization*, 14(3): 407–34.

Anthony, I. (2002) 'Sanctions applied by the European Union and the United Nations', in *SIPRI Yearbook 2002*, Stockholm: SIPRI.

Arnove, A. (2002) *Iraq Under Siege: The Deadly Impact of Sanctions and War*, Cambridge, MA: South Bend Press.

Art, R. J. (1980) 'To what ends military power?' *International Security*, 4(4): 3–35.

Askari, H., Forrer, J., Teegen, H. and Yang. J. (2003) *Economic Sanctions: Examining their Philosophy and Efficacy*, Westport, CT: Praeger.

Ayers, A. J. (2005) 'Sudan's uncivil war: the global-historical constitution of political violence', *Review of African Political Economy*, 37(124): 153–71.

Ayissi, A. and Poulton, R. E. (eds) (2006) *Bound to Cooperate: Conflict, Peace and People in Sierra Leone*, 2nd edn, Geneva: United Nations Institute for Disarmament Research.

Ayittey, G. B. (1999) *Africa in Chaos*, London: Macmillan.

Baldwin, D. A. (1971) 'The power of positive sanctions' *World Politics*, (24)1: 19–38.

— (1985) *Economic Statecraft*, Princeton, NJ: Princeton University Press.

— (1999/2000) 'The sanctions debate and the logic of choice', *International Security*, (24)3: 80–107.

— (2004) 'Sanctions in Political Science', in *International Encyclopedia of the Social & Behavioral Sciences*, 13480–2.

Barber, J. (1979) 'Economic sanctions as a policy instrument,' *International Affairs*, (55)9: 367–84.

Barnett, M. N. (2002) *Eyewitness to a Genocide: The United Nations and Rwanda*, Ithaca, NY: Cornell University Press.

Barret, R. (2008) speech presented at World Conference on Combating Terrorist Financing, Case Western Reserve University, Cleveland, Ohio, 11th April 2008.

Ben-Yehuda, H. and Mishali-Ram, M. (2003) 'The ethnic-state perspective in international crises: a theoretical framework applied to the Arab-Israel conflict 1947–2000', *International Interactions*, (29)1: 1–26.

Bennett, A. and Elman, C. (2007) 'Case study methods in the International Relations subfield', *Comparative Political Studies*, (40) 2: 170–195.

Berdal, M. and Economides, S. (2007) *United Nations Interventionism, 1991–2004*, Cambridge: Cambridge University Press.

Berenskoetter, F. and Williams, M. J. (2007) *Power in World Politics*, London/New York: Routledge.

Berman, E. G. (2000) *Peacemaking in Africa: Capabilities and Culpabilities*, Geneva: United Nations Institute for Disarmament Research.

Bethlehem, D. and Weller, M. (1997) *The Yugoslav Crisis in International Law*, Cambridge: Cambridge University Press.

Biersteker, T. J. and Eckert, S. E. (2006) *Strengthening Targeted Sanctions Through Fair and Clear Procedures*, Providence, RI: Watson Institute for International Studies.

— (eds) (2008) *Countering the Financing of Terrorism*, London/New York: Routledge.

Biersteker, T. J., Eckert, S. E., Halegna, A. and Romaniuk, P. (2005) 'Targeted sanctions and state capacity: towards a framework for national level implementation', in P. Wallensteen and C. Staibano (eds) *International Sanctions: Between Words and Wars in the Global System*, London/New York: Frank Cass, 57–64.

Blake, C. H. and Klemm, N. (2006) 'Reconsidering the effectiveness of international economic sanctions: an examination of selection bias,' *International Politics*, (43)1: 133–49.

Blanchard, J. -M. F. and Ripsman, N. (1999) 'Asking the right question: when do economic sanctions', *Security Studies*, (9)1: 219–53.

Bondi, L. (2002) 'Arms Embargoes: In Name Only?' in D. Cortright and G. A. Lopez (eds) *Smart Sanctions: Targeting Economic Statecraft*, Lanham, MD: Rowman & Littlefield Publishers, 109–24.

'The Bonn-Berlin Process', http://www.smartsanctions.de. (accessed 01/08/2007).

Borgen, C. (2006) *Thawing a Frozen Conflict: Legal Aspects of the Separatist Crisis in Moldova. A Report from the Association of the Bar of the City of*

New York, 06-0045, New York: St. John's Legal Studies Research Paper.

Bosse, G. (2010) 'The EU's relations with Moldova: governance, partnership or ignorance?', *Europe-Asia Studies*, (62)8: 1291–1309.

Bosse, G. and Korosteleva-Polglase, E. (2009) 'Changing Belarus? The limits of EU governance in Eastern Europe and the promise of partnership', *Cooperation and Conflict*, 44: 143–65.

Botan, I. (2009a) 'Ballots of Moldovan citizens from Transnistrian region', http://www.e-democracy.md/en/comments/political/20090214/, *Adept, Association for Participatory Democracy*, 14 February, (accessed 17/11/2009).

— (2009b) 'The Negotiation Process as a Way to Postpone the Solution,' in D. Matveev, G. Selari, E. Bobkova and B. Cseke (eds) *Moldova-Transnistria. Working Together for a Prosperous Future. Negotiation Process*, Chisinau: Cu Drag Publishing House, 116–34.

Boulden, J. (ed.) (2003) *Dealing with Conflict in Africa: The United Nations and Regional Organizations*, New York: Palgrave Macmillan.

Brady, L. J. (1987) 'The Utility of Economic Sanctions as a Policy Instrument,' in D. Leyton-Brown (ed.) *The Utility of International Economic Sanctions*, New York: St. Martin's Press, 297–302.

Brecher, M. (1993) *Crises in World Politics: Theory and Reality*, Oxford, New York, NY: Pergamon Press.

Brecher, M. and James, P. (1986) *Crisis and Change in World Politics*, Boulder, CO: Westview Press.

Brodie, B. (1946) *The Absolute Weapon: Atomic Power and World Order*, New York: Harcourt, Brace and Company.

Brown, M. and Zasloff, J. J. (1998) *Cambodia Confounds the Peacemakers, 1979–1998*, Ithaca, NY: Cornell University Press.

Brzoska, M. and Lopez, G. A (eds) (2009) *Putting the Teeth in the Tiger: Improving the Effectiveness of Arms Embargoes,* Conflict Management, Peace Economics and Development, Bingley: Emerald.

Buchet de Neuilly, Y. (2003) 'The multi-pillar issue of economic sanctions against Serbia', in M. Knodt and S. Princen (eds) *Understanding the European Union's External Relations*, London: Routledge.

Bures, O. (2010) 'Perceptions of the terrorist threat among EU member states', *Central European Journal of International and Security Studies*, (4)1: 51–80.

Bures, O. and Lopez, G. A. (2009) 'The unprecedented embargo: The UN arms sanctions against Iraq, 1990–2004,' in M. Brzoska and G. A. Lopez (eds) *Putting Teeth in the Tiger: Improving the Effectiveness of Arms Embargoes*, Bingley, UK: Emerald, 29–53.

Burnashev, R. and Chernykh, I. (2007) 'Changes in Uzbekistan's military policy after the Andijan events', *China and Eurasia Forum Quarterly*, (5)1: 67–73.

Buzan, B. and Waever, O. (2003) *Regions and Powers: The Structure of International Security*, Cambridge/New York: Cambridge University Press.

Carr, F. and Callan, T. (2002) *Managing Conflict in the New Europe: The Role of International Institutions*, Basingstoke/New York: Palgrave Macmillan.

Castle, S. (2006) 'EU divided over Uzbek sanctions', *The Independent*, 2 November.

Cha, V. D. and Kang, D. C. (2003) *Nuclear North Korea: A Debate on Engagement Strategies*, New York: Columbia University Press.

Chubin, S. (2010) 'The Iranian Nuclear Riddle after June 12', *The Washington Quarterly*, (33)1: 163–72.

Clawson, P. (1993) *How Has Saddam Hussein Survived? Economic Sanctions, 1990–1993*, Washington, DC: Institute for National Strategic Studies, National Defense University.

Colaresi, M. and Thompson, W. R. (2002) 'Strategic rivalries, protracted conflict, and crisis escalation', *Journal of Peace Research*, (39)2: 263–287.

Conroy, R. W. (2000) 'Angola's Agony', in D. Cortright and G. A. Lopez (eds) *The Sanctions Decade: Assessing UN Strategies in the 1990s*, Boulder, CO: Lynne Reinner.

Cordesman, A. H. and Hashim, A.S. (1997) *Iraq: Sanctions and Beyond*, Boulder, CO: Westview Press.

Cortright, D. and Lopez, G. A. (1995) *Economic Sanctions: Panacea or Peacebuilding in a Post-Cold War World?* Boulder, CO: Westview Press.

— (2000) *The Sanctions Decade: Assessing UN Strategies in the 1990s*, Boulder, CO: Lynne Reinner Publishers.

— (2002a) *Sanctions and the Search for Security: Challenges to UN Action*, Boulder, CO: Lynne Reinner Publishers.

— (2002b) *Smart Sanctions: Targeting Economic Statecraft*, Lanham, MD: Rowman & Littlefield Publishers.

— (2005) 'A Sanctions Coodinator: Options for Enhancing Compliance', in P. Wallensteen and C. Staibano (eds) *International Sanctions: Between Words and Wars in the Global System*, London/New York: Frank Cass, 65–74.

— (2007a) 'Strategies and Policy Challenges for Winning the Fight Against Terrorism', in D. Cortright and G. A. Lopez (eds) *Uniting Against Terror: Cooperative Nonmilitary Responses to the Global Terrorist Threat*, Cambridge, MA: MIT Press, 237–74.

— (eds) (2007b) *Uniting Against Terror: Cooperative Nonmilitary Responses to the Global Terrorist Threat*, Cambridge, MA: MIT Press.

Cortright, D., Lopez, G. A., Millar, A. and Gerber-Stellingwerf, L. (2007) 'Global Cooperation Against Terrorism: Evaluating the United Nations Counter-Terrorism Committee', in *Uniting Against Terror: Cooperative Nonmilitary Responses to the Global Terrorist Threat*, Cambridge, MA: MIT Press, 23–50.

Cortright, D., G. A. Lopez and E. S. Rogers (2002) 'Targeted Financial Sanctions: Smart Sanctions That Do Work,' in D. Cortright and G. A. Lopez (eds) *Smart Sanctions: Targeting Economic Statecraft*, Lanham, MD: Rowman & Littlefield Publishers, 23–40.

Cosgrove, E. (2005) 'Examining Targeted Sanctions: Are Travel Bans Effective?' in P. Wallensteen and C. Staibano (eds) *International Sanctions: Between Words and Wars in the Global System*, Abingdon: Frank Cass, 207–28.

Cotonou Agreement (2000) 'Partnership Agreement Between the Members of the African Caribbean and Pacific Groups of States of the One Part, and the European Community and Its Member States, of the Other Part, Signed in [..] on [..] [..] Agreement)', Art. 96 (2000), http://Ec.Europa.Eu/Development/Icenter/Repository/Agr01_en.Pdf.

Council of the European Union, General Affairs and External Relations (2005) 'Press Release 2668th Council Meeting', 9500/05 (Presse 132), Luxemburg.

Crocker, C. A. (2004) *Taming Intractable Conflicts: Mediation in the Hardest Cases*, Washington, DC: United States Institute of Peace Press.

Cronin, P. M. (ed.) (2008) *Double Trouble: Iran and North Korea as Challenges to International Security*, Westport, CT: Praeger Security International.

Crowther, W. (2007) 'Moldova, Transnistria and the PCRM's turn to the West', *East European Quarterly* (XLI)3: 273–304.

Dahl, R. A. (1962) *Who Governs?*, New Haven, Conn: Yale University Press.

Dallaire, R. (2003) *Shake Hands with the Devil: The Failure of Humanity in Rwanda*, Toronto: Random House Canada.

Daniel, D. C.,Taft, P. and Wiharta, S. (2008) *Peace Operations: Trends, Progress, and Prospects*, Washington, DC: Georgetown University Press.

Daoudi, M. S. and Dajani, M. S. (1983) *Economic Sanctions: Ideas and Experience*, London: Routledge and Kegan Paul.

de Vries, A. (2002) 'European Union Sanctions against the Federal Republic of Yugoslavia (1998–2000): a Special Exercise in Targeting', in D. Cortright and G. A. Lopez (eds) *Smart Sanctions: Targeting Economic Statecraft*, Lanham, MD: Rowman & Littlefield Publishers.

de Vries, A. W. and Hazelzet, H. (2005) 'The EU as a New Actor on the Sanctions Scene,' in P. Wallensteen and C. Staibano (eds) *International Sanctions: Between Words and Wars in the Global System*, London/New York: Frank Cass, 95–107.

Dedring, J. (2008) *The United Nations Security Council in the 1990s: Resurgence and Renewal*, Albany, NY: State University of New York Press.

Déme, M. (2005) *Law, Morality and International Armed Intervention: The United Nations and ECOWAS in Liberia*, New York: Routledge.

Diehl, P. F. (1992) 'What Are They Fighting For? The Importance of Issues in International Conflict Research', *Journal of Peace Research,* (29)3: 333–44.

Donovan, J. (2005) 'Uzbekistan: UN, EU Call For International Probe Into Violence', http://www.rferl.org/content/article/1058942.html, *Radio Free Europe – Radio Liberty*, 19 May (accessed 08/02/2010).

Dorussen, H. and Mo, J. (2001) 'Ending economic sanctions: audience costs and rent-seeking as commitment strategies', *Journal of Conflict Resolution*, (45)4: 395–426.

Doxey, M. P. (1971) *Economic Sanctions and International Enforcement*, Oxford: Oxford University Press.

— (1987) *International Sanctions in Contemporary Perspective*, Basingstoke: McMillan Press.

— (2002) 'United Nations Economic Sanctions: Minimizing Adverse Effects on Non-target States,' in D. Cortright and G. A. Lopez (eds) *Smart Sanctions: Targeting Economic Statecraft*, Lanham, MD: Rowman & Littlefield Publishers, 183–200.

— (1999) *The Sanctions Paradox: Economic Statecraft and International Relations*, Cambridge: Cambridge University Press.

Drezner, D. W. (2003a) 'The Hidden Hand of Economic Coercion', *International Organization*, 57: 643–59.

— (2003b) 'How Smart are Smart Sanctions?' *International Studies Review*, (5)1: 107–10.

Drury, C. A. and Y. Li (2006) 'U.S. economic sanction threats against China: failing to leverage better human rights', *Foreign Policy Analysis*, (2)4: 307–24.

Dumasy, T. (2003) 'Belarus's Relations with the European Union: A Western Perspective' in E. A. Korosteleva, C.W. Lawson and R. J. Marsh (eds) *Contemporary Belarus: Between Democracy and Dictatorship*, London/ NY: Routledge, 179–91.

Eberstadt, N. (2007) *The North Korean Economy: Between Crisis & Catastrophe*, New Brunswick: Transaction Publishers.

Edmonds, R. L. (ed.) (2002) *China and Europe Since 1978: A European Perspective*, Cambridge/NY: Cambridge University Press.

Ekengard, A. (2006) *The African Union Mission in Sudan (AMIS): Experiences and Lessons Learned*, FOI Studies in African Security Program.

El-Masri, S. (2008) 'The Hariri Tribunal: politics and International Law', *Middle East Policy*, (XV)3.

Elliott, K. A. (1998) 'The sanctions glass: half full or completely empty?' *International Security*, (23)1: 50–65.

— (2006) *Economic Sanctions as a Foreign Policy Tool*, Institute for International Economics and Center for Global Development, Washington, DC.

Elman, C. (2005) 'Explanatory typologies in qualitative studies of international politics', *International Organization*, (99) 2: 293–326.

Energy Information Administration, O.E.S.f.t.U.G. (2007) 'Libya', http://www. eia.doe.gov/emeu/cabs/Libya/NaturalGas.html (accessed 20/08/2008).

— (2008) 'Russia', http://www.eia.doe.gov/emeu/cabs/Russia/Oil_exports. html (accessed 15/09/2008).

Eriksson, M. (2004) 'EU sanctions: Three Cases of Targeted Sanctions', in C. Staibano and P. Wallensteen (eds) *International Sanctions: Between Words and Wars in the Global System*, London: Frank Cass.

— (2009) 'Rethinking Targeted Sanctions', Ph.D. Dissertation, European University Institute.

Europa House (2010) 'Europa House Tashkent, European Commission's Implementation and Management Support Office in the Republic of Uzbekistan', http://europahouse.uz/joomla2/ (01/12/2010).

European Union (2004b) 'Committee on Legal Affairs and Human Rights', trans Christos Pourgourides, Report Disappeared Persons in Belarus, in 10062.

— 'EU-Belarus Relations', http://eeas.europa.eu/belarus/pdf/belarus_ trade_en.pdf (accessed 15/06/2011).

— 'European Neighbourhood and Partnership Instrument, Belarus. Country Strategy Paper 2007–2013', http://ec.europa.eu/world/enp/pdf/country/ enpi_csp_nip_belarus_en.pdf (2007) (accessed 15/09/2008).

European Union, Council of the European Union (1994) *94/165/CFSP: Council Decision of 15 March 1994 on the Common Position Defined on the Basis of Article J.2 of the Treaty on European Union Concerning the Imposition of an Embargo on Arms, Munitions and Military Equipment on Sudan,* 94/165/CFSP.

— (1995) 95/515/CFSP: Common Position of 20 November 1995, Defined by the Council on the Basis of Article J.2 of the Treaty on European Union, on Nigeria, 95/515/CFSP.

— (1996) 96/746/CFSP: Common Position of 17 December 1996, Defined by the Council on the Basis of Article J.2 of the Treaty on European Union Concerning the Imposition of an Embargo on Arms, Munitions and Military Equipment on Afghanistan, 96/747/CFSP.

— (1998a) Common Position of 30 October 1998, Defined by the Council on the Basis of Article J.2 of the Treaty on European Union, Concerning Nigeria, 98/614/CFSP.

— (1998b) Common Position of 9 July 1998, Defined by the Council on the Basis of Article J.2 of the Treaty on European Union, Concerning Belarus, 98/448/CFSP.

— (1999a) Council Common Position of 16 April 1999, Defined by the Council on the Basis of Article J.2 of the Treaty on European, 1999/261/ CFSP.

— (1999b) Council Decision of 22 February 1999, Repealing Common Position 98/448/CFSP Concerning Belarus, 1999/156/CFSP.

— (2001a) Common Position of 16 July 2001, Concerning a Visa Ban Against Extremists in FYROM, 2001/542/CFSP.

— (2001b) Council Common Position of 8 October 2001, Amending Common Position 96/184/CFSP Concerning Arms Exports to the Former Yugoslavia and Common Position 98/240/CFSP on Restrictive Measures Against the Federal Republic of Yugoslavia, 2001/719/CFSP.

— (2003) Council Common Position 2003/139/CFSP of 27 February 2003, Concerning Restrictive Measures Against the Leadership of the Transnistrian Region of the Moldovan Republic, 2003/139/CFSP.

— (2004a) 'Basic Principles on the Use of Restrictive Measures (Sanctions)', 10198/1/04, Brussels.

— (2004c) Council Common Position 2004/622/CFSP of 26 August 2004,

Amending Common Position 2004/179/CFSP Concerning Restrictive Measures Against the Leadership of the Transnistrian Region of the Moldovan Republic, 2004/622/CFSP.

— (2004d) Council Common Position 2004/661/CFSP of 24 September 2004, Concerning Restrictive Measures Against Certain Officials of Belarus, 2004/661/CFSP.

— (2004e) Council Common Position 2004/698/CFSP of 14 October 2004, Concerning the Lifting of Restrictive Measures Against Libya, 2004/161/CFSP.

— (2004f) Council Common Position 2004/848/CFSP of 13 December 2004, Amending Common Position 2004/661/CFSP Concerning Restrictive Measure Against Certain Officials of Belarus, 2004/848/CFSP.

— (2005a) Common Position 2005/80/CFSP of 31 January 2005, Extending and Amending Common Position 2004/133/CFSP on Restrictive Measures Against Extremists in the Former Yugoslav Republic of Macedonia (FYROM), 2005/80/CFSP.

— (2005b) 'Guidelines on implementation and evaluation of restrictive measures (sanctions) in the framework of the EU Common Foreign and Security Policy', 15114/05, Brussels.

— (2006a) Council Common Position 2006/276/CFSP of 10 April 2006, Concerning Restrictive Measures Against Certain Officials of Belarus and Repealing Common Position 2004/661/CFSP, 2006/276/CFSP.

— (2006b) Council Common Position 2006/29/CFSP of 23 January 2006, Repealing Common Position 96/184/CFSP Concerning Arms Exports to the Former Yugoslavia, 2006/29/CFSP.

— (2006c) Council Common Position 2006/362/CFSP of 18 May 2006, Amending Common Position 2006/276/CFSP Concerning Restrictive Measures Against Certain Officials of Belarus, 2006/362/CFSP.

— (2007a) Council Common Position 2007/173/CFSP of 19 March 2007, Renewing Restrictive Measures Against Certain Officials of Belarus, 2007/173/CFSP.

— (2007b) Council Common Position 2007/734/CFSP of 13 November 2007, Concerning Restrictive Measures Against Uzbekistan, 2007/734/CFSP.

— (2008a) Council Common Position 2008/160/CFSP of 25 February 2008, Concerning Restrictive Measures Against the Leadership of the Transnistrian Region of the Republic of Moldova, 2008/160/CFSP.

— (2008b) Council Common Position 2008/187/CFSP of 3 March 2008, Concerning Restrictive Measures Against the Illegal Government of Anjouan in the Union of Comoros, 2008/187/CFSP.

— (2008c) Council Common Position 2008/611/CFSP of 24 July 2008, Repealing Common Position 2008/187/CFSP Concerning Restrictive Measures Against the Illegal Government of Anjouan in the Union of Comoros, 2008/611/CFSP.

— (2008d) 'Update of the EU Best Practices for the effective implementation of restrictive', 8666/1/08, Brussels.

— (2008e) 'European Union Border Assistance Mission to Moldova and Ukraine – EUBAM', http://www.eubam.org/ (20/08/2008).

— (2009a) Council Common Position 2009/139/CFSP of 16 February 2009, Renewing Restrictive Measures Against the Leadership of the Transnistrian Region of the Republic of Moldova, 2009/139/CFSP.

— (2009b) Council Common Position 2009/314/CFSP of 6 April 2009, Amending Common Position 2006/276/CFSP Concerning Restrictive Measures Against Certain Officials of Belarus, and Repealing Common Position 2008/844/CFSP, 2009/314/CFSP.

— (2009c) Council Common Position 2009/788/CFSP of 27 October 2009, Concerning Restrictive Measures Against the Republic of Guinea, 2009/788/CFSP.

— (2009d) Council Decision 2009/1003/CFSP of 22 December 2009, Amending Common Position 2009/788/CFSP Concerning Restrictive Measures Against the Republic of Guinea, 2009/1003/CFSP.

— (2010a) Council Common Position 2010/639/CFSP of 25 October 2010, Concerning Restrictive Measures Against Certain Officials of Belarus, 2010/639/CFSP.

— (2010b) Council Decision 2010/105/CFSP of 22 February 2009, Renewing Restrictive Measures Against the Leadership of the Transnistrian Region of the Republic of Moldova, 2010/105/CFSP.

— (2010c) Council Decision 2010/186/CFSP of 29 March 2010, Amending Common Position 2009/788/CFSP Concerning Restrictive Measures Against the Republic of Guinea, 2010/186/CFSP.

— (2010d) Council Decision 2010/232/CFSP of 26 April 2010, Renewing Restrictive Measures Against Burma/Myanmar, 2010/232/CFSP.

— (2010e) Council Decision 2010/573/CFSP of 27 September 2009, Renewing Restrictive Measures Against the Leadership of the Transnistrian Region of the Republic of Moldova, 2010/573/CFSP.

— (2010f) Council Decision 2010/638/CFSP of 25 October 2010, Concerning Restrictive Measures Against the Republic of Guinea, 2010/638/CFSP.

— (2008g) *Central Asia Indicative Programme 2007–2010*, http://ec.europa.eu/external_relations/central_asia/rsp/nip_07_10_en.pdf, DG External Relations E/3 (accessed 15/09/2008).

— (2008h) *Regional Strategy Paper for Assistance to Central Asia for the Period 2007–2013*, http://ec.europa.eu/external_relations/central_asia/rsp/07_13_en.pdf, Brussels: European Union (accessed 15/09/2008).

European Union, E.C., Council of the European Union (2005) Council Common Position 2005/792/CFSP of 14 November 2005 Concerning Restrictive Measures Against Uzbekistan, 2005/792/CFSP.

— (2006) Council Common Position 2006/787/CFSP of 13 November 2006, Renewing Certain Restrictive Measures Against Uzbekistan, 2006/787/CFSP.

—   (2007c). 'Sanctions', http://ec.europa.eu/external_relations/cfsp/
        sanctions/index.htm, in Common Foreign and Security Policy (CFSP)
        (accessed 01/08/2007).
Falola, T. (1999) *The History of Nigeria*, Westport, CT: Greenwood Press.
Farral, J. (2007) *United Nations Sanctions and the Rule of Law*, Cambridge:
        Cambridge University Press.
Fearon, J. D. (1994) 'Domestic political audiences and the escalation of
        international disputes', *The American Political Science Review*, (88)3:
        577–92.
—   (1997) 'Signaling foreign policy interests: Tying hands versus sinking
        costs', *The Journal of Conflict Resolution*, (41)1: 68–90.
Findlay, T. (1995) *Cambodia: The Legacy and Lessons of UNTAC*, New York:
        Oxford University Press.
Foley, H. (ed.) (1923) *Woodrow Wilson's Case for the League of Nations*, Princeton,
        NJ: Princeton University Press.
Fudge, J. (1995) *Cargoes, Embargoes, and Emissaries: The Commercial and
        Political Interaction of England and the German Hanse, 1450–1510*,
        Toronto: University of Toronto Press.
Fumagalli, M. (2007) 'Alignments and realignments in Central Asia: the
        rationale and implications of Uzbekistan's rapprochement with Russia',
        International Political Science Review, (28)3: 253-271.
Furley, O. and May, R. (2006) *Ending Africa's Wars: Progressing to Peace*,
        Aldershot/Burlington, VT: Ashgate.
Galtung, J. (1967) 'On the effects of international economic sanctions: with
        examples from the case of Rhodesia', *World Politics*, (19)3: 378–416.
George, A. L. (1971) *The Limits of Coercive Diplomacy; Laos, Cuba, Vietnam*,
        Boston, MA: Little Brown.
George, A. L. and Bennet, A. (2005) *Case Studies and Theory Development in the
        Social Sciences*, Cambridge, MA: MIT Press.
Gerring, J. (2001) *Social Science Methodology: A Criterial Framework*,
        Cambridge/New York: Cambridge University Press.
Gibbons, E. D. (1999) *Sanctions in Haiti: Human Rights and Democracy Under
        Assault*, published with the Center for Strategic and International Studies,
        Washington, D.C., Westport, CT: Praeger.
Giddens, A. (1994) *Sociologia*, Bologna: Il Mulino.
Giumelli, F. (2009) 'Coercing, Constraining and Signaling: Explaining UN and
        EU Sanctions after the Cold War', Ph.D. Dissertation, University of
        Florence.
—   (2010a) 'Measuring the Success of Sanctions. The Case of the EU
        in Uzbekistan', ISA – Annual Convention International Studies
        Associations, New Orleans, LO.
—   (2010b) 'The Restrictive Measures of the European Union: developing
        analytical categories to understand functions and utility of EU sanctions',
        The International Spectator, (45)3.
—   (2011) 'Understanding the effectiveness of targeted sanctions: the case of

the EU in Moldova', *European Foreign Affairs Review*, (16) 3.

Global Terrorism Database (2008) National Consortium for the Study of Terrorism and Responses to Terrorism, http://www.start.umd.edu/data/gtd/ (accessed 15/09/2008).

Goldthorpe, J. H. (1997) 'Current issues in comparative macrosociology: a debate on methodological issues', *Comparative Social Research*, 16: 1–26.

Gunaratna, R. (2002) *Inside Al Qaeda: Global Network of Terror*, New York: Columbia University Press.

Haas, M. (1974) *International Conflicts,* Indianapolis: Bobbs-Merril.

Haass, R. N. (ed.) (1998) *Economic Sanctions and American Diplomacy*, New York: Council on Foreign Relations.

Haass, R. N. and O'Sullivan, M. L. (eds) (2000) *Honey and Vinegar: Incentives, Sanctions and Foreign Policy*, Washington, DC: Brookings Institution Press.

Hacker, F. J. (1976) *Crusaders, Criminals, Crazies: Terror and Terrorism in Our Time*, New York: Norton.

Hare, P. (2005) 'Angola: The End of an Intractable Conflict', in A. C. Crocker (ed.) *Grasping the Nettle: Analyzing Cases of Intractable Conflict*, Washington, DC: United States Institute of Peace Press, 209–30.

Hatzfeld, J. and Coverdale, L. (2005) *A Time For Machetes: The Rwanda Genocide – The Killers Speak*, London: Serpent's Tale.

Hellstrom, J. (2010) *The EU Embargo on China: A Swedish Perspective*, FOI, Swedish Defence Research.

Hensel, P. R. (2001) 'Contentious issues and world politics: territorial claims in the Americas, 1816–1996', *International Studies Quarterly*, (45)1: 81–109.

Herd, G. P. (2005) *Moldova & The Dniestr Region: Contested Past, Frozen Present, Speculative Future?* Central & Eastern Europe Series 05/07, Conflict Studies Research Centre.

Higgins, R. (1993) 'The New United Nations and Former Yugoslavia', *International Affairs*, (69)3: 465–83.

Hill, F. and K. Jones (2006) 'Fear of democracy of revolution: the reaction to Andijon', *The Washington Quarterly*, (29)3: 111–25.

Hoffman, B. (2006) *Inside Terrorism*, New York: Columbia University Press.

House of Lords, Select Committee on Economic Affairs (2007a) 'Chapter 4: Targeted and General EU Sanctions – Burma,' in *Economic Affairs – Second Report*.

— (2007b) *The Impact of Economic Sanctions*, Vol I: Report.

Hovi, J., Huseby, R. and Sprinz, D. F. (2005) 'When do (imposed) economic sanctions work?' *World Politics*, (57)4: 479–99.

Human Rights Watch (2003) 'Belarus,' http://hrw.org/wr2k3/europe4.html, in *World Report 2003* (accessed 15/09/2008).

Human Rights Watch (2006) 'The Andijan Massacre', http://www.hrw.org/campaign/andijan (accessed 15/09/2008).

Hufbauer, G. C., Schott, J. J. and Elliott, K. A. (1990) *Economic Sanctions Reconsidered: History and Current Policy*, 2nd edn, Washington, DC, Upssala: Institute for International Economics.

Hufbauer, G. C., Schott, J. J., Elliott, K. A and Oegg, B. (2007) *Economic Sanctions Reconsidered: History and Current Policy*, 3rd edn, Washington, DC: Peterson Institute for International Economics.

'The Interlaken Process', http://www.smartsanctions.ch. (accessed 01/08/2007).

International Crisis Behavior Project (2008) 8.0, http://www.cidcm.umd.edu/icb/ (accessed 20/08/2008).

International Crisis Group (2005) *Uzbekistan: The Andijon Uprising*, Asia Briefing, 38.

— (2006) *Uzbekistan: Europe's Sanctions Matter*, Asia Briefing, 54.

— (2008a) *Political Murder in Central Asia: No Time to End Uzbekistan's Isolation*, Asia Briefing, 76.

— (2008b) *Somalia: To Move Beyond the Failed State*, Africa Report, 147, Nairobi; Brussels: International Crisis Group.

— (2010a) *Congo: No Stability in Kivu Despite Rapprochement with Rwanda*, Africa Report, 165, Nairobi; Brussels: International Crisis Group.

— (2010b) *Trial by Fire: The Politics of the Special Tribunal for Lebanon*, Middle East Report, 100, International Crisis Group.

Jarabik, B. and Silitski, V. (2008) 'Belarus', in R. Youngs (ed.) *Is the European Union Supporting Democracy in Its Neighbourhood?* Madrid: Fride, 101–20.

Jeffries, I. (2010) *Contemporary North Korea: A Guide to Economic and Political Developments*, London/NY: Routledge.

Jervis, R. (1970) *The Logic of Images in International Relations*, Princeton, NJ: Princeton University Press.

Jones, B. D. (2001) *Peacemaking in Rwanda: The Dynamics of Failure*, Boulder, CO: Lynne Reinner Publishers.

Jones, S. G. (2007) *The Rise of European Security Cooperation*, Cambridge: Cambridge University Press.

'Jose Maria Sison vs. Council of the European Union' (2009), tr. Case T-341/07, Court of First Instance of the European Communities (Seventh Chamber).

Kabia, J. (2009) *Humanitarian Intervention and Conflict Resolution in West Africa: From ECOMOG to ECOMIL*, Farnham, Surrey/Burlington, VT: Ashgate Publishing.

Kaempfer, W. H. and Lowenberg, A. D. (1992) *International Economic Sanctions: A Public Choice Perspective*, Boulder, CO: Westview Press.

— (1999) 'Unilateral versus multilateral sanctions: a public choice perspective,' *International Studies Quarterly*, (43)1: 37–58.

Kasaija, A. P. (2010) 'The UN-led Djibouti peace process for Somalia 2008–2009: results and problems', *Journal of Contemporary African Studies*, (28)3: 261282.

Katagiri, N. (2010) 'Containing the Somali insurgency: learning from the British experience in Somaliland', *African Security Review*, (19)1: 33–45.

Keegan, J. (1994) *A History of Warfare*, New York: Vintage Books.

Keen, D. (2005) *Conflict & Collusion in Sierra Leone*, Oxford/New York: Palgrave.

Keohane, R. O. (1986) *Neorealism and Its Critics*, New York: Columbia University Press.

Keohane, R. O. and Nye, J. S. (1977) *Power and Interdependence: World Politics in Transition*, Boston, MA: Little Brown.

Kerr, D. and Fei, L. (2007) *The International Politics of EU-China Relations*, Oxford: Oxford University Press.

Khadiagala, G. M. (2006) *Security Dynamics in Africa's Great Lakes Region*, Boulder, CO: Lynne Reinner Publishers.

Khan, S. (2010) *Iran and Nuclear Weapons: Protracted Conflict and Proliferation*, London/New York: Routledge.

Kieh, G. K. (2007) *Beyond State Failure and Collapse: Making the State Relevant in Africa*, Lanham, MD: Lexington Books.

King, C. (2000) *The Moldovans – Romania, Russia and the Politics of Culture*, Stanford: Hoover International Press.

King, T. (1999) 'Human rights in European foreign policy: success or failure for post-modern diplomacy?' *European Journal of International Law*, 2: 313–37.

Kirshner, J. (1997) 'The microfoundations of economic sanctions', *Security Studies*, (6)3: 32–64.

Kolsto, P. and Malgin, A. (1998) 'The Transnistrian republic: A case of politicized regionalism', *Nationalities Papers*, (26)1: 103–27.

Kreutz, J. (2004) 'Reviewing the EU arms embargo on China: the clash between value and rationale in the European Security Strategy', *Perspectives*, 22: 43–58.

Kreutz, J. (2005) 'Hard measures by a soft power? sanctions policy of the European Union 1981–2004', *Bonn International Center for Conversion*, Paper 45.

Krivosheev, D. (2003) 'Belarus' External Relations,' in E. A. Korosteleva, C. W. Lawson and R. J. Marsh (eds) *Contemporary Belarus: Between Democracy and Dictatorship*, London/New York: Routledge, 165–78.

Kroslak, D. (2007) *The Role of France in the Rwandan Genocide*, London: Hurst & Co.

Lacy, D. and Niou, E. M. S. (2004) 'A theory of economic sanctions and issue linkage: the roles of preferences, information, and threats', *The Journal of Politics*, (66)1: 25–42.

Lasswell, H. D. and Kaplan, A. (1950) *Power and Society: A Framework for Political Inquiry*, New Haven, CT: Yale University Press.

Lawson, F. H. (1983) 'Using positive sanctions to end international conflicts: Iran and the Arab Gulf countries', *Journal of Peace Research*, (20)4: 311–28.

Leurdijk, D. A. and Venema, A. P. (eds) (1996) *The United Nations and NATO in Former Yugoslavia, 1991–1996: Limits to Diplomacy and Force*, Netherlands Atlantic Commission: Netherlands Institute of International Relations C'lingendael.

Li, Y. and Drury, C. A. (2004) 'Threatening sanctions when engagement would be more effective: attaining better human rights in China', *International Studies Perspectives*, 5: 378–94.

Liddell Hart, B. H. (1947) *The Revolution in Warfare*, New Haven, CT: Yale University Press.

Lindner, R. (2007) 'Neighborhood in Flux: EU-Belarus-Russia: Prospects for the European Union's Belarus Policy', in D. Hamilton and G. Mangott (eds) *The New Eastern Europe: Ukraine, Belarus & Moldova*, Washington, DC: Center for Transatlantic Relations, 55–76.

Lindsay, J. (1986) 'Trade sanctions as policy instruments: a re-examination,' *International Studies Quarterly*, (30)2: 153–73.

Litwak, R. S. (2008) 'Living with ambiguity: nuclear deals with Iran and North Korea', *Survival*, (22)4: 373–85.

Lobiakas, A. (2005) 'Uzbekistan/EU: EU Foreign Ministers Condemn Uzbek Authorities for Andijon Killings,' http://www.rferl.org/content/article/1058965.html, *Radio Free Europe – Radio Liberty*, 23 May (accessed 08/02/2010).

Lopez, G. A. and Cortright, D. (2004) 'Containing Iraq: sanctions worked', *Foreign Affairs*, July/August.

Lutterotti, L.v. (2002) 'The US Extraterritorial Sanctions of 1996 and the EU Reaction,' in S. Griller and B. Weidel (eds) *External Economic Relations and Foreign Policy in the European Union*, Wien/New York: Springer, 237–70.

Lynch, D. (2000) *Russian Peacekeeping Strategies in the CIS: The Cases of Moldova, Georgia and Tajikistan*, New York: St. Martin's Press.

— (ed.) (2005) 'Changing Belarus', *Chaillot Paper*, 85, Paris: European Union Institute for Security Studies.

McNamara, T. E. (2007) 'Unilateral and Multilateral Strategies Against State Sponsors of Terror: A Case Study of Libya, 1979 to 2003', in *Uniting Against Terror: Cooperative Nonmilitary Responses to the Global Terrorist Threat*, Cambridge, MA: MIT Press, 83–122.

Mahoney, J. (2000) 'Strategies of causal inference in small-N analysis', *Sociological Methods & Research*, (28)4: 387–424.

Malan, M. (2002) *Peacekeeping in Sierra Leone: UNAMSIL Hits the Home Straight*, Pretoria: Institute for Security Studies.

Malone, D. (1997) 'Haiti and the International Community: A Case Study', *Survival*, (39)2: 126–46.

Manners, I. (2002) 'Normative Power Europe: a contradiction in terms?', *Journal of Common Market Studies*, (20)2: 235–58.

— (2006a) 'European Union, normative power and ethical foreign policy', in D. Chandler and V. Heins (eds) *Rethinking Ethical Foreign Policy: Pitfalls, Possibilities and Paradoxes*, London: Routledge, 116–36.

— (2006b) 'The Symbolic Manifestation of the European Union's Normative Role in World Politics', in O. Elgstrom and M. Smith (eds) *New Roles for the European Union in International Politics*, London: Routledge, 66–84.

Mansbach, R. W. and Vasquez, J. A. (1981) *In Search of Theory: A New Paradigm for Global Politics*, New York, NY: Columbia University Press.

Martin, L. L. (1992) *Coercive Cooperation: Explaining Multilateral Economic Sanctions*, Princeton, NJ: Princeton University Press.

Martin, L. L. and Laurenti, J. (1997) *The United Nations and Economic Sanctions*, New York: United Nations Association of the United States of America.

Massey, S. and Baker, B. (2009) *Comoros: External Involvement in a Small Island State*, Programme Paper AFP, 1, Chatham House.

Matinuddin, K. (1999) *The Taliban Phenomenon: Afghanistan 1994–97*, Canmbridge: Cambridge University Press.

Matveeva, A. (2006) *EU Stakes in Central Asia*, Chaillot Paper, 91, Paris: European Union Institute for Security Studies.

Melvern, L. (2000) *A People Betrayed: The Role of the West in Rwanda's Genocide*, London/NY: Zed Books.

Mercer, J. (1996) *Reputation and International Politics*, Ithaca, NY: Cornell University Press.

Miers, A. C. and Morgan, C. T. (2002) 'Multilateral Sanctions and Foreign Policy Success: Can Too Many Cooks Spoil the Broth?' *International Interactions*, (28)2: 117–36.

Miklowitz, G. D. (1998) *Masada: The Last Fortress*, Grand Rapids, MI: Eerdmans Books for Young Readers.

Minear, L. (2000) *NATO and Humanitarian Action in the Kosovo Crisis*, Providence, RI: Institute for International Studies.

Mo, J. (1995) 'Domestic institutions and international bargaining: the role of agent veto in Two-Level Games', *The American Political Science Review*, (89)4: 914–24.

Morgan, C. and Miers, A. C. (1999) 'When Threats Succeed: A Formal Model of the Threat and Use of Economic Sanctions'. Annual Meeting of the American Political Science Association, Atlanta, GA.

Morgan, C. T. and Schwebach, V. L. (1996) 'Economic Sanctions as an instrument of foreign policy: the role of domestic politics', *International Interactions*, (36)3: 25–52.

— (1997) 'Fools Suffer Gladly: The Use of Economic Sanctions in International Crises', *International Studies Quarterly*, (47)1: 27–50.

Mueller, J. and Mueller, K. (1999) 'Sanctions of mass destruction', *Foreign Affairs*, (78)3: 43–53.

Mungiu-Pippidi, A. and Munteanu, I. (2009) 'Moldova's "Twitter Revolution"', *Journal of Democracy*, (20)3: 136–42.

Murphy, R. (2007) *UN Peacekeeping in Lebanon, Somalia, and Kosovo: Operational and Legal Issues in Practice*, Cambridge/ New York: Cambridge University Press.

Nantoi, O. (2009) 'Sources and settlement prospects of the Transnistrian conflict', in D. Matveev, G. Selari, E. Bobkova and B. Cseke (eds) *Moldova-Transnistria: Working Together for a Prosperous Future: Negotiation Process*, Chisinau: Cu Drag Publishing House, 160–78.

Naumkin, V. (2006) 'Uzbekistan's State-Building Fatigue', *The Washington Quarterly*, (29)3: 127–40.

Naylor, T. R. (2001) *Economic Warfare: Sanctions, Embargo Busting and Their Human Cost*, Boston, MA: Northeastern University Press.

Nest, M. (2006) *The Democratic Republic of Congo: Economic Dimensions of War and Peace*, Boulder, CO: Lynne Reinner Publishers.

Neukirch, C. (2004) 'The OSCE Mission to Moldova', in *OSCE Yearbook 2003*, Hamburg: The Centre for OSCE Research (CORE), 149–61.

— (2006) 'Managing the Crises – Restarting the Process: The OSCE Mission to Moldova in 2004/2005', in *OSCE Yearbook 2005*, Hamburg: The Centre for OSCE Research (CORE), 139–53.

Newcomb, R. R. (2002) 'Targeted Financial Sanctions: The U.S. Model', in D. Cortright and G. A. Lopez (eds) *Smart Sanctions: Targeting Economic Statecraft*, Lanham, MD: Rowman & Littlefield Publishers.

Niblock, T. (2001) *Pariah States & Sanctions in the Middle East: Iraq, Libya, Sudan*, Boulder, CO/London: Lynne Reinner Publishers.

Nincic, M. (2008) 'Positive Incentives and the Challenge of North Korean and Iranian Nuclear Programs', ISA's 49th Annual Convention, Bridging Multiple Divides, San Francisco, CA: Hilton San Francisco.

Nincic, M. and Wallensteen, P. (1983) *Dilemmas of Economic Coercion: Sanctions in World Politics*, New York: Praeger.

Nmoma, V. (1995) 'Ethnic Conflict, Constitutional Engineering and Democracy in Nigeria', in H. Glickman (ed.) *Ethnic Conflict and Democratization in Africa*, Atlanta, GA: The African Studies Association Press.

Nooruddin, I. (2002) 'Modeling selection bias in studies of sanctions efficacy', *International Interactions*, (28)1: 59–75.

Nossal, R. K. (1989) 'International sanctions as international punishment,' *International Organization*, (43)2: 301–22.

Institution Press.

Oette, L. (2002) 'A Decade of Sanctions against Iraq: Never Again! The End of Unlimited Sanctions in the Recent Practice of the UN Security Council', *European Journal of International Law*, vol. 13, no. 1.

O'Leary, M. (1976) 'The Role of Issues', in J. Rosenau (ed.) *In Search of Global Patterns*, New York: Free Press, 318–25.

Olonisakin, F. (2008) *Peacekeeping in Sierra Leone: The Story of UNAMSIL*, Boulder, CO: Lynne Reiner Publishers.

Opinion Editorial (1994) 'Rwanda's Arms Suppliers,' *The Washington Post*, 15 June.

Osaghae, E. E. (1998) *Crippled Giant: Nigeria Since Independence*, Bloomington and Indianapolis: Indiana University Press.

O'Sullivan, M. (2003) *Shrewd Sanctions: Statecraft and State Sponsors of Terrorism*, Washington, DC/Uppsala: Brookings.

Paes, W. -C. (2009) 'The Challenge of Measuring Success: Yugoslavia Sanctions Decade (1991–2001)', in M. Brzoska and G. A. Lopez (eds) *Putting Teeth in the Tiger: Improving the Effectiveness of Arms Embargoes*, Bingley: Emerald Group Publishing Limited.

Pape, R. A. (1992) 'Coercion and Military Strategy: Why Denial Works and

Punishment Doesn't', *Journal of Strategic Studies*, (15)4: 423–75.

— (1996) *Bombing to Win: Air Power and Coercion in War*, Ithaca, NY: Cornell University Press.

— (1997) 'Why economic sanctions do not work', *International Security*, (22)2: 90–136.

— (1998) 'Why economic sanctions still do not work', *International Security*, (23)1: 66–77.

— (2005) *Dying to Win: The Strategic Logic of Suicide Terrorism*, New York: Random House.

Pedersen, M. B. (2008) *Promoting Human Rights in Burma: A Critique of Western Sanctions Policy*, Lanham, MD: Rowman & Littlefield Publishers.

Popescu, N. (2004) 'Europeanisation and Conflict Resolution: A View from Moldova', *Journal of Ethnopolitics and Minority Issues in Europe*, 1.

— (2005) *The EU in Moldova - Settling Conflicts in the Neighbourhood*, Occasional Paper 60, Paris: European Union Institute for Security Studies.

— (2005/2006) *The EU and Transnistria*, Center for Policy Studies (CPS) International Policy Fellowship Program, Central European University and Open Society Institute.

Portela, C. (2008) 'The Efficacy of Sanctions of the European Union: When and Why Do They Work?', Ph.D. Dissertation, European University Institute.

Power, S. (2002) *'A Problem from Hell': America and the Age of Genocide*, New York: Basic Books.

Preeg, E. H. (1999) *Feeling Good or Doing Good with Sanctions: Unilateral Economic Sanctions and the U.S. National Interest*, Washington, DC: Center for Strategic & International Studies.

Pritchard, C. L. (2007) *Failed Diplomacy: The Tragic Story of how North Korea Got the Bomb*, Washington, DC: Brookings Institution Press.

Protsyk, O. (2004/2005) 'Democratization as a means of conflict resolution in Moldova', *European Yearbook of Minority Issues*, 4.

Prunier, G. (1995) *Rwanda Crisis, 1959–1994*, London: Hurst.

Putnam, R. D. (1988) 'Diplomacy and domestic politics: The logic of two-level game', *International Organization*, (42)3: 427–60.

Radio Free Europe (2004) 'Central Asia Report: 7 April 2004', http://www.rferl.org/content/article/1342159.html, *Radio Free Europe – Radio Liberty*, (4)14 (accessed 08/02/2010).

Ragin, C. C. (1987) *The Comparative Method: Moving Beyond Qualitative and Quantitative*, Berkeley, CA: University of California Press.

— (2000) *Fuzzy-Set Social Science*, Chicago, IL: University of Chicago Press.

— (2006) 'Set Relations in Social Research: Evaluating Their Consistency and Coverage', *Political Analysis*, (14)3: 291–310.

Ralph, J. (2005) 'International Society, the International Criminal Court and American Foreign Policy', *Review of International Studies*, (31)1.

Rashid, A. (2000) *Taliban: Islam, Oil and the New Great Game in Central Asia*, London: I. B. Tauris and Co.

—   (2001) *Taliban: Militant Islam, Oil and Fundamentalism in Central Asia*, New Haven/London: Yale University Press.

Rettman, A. (2011) 'EU imposes visa ban on Belarus, threatens economic measures', *Euobserver.com*, 31 January.

Riedel, B. (2007) 'Al Qaeda strikes back', *Foreign Affairs*, (86)3.

Rodkiewicz, W. (2008) 'The frozen conflict in Transnistria: a chance for agreement?', *Center for Eastern Studies Commentary*, 2.

Rogers, E. S. (1996) 'Using economic sanctions to control regional conflicts', *Security Studies*, (5)4: 43–72.

Rothman, T. (2007) 'A state's choice: nuclear policy in a changing world between Libya and North Korea', *Defence & Security Analysis*, (23)3: 297–313.

Roy, J. (1997) 'The Helms-Burton Law: development, consequences, and legacy for Inter-American and European-US Relations', *Journal of Inter-American Studies and World Affairs*, (39)3: 77–108.

Rudling, P. A. (2008) 'Belarus in the Lukashenka Era: National Identity and Relations with Russia', in O. Schmidtke and S. Yekelchyk (eds) *Europe's Last Frontier? Belarus, Moldova, and Ukraine Between Russia and the European Union*, New York: Palgrave Macmillan, 55–77.

Rummel, R. J. (1963) 'Dimensions of Conflict Behavior within and between Nations', *General System Yearbook*, vol. 8, 1–50.

—   (1966) 'Dimensions of Conflict Behavior within Nations, 1946–1959', *The Journal of Conflict Resolution*, (10)1: 65–73.

Runner, P. (2009) 'EU Ministers drop Iran group from terror list', *Euobserver.com*, 26 January.

Sadat, L. (2002) *The International Criminal Court and the Transformation of International Law: Justice for the New Millennium*, Ardsley, NY: Transnational Publishers.

Safa, O. (2006) 'Lebanon Springs Forward', *Journal of Democracy*, (17)1.

Safonov, A. (2009) 'Transnistrian's Path', in D. Matveev, G. Selari, E. Bobkova and B. Cseke (eds) *Moldova-Transnistria. Working Together for a Prosperous Future. Negotiation Process*, Chisinau: Cu Drag Publishing House, 179–197.

Sagan, S. D. (1993) *The Limits of Safety*, Princeton, NJ: Princeton University Press.

—   (2006) 'How to keep the bomb from Iran', *Foreign Affairs*, (85)5: 45–59.

Salem, P. (2006) 'The future of Lebanon', *Foreign Affairs*, (85)6.

Sartori, G. (1970) 'Concept misinformation in comparative politics', *American Political Science Review*, (64)4.

—   (ed.) (1984) *Concepts: A Systematic Analysis*, Beverly Hills: Sage.

Schelling, T. C. (1960) *The Strategy of Conflict*, Cambridge, MA: Harvard University Press.

Schmid, A. P. and Jongman, A. J. (1988) *Political Terrorism: A New Guide to Actors, Authors, Concepts, Data Bases, Theories, and Literature*, Amsterdam: Transaction Books.

Schneider, B. R. and Post, J. M. (eds) (2003) *Know The Enemy: Profiles of Adversary Leaders and Their Strategic Cultures*, 2nd edn, Maxwell Air

Force Base, Alabama: USAF Counterproliferation Center.

Schwebach, V. L. (2000) 'Sanctions as Signals: A Line in the Sand or a Lack of Resolve?' in Chan Steve and C. A. Drury (eds) *Sanctions as Economic Statecraft: Theory and Practice*, Basingstoke: McMillan Press.

Selari, G. (2009) 'Moldova and Transnistria: The Regional Economic Dimension', in D. Matveev, G. Selari, E. Bobkova and B. Cseke (eds) *Moldova-Transnistria. Working Together for a Prosperous Future: Economic Aspects*, Chisinau: Cu Drag Publishing House, 136–48.

Senyuva, O. (2010) 'Parliamentary elections in Moldova, April and July 2009', *Electoral Studies*, (29)1: 190–95.

Shambaugh, G. E. (1999) *States, Firms, and Power: Successful Sanctions in United States Foreign Policy*, Albany, NY: State University of New York Press.

Simons, G. L. (2003) *Libya and the West: From Independence to Lockerbie*, London: Centre for Libyan Studies.

Smith, A. (1995) 'The success and use of economic sanctions', *International Interactions*, (21)3: 229–45.

Smith, J. D., Federal Deposit Insurance Corporation (2008) 'Panel 4: Key Developments in Enforcement and Asset Seizure', in *World Conference on Combating Terrorist Financing*, Cleveland, OH: Frederick K. Cox, International Law Center, Case Western University.

Smith, K. E. (2006) 'The Limits of Proactive Cosmopolitanism: the EU and Burma/Myanmar, Cuba and Zimbabwe', in O. Elgstrom and M. Smith (eds) *The European Union's Roles in International Politics: Concepts and Analysis*, New York: Routledge/ECPR Studies in European Political Science.

Smith, M. (1999) *Burma: Insurgency and the Politics of Ethnicity*, London: Zed Books.

Soares, C. (2007) 'EU lifting of Uzbek travel ban greeted with dismay', *The Independent*, 17 October, 24.

Sørbø, G. M. (2010) 'Local violence and international intervention in Sudan', *Review of African Political Economy*, (37)124: 173–86.

SIPRI (2008) SIPRI Arms Transfers Database, SIPRI, http://www.sipri.org/contents/armstrad/at_db.html (accessed 15/09/2008).

'The Stockholm Process', http://www.smartsanctions.se (accessed 01/08/2007).

Svensson, E. (2008) *The African Union's Operations in the Comoros: MAES and Operation Democracy*, Defense Analysis, FOI, Swedish Defence Research.

Tang, S. C. (2005) 'The EU's policy towards China and the arms embargo', *Asia Europe Journal*, 3: 313–21.

Tanter, R. (1966) 'Dimensions of Conflict Behavior within and between nations, 1958-1960', *The Journal of Conflict Resolution*, (10)1, 41–64.

Tarock, A. (2006) 'Iran's Nuclear Programme and the West', *Third World Quarterly*, (27)4: 645–64.

Tocci, N. (2007) *The EU and Conflict Resolution: Promoting Peace in the Backyard*, London, New York: Routledge.

— (ed.) (2008) *Who is a Normative Foreign Policy Actor?* Brussels: Centre for European Policy Studies.

Tostensen, A. and Bull, B. (2002) 'Are Smart Sanctions Feasible?', *World Politics*, (54)3: 373–403.

Traynor, I. (2007) 'Germany pushes for lifting of EU sanctions on Uzbekistan', *The Guardian*, 14 May, 22.

Trenin, D. (2006) 'Russia leaves the West', *Foreign Affairs*, (85)4: 87.

Tsebelis, G. (1990) 'Are sanctions effective? A game-theoretic analysis', *Journal of Conflict Resolution*, (34)1: 3–28.

UNICEF (1998) 'Situation Analysis of Children and Women in Iraq', http://www. childinfo.org/Other/Iraq_sa.pdf, in *Unicef Report* (accessed 01/08/2007).

United Nations 'Impact of Sanctions', http://ochaonline.un.org/HumanitarianIssues/ ImpactofSanctions/tabid/1201/language/en-US/Default.aspx, Office for the Coordination of Humanitarian Affairs, OCHA (accessed 30/08/2008).

United Nations (1945) *Charter of the United Nations*.

United Nations, Economic and Social Council (1997) 'The relationship between economic sanctions and respect for economic, social and cultural rights', http://www.unhchr.ch/tbs/doc.nsf/0/974080d2db3ec66d802565c5003b2 f57?Opendocument (1997) (accessed 01/08/2007)

United Nations, Security Council, International Commission on Inquiry (1998a) 'Letter Dated 18 November 1998 from the Secretary-General Addressed to the President of the Security Council', S/1998/1096.

United Nations, Security Council (1991a) *Resolution 687 (1991)*, S/RES/687.

— (1991b) Resolution 713 (1991), S/RES/713.

— (1992a) Resolution 731 (1992), S/RES/731.

— (1992b) Resolution 748 (1992), S/RES/748.

— (1992c) Resolution 788 (1992), S/RES/788.

— (1993a) Resolution 864 (1993), S/RES/864.

— (1993b) Resolution 872 (1993), S/RES/872.

— (1993c) Resolution 883 (1993), S/RES/883.

— (1994) Resolution 918 (1994), S/RES/918.

— (1995a) Resolution 1011 (1995), S/RES/1011.

— (1995b) Resolution 997 (1995), S/RES/997.

— (1996) Letter Dated 1 February 1996 from the Chairman of the Security Council Committee Established Pursuant to Resolution 918 (1994) Concerning Rwanda Addressed to the President of the Security Council, S/1996/82.

— (1997a) Resolution 1127 (1997), S/RES/1127.

— (1997b) Resolution 1132 (1997), S/RES/1132.

— (1998b) Resolution 1156 (1998), S/RES/1156.

— (1998c) Resolution 1173 (1998), S/RES/1173.

— (1999) Resolution 1267 (1999), S/RES/1267.

— (2001) Resolution 1363 (2001), S/RES/1363.

— (2002a) Resolution 1388 (2002), S/RES/1388.

— (2002b) Resolution 1390 (2002), S/RES/1390.

— (2003a) Resolution 1483 (2003), S/RES/1483.
— (2003b) Resolution 1493 (2003), S/RES/1493.
— (2004a) Resolution 1526 (2004), S/RES/1526.
— (2004b) Resolution 1556 (2004), S/RES/1556.
— (2005) Resolution 1636 (2005), S/RES/1636.
— (2006a) Resolution 1718 (2006), S/RES/1718.
— (2006b) Resolution 1730 (2006), S/RES/1730.
— (2006c) Resolution 1737 (2006), S/RES/1737.
— (2007c) Resolution 1747 (2007), S/RES/1747.
— (2008c) Resolution 1823 (2008), S/RES/1823.
— (2008d), United Nations Assistance Mission for Rwanda (UNAMIR), Department of Peacekeeping Operation (DPKO), http://www.un.org/Depts/dpko/co_mission/unamir.htm (accessed 20/08/2008).
— (2008d) United Nations Assistance Mission for Iraq – UNAMI, http://www.uniraq.org (accessed 20/08/2008).
— (2008e) United Nations Monitoring, Verification and Inspection Commission – UNMOVIC, http://www.unmovic.org/ (accessed 20/08/2008).
— (2010a) Resolution 1929 (2010), S/RES/1929.
— (2010b) Resolution 1952 (2010), S/RES/1952.
United Nations, Security Council, Sanctions Committee (2007a) 'Letter dated 15 November 2007 from the Chairman of the Security Council Committee established pursuant to resolution 1267 (1999) concerning Al-Qaida and the Taliban and associated individuals and entities addressed to the President of the Security Council', S/2007/677.
— (2007b) 'Letter dated 2 October 2007 from the Chairman of the Security Council Committee established pursuant to resolution 1591 (2005) concerning the Sudan addressed to the President of the Security Council', S/2007/584.
— (2008a) 'Letter dated 13 May 2008 from the Chairman of the Security Council Committee established pursuant to resolution 1267 (1999) concerning Al-Qaida and the Taliban and associated individuals and entities addressed to the President of the Security Council'.
— (2008b) 'Letter dated 31 December 2007 from the Chairman of the Security Council Committee established pursuant to resolution 918 (1994) concerning Rwanda addressed to the President of the Security Council', S/2007/782.
United Nations, E.a.S. (2006). *Report of the United Nations High Commissioner for Human Rights and Follow Up to the World Conference on Human Rights. Report of the Mission to Kyrgyzstan by the Office of the United Nations High Commission for Human Rights (OHCHR) Concerning the Events in Andijan, Uzbekistan*, 13–14 May 2005 ed., Commission on Human Rights, E/CN.4/2006/119.
United Nations, S.C. 'Focal Point for De-listing established pursuant to Security Council', http://www.un.org/sc/committees/dfp.shtml, in *UN Security*

Council Sanctions Committees (accessed 15/09/2008).

United Nations, Security Council http://www.un.org/Docs/sc/committees/ AngolaTemplate.htm, in *Security Council Committee Concerning the Situation in Angola Pursuant to Resolution 864 (1993)* (accessed 01/08/2008).

United Nations, Security Council http://www.un.org/Docs/sc/committees/ IraqKuwait/IraqSanctionsCommEng.htm, in *Security Council Committee Established Pursuant to Resolution 661 (1990) Concerning the Situation Between Iraq and Kuwait* (accessed 20/08/2008).

United Nations, Security Council (2011) *The Consolidated List Established and Maintained by the 1267 Committee with Respect to Al-Qaida, Usama Bin Laden, and the Taliban and Other Individuals, Groups, Undertakings and Entities Associated with Them*, http://www.un.org/sc/committees/1267/ pdf/consolidatedlist.pdf (accessed 15/02/2011).

Vahl, M. (2005a) 'The Europeanisation of the Transnistrian Conflict', *EuroJournal. org – Journal of Foreign Policy of Moldova*, no. 6.

— (2005b) 'The Europeanization of the Transnistrian Conflict', CEPS Policy Brief, 73, Brussels: Centre for European Policy Studies.

Vahl, M. and Emerson, M. (2004) 'Moldova and the Transnistrian Conflict', *Journal of Ethnopolitics and Minority Issues in Europe*, 1.

van Bergeijk, P. A. G. (1994) *Economic Diplomacy, Trade, and Commercial Policy : Positive and Negative Sanctions in a New World Order*, Aldershot, Brookfield, VT: Edward Elgar.

Vandewalle, D. (2006) *A History of Modern Libya*, Cambridge/New York: Cambridge University Press.

— (2007) Storia Della Libia Contemporanea, Roma: Salerno Editrice.

Vasquez, J. A. (1993) *The War Puzzle*, Cambridge: Cambridge University Press.

Vines, A. (2003) 'Monitoring UN sanctions in Africa: the role of panels of experts', in T. Findlay (ed.) *Verification Yearbook 2003*, London: VERTIC, 247–63.

von Braunmühl, C. and Kulessa, M. (1995) *The Impact of UN Sanctions on Humanitarian Assistance Activities*, A Report on a Study Commissioned by the United Nations Department of Humanitarian Affairs Berlin: Gesellschaft für Communication Management Interkultur Training.

Wagemann, C. (2008) 'Qualitative Comparative Analysis', SISP 2008 – XXIII Annual Conference Società Italiana Di Scienza Politica, Pavia.

Wagner, H. R. (1988) 'Economic interdependence, bargaining power, and political influence', *International Organization*, (42) 3: 461–83.

Walker, P. (1995) 'How to keep sanctions in proportion', *Financial Times*, 18 May.

Wallensteen, P. (2007) *Understanding Conflict Resolution: War, Peace, and the Global System*, 2nd edn, London, Thousand Oaks, CA: Sage Publications.

Wallensteen, P. and C. Staibano, (eds.) (2005) *International Sanctions: Between Words and Wars in the Global System*, London, New York: Frank Cass.

Walter, B. F. (2004) 'Does Conflict Beget Conflict? Explaining Recurring Civil War', *Journal of Peace Research*, (41)3: 371–88.

Waltz, K. N. (1979) *Theory of International Politics*, New York, NY: McGraw-Hill.

— (1996) 'International Politics is not Foreign Policy', *Security Studies*, (6)1: 54–57.

Weir, F. (2006) 'Status quo wins in Belarus', *Christian Science Monitor*, 21 March, 608–18.

Weiss, T. G., Cortright, D., Lopez, G. A. and Minear, L. (eds) (1997) *Political Gain and Civilian Pain: Humanitarian Impact of Economic Sanctions*, Lanham, MD: Rowman and Littlefield Publishers.

'What the European Union could bring to Belarus', http://eeas.europa.eu/delegations/belarus/documents/eu_belarus/non_paper_1106.pdf (2006) (accessed 15/09/2008).

Wolfer, A. (1962) *Discord and Collaboration: Essays on International Politics*, Baltimore, MD: Johns Hopkins Press.

Wouters, J. and Naert, F. (2001) 'How Effective is the European Security Architecture? Lessons from Bosnia and Kosovo', *International And Comparative Law Quarterly*, 50: 540–76.

'Yassin, Abdullah Kadi and Barakaat, Al, International Foundation vs. Council of the European Union' (2008), tr. Joined Cases C-402/05 and C-415/05 P, Court of Justice.

Zaidi, S. (1997) 'Humanitarian Effects of the Coup and Sanctions in Haiti', in T. G. Weiss, D. Cortright, G. A. Lopez and L. Minear (eds) *Political Gain and Civilian Pain: Humanitarian Impacts of Economic Sanctions*, Lanham, MD: Rowman and Littlefield Publishers, 189–214.

Zurawski vel Grajewski, P. (2005) 'Belarus: The Unrecognized Challenge', in D. Lynch (ed.) *Changing Belarus*, Paris: European Union Institute for Security Studies, 79–96.

| appendices

APPENDIX I – Cases distributed per logic

Type	N	Episodes	
Coercing	10	EU/Iran – 2010 EU/US – 1996 to present EU/Belarus – 2007 to present EU/Libya – 2004 to present	UN/1267 – 1999 to 2001 UN/Yugoslavia – 1994 to 1996 UN/Eritrea – 2009 to present UN/Libya – 1993 to 1999 UN/Iran – 2006 to present UN/DPRK – 2009 to present
Constraining	22	EU/Bosnia & Herzegovina – 2001 to 2006 EU/Milosevic – 2000 to present EU/ICTY – 2001 to present EU/Zimbabwe – 2002 to present EU/Transnistria – 2003 to 2010 EU/Guinea – 2009 to present EU/Burma/Myanmar – 2007 to present EU/FRY – 1998 to 2000	UN/Bosnian-Serbs – 1994 to 1996 UN/Haiti – 1993 to 1994 UN/Liberia – 2001 to 2003 UN/Cote d'Ivoire – 2004 to present UN/Iraq – 1991 to 2003 UN/Liberia – 2003 to present UN/Sierra Leone – 2000 to 2003 UN/Cambodia – 1992-1993 UN/Unita – 1999 to 2002 UN/Iraq – 1990 to 1991 UN/Iraq – 2003 to present UN/1267 – 2002 to present UN/Somalia – 2008 to present UN/Yugoslavia – 1992 to 1994

Type	N		Episodes
Signalling	38	EU/Belarus – 1998 to 1999 EU/Belarus – 2004 to 2007 EU/Comoros – 2008 to 2008 EU/FYROM – 2001 to 2009 EU/Nigeria – 1993 to 1998 EU/Uzbekistan – 2005 to 2009 EU/Transnistria – 2010 to present EU/China – 1989 to present EU/FRY – 1996 to 1998 EU/Nigeria – 1998 to 1999 EU/Afghanistan – 1996 to 1999	UN/Haiti – 1993 to 1993 UN/Sudan – 1996 to 1996 UN/Sierra Leone – 2003 to 2010 UN/Libya – 1999 to 2003 UN/Libya – 1992 to 1993 UN/Ethiopia-Eritrea – 2000 to 2001 UN/Liberia – 1992 to 2001 UN/Sierra Leone – 1997 to 1998 UN/Sierra Leone – 1998 to 2000 UN/Hariri – 2005 to present UN/Somalia – 1992 to 2008 UN/Unita – 1993 to 1999 UN/DRC – 2003 to present UN/Lebanon – 2006 to present
Signalling	38	EU/Burma/Myanmar – 1991 to 2007 EU/DRC – 1993 to 2003 EU/Sudan – 1994 to 2004 EU/Sudan – 2004 to 2005 EU/Indonesia – 1999 to 2000 EU/Libya – 1999 to 2004	UN/Sudan – 2004 to 2005 UN/Sudan – 2005 to present UN/Yugoslavia – 1991 to 1992 UN/Kosovo – 1998 to 2001 UN/Rwanda – 1994 to 1995 UN/Rwanda – 1995 to 2008 UN/DPRK – 2006 to 2009

APPENDIX II – Coefficient of threat, ascending

N	Case	
1	UN/DRC – 2003 to present	0.00
2	EU/Zimbabwe – 2002 to present	0.05
3	UN/Ethiopia-Eritrea – 2000 to 2001	0.05
4	UN/Cote d'Ivoire – 2004 to present	0.05
5	UN/Rwanda – 1994 to 1995	0.05
6	UN/Rwanda – 1995 to 2008	0.05
7	EU/China – 1989 to present	0.11
8	EU/Nigeria – 1993 to1998	0.11
9	EU/Nigeria – 1998 to 1999	0.11
10	EU/Uzbekistan – 2005 to 2009	0.11
11	UN/Unita – 1993 to 1999	0.11
12	UN/Somalia – 1992 to 2008	0.11
13	EU/Burma/Myanmar – 1991 to 2007	0.16
14	EU/Burma/Myanmar – 2007 to present	0.16
15	EU/Comoros – 2008 to 2008	0.16
16	EU/DRC – 1993 to 2003	0.16
17	EU/Indonesia – 1999 to 2000	0.16
18	EU/Sudan – 1994 to 2004	0.16
19	UN/Liberia – 1992 to 2001	0.16

N	Case	
20	UN/Sierra Leone – 1997 to 1998	0.16
21	UN/Cambodia – 1992 to 1993	0.16
22	EU/Milosevic – 2000 to present	0.21
23	UN/Sudan – 2004 to 2005	0.21
24	EU/Bosnia & Herzegovina – 2001 to 2006	0.26
25	UN/Libya – 1999 to 2003	0.26
26	UN/Sudan – 2005 to present	0.26
27	EU/Libya – 1999 to 2004	0.26
28	EU/Afghanistan – 1996 to 1999	0.32
29	EU/Guinea – 2009 to present	0.32
30	UN/Sierra Leone – 2003 to 2010	0.32
31	UN/Iraq – 1991 to 2003	0.37
32	UN/Sierra Leone – 1998 to 2000	0.37
33	UN/Sudan – 1996 to 1996	0.37
34	UN/DPRK – 2006 to 2009	0.37
35	EU/Belarus – 1998 to 1999	0.42
36	EU/Belarus – 2004 to 2007	0.42
37	EU/FRY – 1996 to 1998	0.42
38	EU/FYROM – 2001 to 2009	0.42
39	UN/Liberia – 2003 to present	0.42
40	UN/Haiti – 1993 to 1993	0.42

N	Case	
41	UN/Hariri – 2005 to present	0.42
42	EU/ICTY – 2001 to present	0.47
43	EU/Sudan – 2004 to 2005	0.47
44	UN/Lebanon – 2006 to present	0.47
45	UN/1267 – 1999 to 2001	0.53
46	UN/Kosovo – 1998 to 2001	0.53
47	EU/Transnistria – 2003 to 2010	0.58
48	EU/Transnistria – 2010 to present	0.58
49	UN/Liberia – 2001 to 2003	0.58
50	UN/Sierra Leone – 2000 to 2003	0.58
51	UN/Haiti – 1993 to 1994	0.58
52	EU/Libya – 2004 to present	0.58
53	EU/Belarus – 2007 to present	0.63
54	EU/Iran – 2010	0.63
55	UN/Unita – 1999 to 2002	0.63
56	UN/Iran – 2006 to present	0.63
57	UN/Eritrea – 2009 to present	0.63
58	UN/Yugoslavia – 1994 to 1996	0.63
59	EU/US – 1996 to present	0.68
60	UN/Iraq – 2003 to present	0.68
61	UN/Somalia – 2008 to present	0.68

N	Case	
62	UN/1267 – 2002 to present	0.74
63	UN/DPRK – 2009 to present	0.74
64	UN/Yugoslavia – 1991 to 1992	0.79
65	UN/Yugoslavia – 1992 to 1994	0.79
66	UN/Bosnian-Serbs – 1994 to 1996	0.79
67	UN/Libya – 1992 to 1993	0.89
68	UN/Libya – 1993 to 1999	0.89
69	EU/FRY – 1998 to 2000	0.95
70	UN/Iraq – 1990 to 1991	1.00

APPENDIX III – Coefficient of salience, ascending

N	Case	
1	EU/Burma/Myanmar – 1991 to 2007	0.00
2	EU/Comoros – 2008 to 2008	0.00
3	EU/Sudan – 1994 to 2004	0.00
4	UN/Ethiopia-Eritrea – 2000 to 2001	0.00
5	UN/Sierra Leone – 1997 to 1998	0.00
6	UN/Somalia – 1992 to 2008	0.00
7	UN/Eritrea – 2009 to present	0.00
8	UN/Sudan – 1996 to 1996	0.00
9	EU/Belarus – 2004 to 2007	0.17
10	EU/DRC – 1993 to 2003	0.17
11	EU/Transnistria – 2003 to 2010	0.17
12	EU/Transnistria – 2010 to present	0.17
13	UN/Liberia – 1992 to 2001	0.17
14	UN/Liberia – 2001 to 2003	0.17
15	UN/1267 – 1999 to 2001	0.17
16	UN/Rwanda – 1994 to 1995	0.17
17	EU/Sudan – 2004 to 2005	0.33
18	UN/Sierra Leone – 1998 to 2000	0.33
19	UN/Haiti – 1993 to 1993	0.33

N	Case	
20	UN/Haiti – 1993 to 1994	0.33
21	UN/Hariri – 2005 to present	0.33
22	EU/Libya – 1999 to 2004	0.33
23	EU/Afghanistan – 1996 to 1999	0.50
24	EU/Belarus – 1998 to 1999	0.50
25	EU/Uzbekistan – 2005 to 2009	0.50
26	EU/Burma/Myanmar – 2007 to present	0.67
27	EU/FYROM – 2001 to 2009	0.67
28	EU/ICTY – 2001 to present	0.67
29	EU/Nigeria – 1993 to 1998	0.67
30	UN/Unita – 1993 to 1999	0.67
31	UN/DRC – 2003 to present	0.67
32	UN/Sierra Leone – 2003 to 2010	0.67
33	UN/Cote d'Ivoire – 2004 to present	0.67
34	UN/Cambodia – 1992 to 1993	0.67
35	EU/Libya – 2004 to present	0.67
36	EU/Belarus – 2007 to present	0.67
37	EU/China – 1989 to present	0.83
38	EU/Guinea – 2009 to present	0.83
39	EU/Indonesia – 1999 to 2000	0.83

N	Case	
60	EU/FRY – 1998 to 2000	1.00
61	EU/Bosnia & Herzegovina – 2001 to 2006	1.00
62	EU/Milosevic – 2000 to present	1.00
63	UN/Unita – 1999 to 2002	1.00
64	UN/Liberia – 2003 to present	1.00
65	UN/Sierra Leone – 2000 to 2003	1.00
66	UN/Lebanon – 2006 to present	1.00
67	UN/Sudan – 2005 to present	1.00
68	UN/Bosnian-Serbs – 1994 to 1996	1.00
69	UN/Kosovo – 1998 to 2001	1.00
70	UN/Rwanda – 1995 to 2008	1.00

N	Case	
40	EU/Iran – 2010	0.83
41	EU/Nigeria – 1998 to 1999	0.83
42	EU/US – 1996 to present	0.83
43	EU/Zimbabwe – 2002 to present	0.83
44	UN/Iraq – 1990 to 1991	0.83
45	UN/Iraq – 1991 to 2003	0.83
46	UN/Iraq – 2003 to present	0.83
47	UN/1267 – 2002 to present	0.83
48	UN/Libya – 1992 to 1993	0.83
49	UN/Libya – 1993 to 1999	0.83
50	UN/Libya – 1999 to 2003	0.83
51	UN/Iran – 2006 to present	0.83
52	UN/Somalia – 2008 to present	0.83
53	UN/Sudan – 2004 to 2005	0.83
54	UN/Yugoslavia – 1991 to 1992	0.83
55	UN/Yugoslavia – 1992 to 1994	0.83
56	UN/Yugoslavia – 1994 to 1996	0.83
57	UN/DPRK – 2006 to 2009	0.83
58	UN/DPRK – 2009 to present	0.83
59	EU/FRY – 1996 to 1998	1.00

APPENDIX IV – Coefficient of complexity, ascending

N	Case	
1	UN/Sierra Leone – 2003 to 2010	0.07
2	EU/Bosnia & Herzegovin – 2001 to 2006	0.17
3	EU/Milosevic – 2000 to present	0.17
4	UN/Libya – 1999 to 2003	0.17
5	EU/Libya – 1999 to 2004	0.17
6	EU/Libya – 2004 to present	0.17
7	EU/Belarus – 2007 to present	0.20
8	EU/ICTY – 2001 to present	0.20
9	EU/Nigeria – 1998 to 1999	0.20
10	UN/DPRK – 2006 to 2009	0.20
11	EU/Belarus – 1998 to 1999	0.23
12	EU/FYROM – 2001 to 2009	0.23
13	EU/Transnistria – 2010 to present	0.23
14	EU/US – 1996 to present	0.23
15	UN/Libya – 1992 to 1993	0.23
16	UN/Libya – 1993 to 1999	0.23
17	EU/FRY – 1996 to 1998	0.27
18	UN/DPRK – 2009 to present	0.27
19	EU/Uzbekistan – 2005 to 2009	0.30
20	EU/China – 1989 to present	0.33
21	EU/Comoros – 2008 to 2008	0.33
22	UN/1267 – 1999 to 2001	0.33
23	UN/Haiti – 1993 to 1993	0.33
24	EU/Belarus – 2004 to 2007	0.37
25	EU/Zimbabwe – 2002 to present	0.37
26	UN/Eritrea – 2009 to present	0.37
27	UN/Yugoslavia – 1994 to 1996	0.37
28	UN/Liberia – 2003 to present	0.40
29	EU/Nigeria – 1993 to 1998	0.43
30	UN/Sierra Leone – 2000 to 2003	0.43
31	EU/Iran – 2010	0.47
32	UN/Cambodia – 1992 to 1993	0.47
33	UN/Iran – 2006 to present	0.47
34	UN/Iraq – 2003 to present	0.50
35	UN/Hariri – 2005 to present	0.50
36	UN/Sudan – 1996 to 1996	0.53
37	UN/Bosnian-Serbs – 1994 to 1996	0.53
38	UN/Iraq – 1991 to 2003	0.57
39	UN/Haiti – 1993 to 1994	0.57

N	Case	
40	EU/FRY – 1998 to 2000	0.60
41	EU/Transnistria – 2003 to 2010	0.60
42	EU/Burma/Myanmar – 2007 to present	0.63
43	EU/Guinea – 2009 to present	0.63
44	UN/Iraq – 1990 to 1991	0.63
45	UN/1267 – 2002 to present	0.63
46	UN/Rwanda – 1995 to 2008	0.63
47	EU/DRC – 1993 to 2003	0.67
48	EU/Indonesia – 1999 to 2000	0.73
49	UN/Liberia – 2001 to 2003	0.77
50	UN/Kosovo – 1998 to 2001	0.77
51	EU/Sudan – 2004 to 2005	0.80
52	UN/DRC – 2003 to present	0.80
53	UN/Somalia – 2008 to present	0.80
54	EU/Burma/Myanmar – 1991 to 2007	0.83
55	UN/Ethiopia-Eritrea – 2000 to 2001	0.83
56	UN/Sierra Leone – 1997 to 1998	0.83
57	EU/Afghanistan – 1996 to 1999	0.87
58	EU/Sudan – 1994 to 2004	0.87
59	UN/Cote d'Ivoire – 2004 to present	0.87

N	Case	
60	UN/Lebanon – 2006 to present	0.87
61	UN/Sudan – 2004 to 2005	0.87
62	UN/Sudan – 2005 to present	0.87
63	UN/Rwanda – 1994 to 1995	0.87
64	UN/Liberia – 1992 to 2001	0.90
65	UN/Sierra Leone – 1998 to 2000	0.90
66	UN/Yugoslavia – 1991 to 1992	0.90
67	UN/Yugoslavia – 1992 to 1994	0.90
68	UN/Unita – 1993 to 1999	0.93
69	UN/Unita – 1999 to 2002	0.93
70	UN/Somalia – 1992 to 2008	1.00

APPENDIX V – Episodes combination

	Episodes	
1	UN/Bosnian-Serbs – 1994 to 1996 UN/Somalia – 2008 to present EU/FRY – 1998 to 2000 UN/Yugoslavia – 1992 to 1994 UN/Unita – 1999 to 2002 UN/Yugoslavia – 1991 to 1992 UN/Iraq – 1990 to 1991 UN/Kosovo – 1998 to 2001 UN/1267 – 2002 to present UN/Iraq – 2003 to present	10
2	UN/Haiti – 1993 to 1994 UN/Liberia – 2001 to 2003 EU/Transnistria – 2003 to 2010	3
3	UN/Eritrea – 2009 to present EU/Transnistria – 2010 to present UN/1267 – 1999 to 2001	3
4	EU/Belarus – 1998 to 1999 UN/Haiti – 1993 to 1993 EU/Belarus – 2004 to 2007 UN/Hariri – 2005 to present EU/Comoros – 2008 to 2008 EU/Libya – 1999 to 2004 EU/Uzbekistan – 2005 to 2009	7
5	UN/DPRK – 2006 to 2009 EU/FYROM – 2001 to 2009 EU/Bosnia & Herzegovina – 2001 to 2006 EU/Nigeria – 1993 to 1998 EU/Milosevic – 2000 to present EU/China – 1989 to present EU/ICTY – 2001 to present EU/FRY – 1996 to 1998 EU/Zimbabwe – 2002 to present EU/Nigeria – 1998 to 1999 UN/Liberia – 2003 to present UN/Sierra Leone – 2003 to 2010 UN/Cambodia – 1992 to 1993 UN/Libya – 1999 to 2003	14

	Episodes		
6	UN/Iraq – 1991 to 2003 EU/Guinea – 2009 to present EU/Burma/Myanmar – 2007 to present UN/Cote d'Ivoire – 2004 to present EU/Indonesia – 1999 to 2000 UN/Unita – 1993 to 1999	UN/DRC – 2003 to present UN/Lebanon – 2006 to present UN/Sudan – 2004 to 2005 UN/Sudan – 2005 to present UN/Rwanda – 1995 to 2008	11
7	UN/DPRK – 2009 to present EU/Iran – 2010 EU/Belarus – 2007 to present EU/US – 1996 to present UN/Libya – 1993 to 1999	UN/Iran – 2006 to present UN/Yugoslavia – 1994 to 1996 UN/Sierra Leone – 2000 to 2003 UN/Libya – 1992 to 1993 EU/Libya – 2004 to present	10
8	UN/Sudan – 1996 to 1996 EU/Afghanistan – 1996 to 1999 EU/Burma/Myanmar – 1991 to 2007 EU/DRC – 1993 to 2003 EU/Sudan – 1994 to 2004 EU/Sudan – 2004 to 2005	UN/Ethiopia-Eritrea – 2000 to 2001 UN/Liberia – 1992 to 2001 UN/Sierra Leone – 1997 to 1998 UN/Sierra Leone – 1998 to 2000 UN/Somalia – 1992 to 2008 UN/Rwanda – 1994 to1995	12

APPENDIX VI – Number of articles

Case	Date of imposition	Financial Times	Economist	NY Times	Sum of Articles	Level of Attention
EU/Afghanistan – 1996 to 1999	12/17/1996	215	77		292	2
EU/Belarus – 1998 to 1999	7/9/1998	226	53		279	2
EU/Belarus – 2004 to 2007	9/24/2004	142	24		166	1
EU/Belarus – 2007 to present	3/19/2007	259	68		327	2
EU/Burma/Myanmar – 1991 to 2007	7/1/1991	126	42		168	1
EU/Burma/Myanmar – 2007 to present	11/19/2007	422	88		510	3
EU/China – 1989 to present	6/27/1989	3361	691		4052	3
EU/Comoros – 2008 to 2008	3/3/2008	3	3		6	1
EU/DRC – 1993 to 2003	4/7/1993	98	43		141	1
EU/FRY – 1996 to 1998	2/26/1996	928	175		1103	3
EU/FRY – 1998 to 2000	3/19/1998	845	127		972	3
EU/Bosnia & Herzegovina – 2001 to 2006	10/8/2001	323	1		324	2
EU/Milosevic – 2000 to present	1/24/2000	1008	190		1198	3
EU/FYROM – 2001 to 2009	7/16/2001	177	289		466	2
EU/Guinea – 2009 to present	10/27/2009	301	57		358	2
EU/ICTY – 2001 to present	2/26/2001	149	6		155	1
EU/Indonesia – 1999 to 2000	9/16/1999	260	58		318	2
EU/Iran – 2010 to present	26/7/2010	2488	508		2996	3
EU/Nigeria – 1993 to 1998	11/1/1993	530	90		620	3

Case	Date of imposition	Financial Times	Economist	NY Times	Sum of Articles	Level of Attention
EU/Nigeria – 1998 to 1999	10/30/1998	638	113		751	3
EU/Sudan – 1994 to 2004	3/15/1994	134	66		200	2
EU/Sudan – 2004 to 2005	1/9/2004	189	2		191	1
EU/Transnistria – 2003 to 2010	2/27/2003	76	0		76	1
EU/Transnistria – 2010 to present	2/22/2010	126	0		126	1
EU/US – 1996 to present	11/22/1996	379	2479		2858	3
EU/Uzbekistan – 2005 to 2009	11/14/2005	187	42		229	2
EU/Zimbabwe – 2002 to present	2/18/2002	1001	156		1157	3
UN/Unita – 1993 to 1999	9/15/1993	269		136	405	2
UN/Unita – 1999 to 2002	5/7/1999	248		82	330	2
UN/DRC – 2003 to present	7/28/2003	215		12	227	1
UN/Ethiopia-Eritrea – 2000 to 2001	5/17/2000	99		65	164	1
UN/Iraq – 1990 to 1991	8/6/1990	1135		335	1470	3
UN/Iraq – 1991 to 2003	4/3/1991	6002		2930	8932	3
UN/Iraq – 2003 to present	5/22/2003	6002		5056	11058	3
UN/Liberia – 1992 to 2001	11/19/1992	77		48	125	1
UN/Liberia – 2001 to 2003	3/17/2001	110		43	153	1
UN/Liberia – 2003 to present	12/22/2003	258		214	472	3
UN/Sierra Leone – 1997 to 1998	10/8/1997	103		59	162	1
UN/Sierra Leone – 1998 to 2000	6/5/1998	159		59	218	1

Case	Date of imposition	Financial Times	Economist	NY Times	Sum of Articles	Level of Attention
UN/Sierra Leone – 2000 to 2002	7/5/2000	273		156	429	2
UN/Sierra Leone – 2002 to 2010	12/4/2002	228		71	299	2
UN/Cote d'Ivoire – 2004 to present	11/15/2004	225		162	387	2
UN/1267 – 1999 to 2001	10/15/1999	84		125	209	1
UN/1267 –2002 to present	1/16/2002	614		377	991	3
UN/Cambodia – 1992 to 1993	11/30/1992	236		180	416	2
UN/Haiti – 1993 to 1993	6/16/1993	120		411	531	3
UN/Haiti – 1993 to 1994	10/13/1993	128		455	583	3
UN/Hariri – 2005 to present	10/31/2005	151		90	241	1
UN/Lebanon – 2006 to present	8/11/2006	948		666	1614	3
UN/Libya – 1992 to 1993	3/31/1992	420		122	542	3
UN/Libya – 1993 to 1999	11/11/1993	318		150	468	3
UN/Libya – 1999 to 2003	4/5/1999	343		94	437	2
UN/Iran – 2006 to present	12/23/2006	2868		1439	4307	3
UN/Somalia – 1992 to 2008	1/23/1992	98		53	151	1
UN/Somalia – 2008 to present	11/20/2008	278		271	549	3
UN/Eritrea – 2009 to present	12/23/2009	43		13	56	1
UN/Sudan – 1996 to 1996	4/26/1996	143		80	223	1
UN/Sudan – 2004 to 2005	7/30/2004	256		62	318	2
UN/Sudan – 2005 to present	3/29/2005	450		229	679	3

Case	Date of imposition	Financial Times	Economist	NY Times	Sum of Articles	Level of Attention
UN/Yugoslavia – 1991 to 1992	9/25/1991	891		496	1387	3
UN/Yugoslavia – 1992 to 1994	5/30/1992	1126		657	1783	3
UN/Yugoslavia – 1994 to 1996	9/23/1994	1187		394	1581	3
UN/Bosnian-Serbs – 1994 to 1996	9/23/1994	1976		3000	4976	3
UN/Kosovo – 1998 to 2001	3/31/1998	854		70	924	3
UN/Rwanda – 1994 to 1995	5/17/1994	119		98	217	1
UN/Rwanda – 1995 to 2008	8/16/1995	353		466	819	3
UN/DPRK – 2006 to 2009	10/14/2006	1082		562	1644	3
UN/DPRK – 2009 to present	6/12/2009	760		390	1150	3
EU/Libya – 1999 to2004	6/16/1999	356	65		421	2
EU/Libya – 2004 to present	10/14/2004	609	117		726	3

| index

www.ingramcontent.com/pod-product-compliance
Lightning Source LLC
Chambersburg PA
CBHW072121020426
42334CB00018B/1670